ADOBE®
FLASH® PLATFORM
FROM START TO FINISH

WORKING COLLABORATIVELY USING **ADOBE® CREATIVE SUITE® 5**

AARON PEDERSEN

JAMES POLANCO

DOUG WINNIE

Adobe Flash Platform from Start to Finish:
Working Collaboratively Using Adobe Creative Suite 5

Aaron Pedersen, James Polanco, and Doug Winnie

This Adobe Press book is published by Peachpit.

Peachpit
1249 Eighth Street
Berkeley, CA 94710
510/524-2178
510/524-2221 (fax)

Peachpit is a division of Pearson Education.
For the latest on Adobe Press books, go to www.adobepress.com
To report errors, please send a note to errata@peachpit.com

Acquisitions Editor: Victor Gavenda
Project Editor: Susan Rimerman
Production Editor: Cory Borman
Developmental Editor: Kim Wimpsett
Copy Editor: Cathy Caputo
Cover Design: Mimi Heft
Interior Design and Composition: Kim Scott, Bumpy Design
Indexer: James Minkin

ISBN-13: 978-0-321-68071-6
ISBN-10: 0-321-68071-5

9 8 7 6 5 4 3 2 1

Printed and bound in the United States of America

DEDICATIONS

I would like to dedicate this book to those friends, families, and colleagues who have made the largest impact on my life and who have supported me throughout my career.

To my mother, for always reminding me to take a step back and "smell the roses."

To my father, for always encouraging me to go further and to pursue my dreams.

To my brothers, for their friendship and for always being there to share the great experiences in life.

To Granny and Grandpa, for being my motivation for staying out of trouble and for reaching for the stars.

To my coauthors, James and Doug; thank you for pushing me to new bounds and allowing me to be part of this milestone. And thank you for your great friendship.

To Kevin Clerici, thanks for being my long-time friend and editor and for being one of my motivation when I write.

To Kyle Arteaga and Dave Kramer, without your guidance I would not be where I am today. Thank you!

To Dennis Maloney and Dan Foley for taking a chance on a little whippersnapper and giving me the opportunity to succeed in this profession.

To my wife, Ashley, thank you for always understanding my high-energy mind and supporting my wild ideas. You are my best friend. I promise with the book finished, my weekends are yours (at least until my next bright idea).

—Aaron Pedersen

This book is dedicated to my family, friends, and co-workers; without you, this opportunity would never have been realized.

To Doug and Aaron, for hours, nay days, nay weeks, talking about process and practices, I am glad to have such friends who share my same geek-filled interests.

To our cats (yes, all three authors are cat people) Pretty, Simon, and Kaylee for distracting me when needed and reminding me there are better things than sitting in front of a monitor.

To Jeevan, for providing me with your guidance and opening doors into this awesome industry.

To the Brady Bunch team, for showing me how to make an amazing vision a reality when few expected us to do so.

To Pierre, for putting your trust in my then unproven abilities and allowing me to lead such an amazing project.

To my parents, who I am sure worried much for me over the years, but you always provide me with amazing insight, guidance, trust, and love.

To Christina, my lovely wife, thank you so much for supporting me in this and all my endeavors; it means more to me than I could ever express in words.

—James Polanco

For all of the sacrifices we have endured over the writing of this book and for the creation of Creative Suite 5, I'd like to dedicate this book to my family and friends.

To Aaron and James, for making the creation of this book a fun experience and for their wonderful friendship.

To our cats Hoover, BeBe, and "Big Girl" for sitting on my lap, keeping me warm and entertained.

To Tim, for making technology a passion that brings me fulfillment every day.

To Janet, for showing how art, design, and beauty have a place in everything, including technology.

To Mike, my husband and best friend, who makes me smile every day, no matter where we are, and inspires me to do great things. Thanks, Groovy Dude.

—Doug Winnie

ACKNOWLEDGMENTS

The ideas and best practices in this book were conceived over many years of experience and with the inspiration and ideas of many people who we have been fortunate enough to brush shoulders with over our careers. I would like to acknowledge a few: James Polanco, Doug Winnie, Matt Doyal, Dennis Maloney, Dan Foley, Ruthie Winig, Matt Macchia, Natalie Pietrykowski, Dave Kramer, Kyle Arteaga, Ron Reimann, Aaron Lange, Greg Collins, Chris Stone, John Wells, Tony Mowers, Clay Graham, Daniel Billotte, Rachel Roth, Ernesto Johnson, Chris Yap, Kristen Jarin, Kevin Elliot, Ann Gladstone, Dave Grijalva, Mani White, and the rest of DHAP Digital. And of course, we can't forget about Adobe Press: Thank you for giving us the opportunity to write this book, and thank you to all the team members who helped make this book a success.

—Aaron Pedersen

Attempting to consolidate all the good ideas and why we should use them, and to understand all the bad ideas and how we should avoid them, was inspired by the amazing work of many of my colleagues throughout the years. Unfortunately, there are too many amazing people to list here, but I would like to call out a few people: Jeevan Nair, Curt Swayne, Chad Campbell, Reagan Smith, Boaz Englesberg, Tom Higgins, Chris Campbell, Larry Gonzales, Marni Sweetland, John Koch, Don Booth, Jonathan Duran, Hank Hansen, Larry McLister, Heidi Williams, Dexter Reid, Tanya Dimalsky, Gabe Chua, David Zuckerman, Narciso Jaramillo, Mike Morearty, Chris Saari, Sho Kuwamoto, Mark Anders, David Wadhwani, Rebecca Hyatt, Ely Greenfield, Matt Chotin, Deepa Subramaniam, Tim Strickland, Sami Iwata, Chris Walcott, Josh Kebble-Wyen, Christopher Morin, Maer Ben-Yisrael, Ann Haas, Rachel Roth, Mani White, Ernesto Johnson, Chris Yap, Matt Boris, and Pierre Tehrany. This is just a handful of the talented people who I have had the privilege to work and learn from. Thank you to all the folks at Adobe for making such great products. And finally, a special thank-you to Victor Gavenda, Susan Rimerman, Kim Wimpsett, Cory Borman, and everyone at Adobe Press for making this book a reality; it's been a pleasure and a privilege.

—James Polanco

All the material in this book wouldn't be possible without the contribution of the thousands of people at Adobe who make the Flash Platform and Creative Suite 5 possible. A few people at Adobe in particular I'd like to acknowledge are Dani Beaumont, Doug Benson, Bruce Bowman, Mike Chambers, Matt Chotin, Greg DeMichillie, Aaron Dolberg, Madhura Dudhgaonkar, Scott Fegette, Devin Fernandez, Ben Forta, Richard Galvan, Ely Greenfield, Bill Heil, Steve Heintz, Lea Hickman, Susan Lally, Adam Lehman, David Macy, John Nack, Ted Patrick, Greg Rewis, Merline Saintil, Andrew Shorten, Ryan Stewart, Deepa Subramaniam, Frances Thomas, Cory West, Heidi Williams, and the entire Adobe Flash Catalyst CS5, Flash Professional CS5, Flash Builder 4, Flex 4, Dreamweaver CS5, Fireworks CS5, and BrowserLab teams—all of which are too long to list, but each team member knows how passionate and appreciative I am of their hard work and sacrifices. Special thanks to Chris Stone who created some of the template design files for this book for user workflows and wireframes. Also a shout-out to all of my old team members at DHAP Digital and DigitalThink—thank you!

—Doug Winnie

Contents

PART II ▪ PLANNING

PART V ▪ BUILD AND RELEASE

PART VI ▪ MAINTENANCE

ABOUT THE AUTHORS

Aaron Pedersen

Aaron Pedersen is a Web application architect and the cofounder of DevelopmentArc. He brings more than a decade of experience working with many startup and Fortune 500 companies. Aaron currently focuses on user interface technologies such as the Adobe Flash Platform (Adobe Flex, AIR) and JavaScript. He believes that up-front planning, team cooperation, and established team workflows are the key to the success of any Web application for today's Web environment.

Currently Aaron resides in San Francisco and in his spare time enjoys hiking with his lovely wife Ashley, snowboarding in the backcountry of Colorado with his brothers, and shooting photography every step of the way.

James Polanco

James is a Web application architect and cofounder of DevelopmentArc, which focuses on the Flash Platform (Flash, AIR, Flex, and so on). He has been dabbling with Flash since the beginning but became serious about development and research with the release of Flash MX. Over the years, James has focused primarily on ActionScript development, design patterns, and component implementations, which became a natural fit for Flex development and Web application planning and architecture.

James has been involved with projects such as Scion.com, Lexus.com, Toyota.com, Libsyn Podcast Analytics Dashboard, Fake Science Music Store, ILM The show, Adobe kuler, Nortel's Energy Efficiency Calculator, Adobe WorkflowLab, and many other projects and applications for startups to Fortune 500 companies. He is an avid blogger, author, speaker, and researcher focusing on technology implementations, best practices, and analysis of Web-enabled tools and technologies. When he has free time (which is rare nowadays), he is also a DJ, producer, snowboarder, and amateur rock climber.

Doug Winnie

Doug Winnie is the principal product manager for Adobe Flash Catalyst, Flash Platform Workflow, and WorkflowLab. He is responsible for the integration and collaborative workflows between designers and developers using the Adobe Flash Platform and between Adobe's Flash tools (Flash Professional, Flash Catalyst, and Flash Builder).

Doug is also an instructor at San Francisco State University teaching HTML/Ajax Web design with Dreamweaver, ActionScript programming, working with XML data, and Flex application design and development with Flash Catalyst and Flash Builder. He also hosts the Adobe TV show *ActionScript 1:1 with Doug Winnie*.

In his spare time, Doug is an active gamer and all-around geek collecting classic computer games. He enjoys hobbyist music composition, video production, and game development. Doug is currently writing and building his own role-playing game in Flash.

Introduction

Adobe provides a deep ecosystem based around Flash Player. This ecosystem has been coined the *Flash Platform*, and it consists of a series of Adobe tools, technologies, and services.

Creating projects for the Flash Platform is an exciting process, yet it is often a daunting experience for everyone involved. Adobe is constantly evolving the platform to provide new and powerful features that not only give creators more control but also provide the ability for team members to work together more efficiently. Adobe Creative Suite 5 has introduced many new features and improvements to help teams work together so that the final product, be it a Web site, a banner ad, a desktop application, or a mobile game, is the best that it can be. By taking advantage of both Creative Suite 5 and the Flash Platform, project teams have the potential to build amazing applications, yet tools alone cannot guarantee that a project will be successful.

In this book, we examine why projects are not always successful and how to avoid many of these issues. We will look at key areas that can breed both success and the potential for failure. You will learn how to plan and execute all aspects of your project, from initial concept to the time your users no longer need your application. We will also spend a lot of time showing you cool new (and existing) features in Creative Suite 5 and the Flash Platform that can help improve your creation experience to give your project the power to succeed.

WHO THIS BOOK IS FOR

This book is for the entire project team that is looking to adopt and build projects using Adobe's CS5 and Flash Platform technologies. This includes teams of one to teams that span departments and companies. Our goal is to provide information about the Flash Platform project creation process for everyone on your team. This includes executive management, project management, design, development, testing, and deployment.

One of the keys to success is making sure that everyone involved with a project, including your customers, are "on the same page" throughout the entire process. If the entire process is not understood, then these unknown areas pose the most risk to hindering your project's success. We hope to shed light on all of these areas so that you and your team are prepared as much as possible.

WHO THIS BOOK ISN'T FOR

In this book we cover a lot of different and important subjects, yet we could not write a book that covers every topic needed for every person who wants to use the Flash Platform. If you are looking learn how to design and develop Flex and Flash for the first time, this is not the book for you. We make the assumption that you and your team are familiar with creating Flash-based content.

If you are looking for a book that examines a specific Creative Suite 5 tool or Flash Platform technology in-depth, then this book is not for you. We cover a lot of the tools and technologies as deeply as possible, but our goal is to focus more on highlighting important features and processes to help your team succeed, not master one specific tool.

If you are looking to learn the basics of Creative Suite 5, then this book is not for you. Similar to Flash and Flex, we cover a lot of ground, but we are assuming that you are familiar with using many of the tools included with Creative Suite.

HOW THIS BOOK IS ORGANIZED

Because we are writing a book that covers the Flash Platform project process from beginning to end, we have broken the book down into six phases: Overview, Planning, Design, Development, Build and Release, and Maintenance.

- **Overview.** We examine why projects fail, what makes up a project, who is involved in your project, and how the project proceeds over time.

- **Planning.** We cover the overall process for how to plan and execute your project, organize your requirements, set expectations for everyone involved, and make sure everyone is in agreement throughout the entire life of your project.

- **Design.** We discuss how to plan for design, who is involved in the design process, what the design team requires, and how to collaborate seamlessly with everyone involved in the project.

- **Development.** We talk about the planning process for development, who is involved in the development process, what the development team requires, and how to collaborate seamlessly with everyone involved in the project.

- **Build and Release.** We examine what the build and release process is, who is involved, how to plan for build and release, and how this process is important for guaranteeing the quality of your project.

- **Maintenance.** Just because your project has launched doesn't mean that you and your team's involvement is done. We look at common issues that arise post-release and how to support your project's growth and improvement over time.

It is important to note that we have written the chapters in a linear order, but we realize that many of these phases will overlap during the actual project. This is especially true for those teams that employ iterative processes such as Agile or Extreme Programming. Throughout the book we will examine how each phase interacts and often overlaps with other phases.

In each chapter, you will be presented with terms that are relative to the topic at hand. We have compiled a list of definitions of these terms in the glossary at the end of the book.

HOW TO CONTACT US

If you have questions about the processes outlined in the book or are looking for more details, we recommend checking out our Web sites.

You can find James and Aaron's blog at *http://www.developmentarc.com*. You can find Doug's blog at *http://www.adobe.dougwinnie.com*. You can also follow all three of the authors on Twitter:

Aaron: @aaronpedersen
James: @jamespolanco
Doug: @sfdesigner

PART I

OVERVIEW

CHAPTER 1

Why Projects Fail

You may be reading this book for a variety of reasons, but the primary one is to ensure that your future projects are as successful as possible. Like with many things, though, you need to define what "success" really means. In this chapter, we'll review some of the factors that can turn projects south. We'll also introduce a workflow using Adobe software and technologies that can help address common project issues before they happen.

WHAT FAILURE LOOKS LIKE

Before you can define what a successful project is, you need to understand what a "failed" project looks like. You can define failure in several ways. In fact, a failed project might have launched successfully and may have even met all of the customer's requirements, but it still could be a complete failure. This kind of failure is common in this industry—on the surface a project seems fine, but behind the scenes everything and everyone are in a complete shambles. This can spell doom for the individual, team, or agency that worked on the failed project.

This section explores the three main ways a project can fail.

Over budget. We generally are in business to make money or to ensure that we have enough money to do other things, and one of the clearest definitions of failure is when a project is *over budget*. Being over budget can result from a number of issues, including accepting ongoing changes that were not initially planned for, adding developers or designers that were not originally accounted for, or requiring more expensive resources to complete complex tasks that weren't anticipated. Although one over-budget project might not spell doom for a company, if it becomes a regular occurrence it can lead to disaster, especially for smaller companies or for freelancers. Over-budget projects can be avoided by thoughtfully examining how you or your team will complete the steps of your project. We'll review some key ways to do this throughout the book.

Over time. Another indication of project failure is when the project is late, or is *over time*. Missing a project deadline—whether it's to hand over project materials or to deploy a project live to a server—can be disastrous to your relationship with the customer or client. And often these types of failures are due to external factors beyond your control. Numerous times, external vendors, subcontractors, or even clients themselves are late to deliver critical milestones that can impact your ability to deliver an overall project. Through defining clear communication channels and establishing a consistent project management role

in your team, you can avoid these issues. In future chapters, this book will discuss how to keep your client engaged and present throughout your project.

Under quality. The final major type of failed project is when the project is delivered on time, within budget, but is of subpar quality, sometimes referred to as *under quality*. Too often, projects get rushed to delivery to meet client requirements, are buggy, have performance issues, or are impossible to maintain after they are delivered. Quality is one of the hardest project factors to accurately measure since it is very subjective, but this book will help you define clear quality goals that can help you meet this critical project requirement.

To help you understand more about project dynamics, here is a metaphor a former colleague taught us: Imagine that the resources, budget, schedule, and quality of your project are represented as a single loop of string. You can pull this loop in multiple directions to give in one area or take in another, but the length of the string never changes. Because of this, you can pull in one direction only so far while maintaining the other forces of the project. The only way to do more with that string is to make the string longer—by adding more money, people, tools, or technologies or by adjusting what is actually being built. If you try to pull the string too hard in one direction with the same amount of constraints, your string will snap, which is what will happen with your team if you don't consider their quality of life when working on a project.

STATE OF THE THREE TS: TECHNOLOGY, TOOLS, AND TEAMS

There are many reasons you might go over budget, go over time, or have subpar quality, but often it's attributable to some snafu of the three Ts: technology, tools, and teams. It's important to know how these things can affect your project. This section gives you an overview of the three Ts, and you'll learn more about them throughout the book.

Technology. A big contributor to failed projects is when customers or clients don't understand that the technology behind the scenes has adapted or changed. The Adobe Flash Platform has evolved significantly from the days of simple Flash animation, but a lot of clients and customers don't fully understand that. Even within the interactive design and development world, there is misconception about what Flash can and cannot do. This book will clearly describe what exactly the Flash Platform is, how it can be used, and how you can effectively build applications for it.

Tools. With each release of Adobe Flash Player, Adobe AIR, Adobe Creative Suite, and other tools, Adobe adds new workflows and makes existing workflows easier and more efficient. Although your team may have found workarounds and other ways to navigate some of the inefficient gaps that existed in earlier versions of Creative Suite or with earlier Macromedia software, it is important to have someone on your team keep up-to-date on the latest version of the software to see whether there are true efficiency gains that can help your team.

If your team decides to request new versions of software, you need to consider the big picture. Although a software purchase may seem difficult or costly now, the resulting efficiency gains and increased success with projects, team motivation, and client satisfaction can lead to better opportunities and more profitability. Whenever a new version of Creative Suite is released, it represents a significant amount of workflow improvements that can be difficult to fully understand. This book will discuss features of Creative Suite that are relevant for building interactive projects using the Flash Platform—from planning to deployment.

Teams. Be sure to listen to your team—they will give you direct and indirect feedback if they are overworked. Overextending your team or not giving them interesting work or exciting challenges can result in absenteeism, lateness, slowness to fix bugs, and general low productivity. For example, one team member we know was routinely tasked with the same mundane, boring, and technically complex work. Instead of giving him the opportunity to stretch his legs and work on something new and challenging, the same

work was sent his way all the time. "But he already knows how to do the work" was always the rationale. Until he left the company because he was bored and not challenged. This demonstrates two important principals of team management: always keep your team engaged and excited about the challenges that lie ahead, and always make sure that knowledge of your project is shared across team members, in case someone leaves.

Another important dynamic of a successful team is maintaining balance for your management team. Failed projects are often the result of a communication breakdown of some sort, either within team or with the customer or client. The knee-jerk reaction can be to compel your management team to pay more attention to the areas of failed communication. But a good project manager knows to balance the needs of their internal team with the customer's expectations. If there are problems among the internal team members—misunderstandings over how a feature should be built, poor communication, or unclear client requests, for example—then the manager will be forced to draw their attention to those internal issues. What can happen is that the client or customer is unattended, and therefore the project manager is not able to communicate effectively with them and is not able to focus on the important details that are expected, resulting in higher risk of a failed project.

HOW TO DELIVER SUCCESSFUL PROJECTS

That brings us to this section and, frankly, the reason why you picked up this book in the first place: How can you ensure that your projects are more successful for your customers and increase the efficiency and satisfaction of your team? Throughout this book, we'll explain in depth how to tackle your projects and provide some best practices using Adobe software and technologies that can help. The Flash Platform and Creative Suite are broad tools, and a ton of information is available that spans extensive industries. This book will take aspects from all of these products and present a workflow that integrates everything together.

The cornerstone of the approach is not to consider planning as a task or requirement that you do at the beginning of your project, but as an ongoing process throughout the entire project. Planning—and the information it can provide you—should be considered a partner or collaborator. Few people enjoy the rigors of project planning, but that is because it has been devoid of true context that makes it exciting and gives it life as you build and create your project.

Next, it is important for everyone on the project, including your client, to understand his or her role in bringing everything together. Often, some individuals feel that they are the "core" of the project, while others feel that they aren't adding significant value. For everyone to understand the interconnectedness of each person's contribution to the project, you need to show the network that exists among your team members and how each individual is critical to the project's success. By clearly defining these roles and networks, you can build strong avenues of communication between everyone on the team with clear understanding as to why these lines of communication are critical to the success of the project. With strong communication lanes established, teams can collaborate on given tasks to ensure full team transparency and provide the necessary feedback required.

When it comes to actually sitting down and getting to work, the next step is to learn how to successfully take advantage of the hundreds of features that are part of Adobe's vast set of tools. These include the new capabilities of the Flash Platform, Creative Suite 5, and the new CS Live bundle of services such as CS Review, Adobe Story, and Acrobat.com. Creative Suite 5 also introduces Adobe Flash Catalyst CS5 and now includes Adobe Flash Builder 4 (formerly called Adobe Flex Builder). With such an expanded set of tools and capabilities, it can be easy to become overwhelmed and lost. This book will focus on how you and your team can use these features to increase your efficiency in building interactive and creative projects.

So, let's get started and discuss the various types of projects you can create with Creative Suite and the Flash Platform.

CHAPTER 2

The Project Spectrum

Before we define the specifics of project processes and workflows, let's talk about the projects themselves. With the Flash Platform, you can create projects of varying sizes, complexities, and features. What you'll find, though, is that as you work with more and more projects, they tend to be placed on a spectrum instead of being in specific buckets.

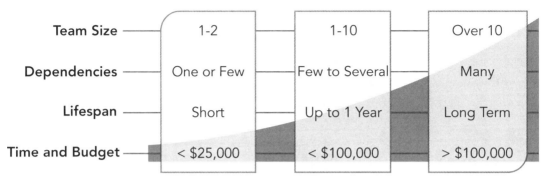

Team Size	1-2	1-10	Over 10
Dependencies	One or Few	Few to Several	Many
Lifespan	Short	Up to 1 Year	Long Term
Time and Budget	< $25,000	< $100,000	> $100,000

Figure 2-1 The project spectrum

This project spectrum, shown in **Figure 2-1**, considers several factors to help define the differences between projects. These include the following:

- Team size
- Dependencies, either external, internal, or based on technologies
- Project lifespan
- Time and budget considerations

You can consider this spectrum as a way to map out overall project complexity and see where your project exists on the overall spectrum. We'll be using this as a guide throughout this chapter.

Each category on the spectrum outlines typical values that would constitute smaller or larger projects. For example, a project that has a small team size could still have a large external technology dependency that should be considered when planning your project. Having a number of external dependencies can also affect communication with your client. Use this as a guide to help map out your project requirements.

In this chapter, we'll review a few points along the continuum line and give examples of each type of project. Just to note, the projects discussed here are generalizations and might not completely map to your projects; however, you can use these examples as guideposts to help identify issues or items that may apply to your own project.

SMALL PROJECTS

Let's start at the small end of the project spectrum (see **Figure 2-2**), with projects that can be completed with a rather quick turnaround from days to a few weeks. Projects such as advertising widgets, banner ads, or projects that have very focused uses may fall into this category. Also, maintenance projects or expansions of existing projects—such as adding incremental features to an product or application—would be included here.

LARGE PROJECTS IN DISGUISE

We have encountered several projects that were pitched as small projects, but when we reviewed all of the requirements and the creative work involved, we determined that they were much larger than expected.

When doing your initial review of the project size, just like a book, don't judge it by its cover, and don't build an estimate from a casual review. You should gather full project requirements that can be used to create accurate estimates and get your project planning off to a healthy and sustainable rate.

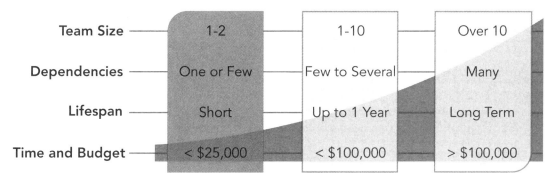

Figure 2-2 Characteristics of small projects along the project spectrum

Small projects typically require a handful of design and development resources. But some small projects can have large teams depending on the number of dependencies there are in the project, such as with advertising widgets where there are many stakeholders, contributors, and technological moving pieces.

Banner ads are one of the best examples of a small project. They typically have very limited feature sets, are physically small in dimension, are small in file size, and have a limited life span. Because of these characteristics, you will find that these projects don't require extensive architecture development or reusable frameworks; that is because once it is created, there are few instances where it will need to be modified or reused. They are developed, used, and then tossed away.

MEDIUM PROJECTS

Moving up the spectrum, medium-sized projects tend to have longer calendars for design and development, typically from a few weeks to several months (see **Figure 2-3**). Accordingly, the size of your design, development, and external stakeholder teams are larger—anywhere from a couple of people developing an individual project to teams of a dozen or more people working across companies or organizations in a larger company.

What you'll commonly find in medium-sized projects, along with the expanded feature set of the product itself, is that the project will live on beyond the initial release. Projects of this size have more attention placed on reusable architectures, modular design,

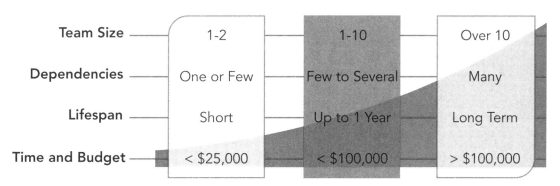

Figure 2-3 Characteristics of medium projects along the project spectrum

or support for administrative back-end interfaces to manage content. They also are built on existing company or external technologies such as content management systems, learning management systems, or existing databases. Because the product will have a longer life span, your project planning will need to consider not just the initial versions of the project but also the future directions the project will take. The future of the project will be an important consideration as you do your initial architecture to ensure that what you do today will efficiently scale to what is required tomorrow.

Typical projects in this category include content-managed Web sites, multistaged ad campaigns, promotional interactive Web sites, casual games, and desktop or browser-based applications. An example of a desktop application that was a medium-sized project to build is Adobe WorkflowLab.

The initial version of Adobe WorkflowLab took approximately two months to fully complete from concept to delivery. It was designed and developed by the authors of this book, so the internal team was rather small, but there were about a dozen or so external contributors or stakeholders who facilitated critical requirements of the project that were external to core design and development. In addition, it was known from the beginning that the project would expand and grow after the initial version, so during the planning process we mapped out features and noted where these features would most likely go in future versions. Also, when we designed and developed features for the

initial version, if we anticipated design or functional changes, we noted them but kept going with the original specification to keep on schedule and to ensure that the developers and designers understood how the feature would likely change in a future version.

LARGE PROJECTS

On the other end of the spectrum are large projects, which can typically take anywhere from several months to even several years (see **Figure 2-4**). These projects usually have a large core set of designers and developers who handle the creation of the project, which can have multiple delivery schedules planned out in long-term road maps.

Examples of large projects are the development of Adobe Buzzword and the rest of the Adobe Acrobat .com suite of online services. When you consider the internal development milestones required for development, setting up programs for prerelease testing by a private set of the general public, public betas, initial releases, and follow-up revisions and expansion, it clearly makes sense why these are large projects.

Other examples of large projects are Web sites or Web applications that have extensive technology dependencies that add to the overall complexity of the project, as well as projects that have mission-critical requirements that must have perfect execution and redundancy. An example of a large project could be

ADOBE WORKFLOWLAB

Adobe WorkflowLab is a desktop utility used for mapping out project workflows. In addition, WorkflowLab helps new designers and developers learn about best practices for using Adobe software and technology, resulting in better success with projects. This book will refer to WorkflowLab extensively and will map out workflows and best practices based on the WorkflowLab project model. Workflows from this book are also available as downloads from the book's Web site for use in WorkflowLab.

MEDIUM IN DESIGN OR MEDIUM IN DEVELOPMENT?

Medium projects tend to swing heavily on either the design or development side of the spectrum. When you are doing your initial review of a project, you should have stakeholders from both design and development at the table. Architects can miss an initial design assessment, and creative or art directors can miss technical complexity mostly because these areas don't match their expertise. So, be sure to have a balanced business development and project review team at your disposal.

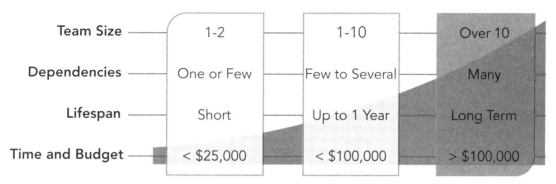

Team Size	1-2	1-10	Over 10
Dependencies	One or Few	Few to Several	Many
Lifespan	Short	Up to 1 Year	Long Term
Time and Budget	< $25,000	< $100,000	> $100,000

Figure 2-4 Characteristics of large projects along the project spectrum

---

THE WIZARD BEHIND THE CURTAIN

Sometimes we have undertaken projects that seem like relatively complex medium-sized projects, such as a consumer Web site or a collaborative educational application, but when we dug through the layers and discovered the sometimes scary technological dependences behind them, our medium project turned into a multiyear behemoth. Even if your team or company is working on only a portion of the overall project, it is critical that you have someone in your management team who understands all of the external dependencies for the project because if one of these external stakeholders is late or delivers a faulty or buggy deliverable, it can add risk of failure to your role on the project and can also cascade that risk to other projects in your pipeline. In this case, ignorance is certainly not bliss.

---

a Web site that combines inventory management, marketing, advertising, and other extensive amounts of business logic such as an automotive Web site with car configurators, used-car search engines, and other similar features. Mission-critical applications can include medical, legal, or government applications or enterprise dashboards for finance and banking. On the consumer side, examples include broadly used online services such as search engines, simultaneous multiuser applications, or video distribution services and applications.

One final characteristic that can make a seemingly medium-sized project into a large one is when you consider how the application will be distributed. If you are creating an online service or Web application that will be deployed on the browser, you most likely have a medium-sized project. If you want to distribute that to the desktop across operating systems and as a mobile application for multiple devices, you have

potentially moved up to a large project. In this book, we'll review how to understand and mitigate project scope changes based on delivery methods using the Flash Platform.

NOT ALL PROJECTS ARE THE SAME

As we mentioned in the introduction to this chapter, these project types are just guideposts for you to use when doing your initial review of your proposed projects. They don't fit all use cases, but the points outlined in this chapter will help you understand more of the behind-the-scenes complexity that your projects could potentially be hiding.

In the next chapter, we'll start introducing roles involved in the design and development process, and then we'll jump into the high-level steps that these roles will complete in a project.

CHAPTER 3

Understanding Roles in a Project

As the saying goes: "Use the right tool for the right job." When considering your interactive project or application, you need to have a similar mantra: "Use the right role for the right task." Roles on a project can cover several different disciplines or activities that are common on interactive projects.

A single person can have multiple roles on a project. This is common with small teams, especially for the solo "jack-of-all trades" that needs to do everything. Depending on the vastness of the project, you may find that roles can be specialized into more focused work or potentially outsourced to a subcontractor or external team.

This chapter will define the important roles on a team that is creating a Flash Platform project, and it will explain the disciplines underneath each role to help you match the "role" with the "task."

EXTERNAL ROLES

A couple of roles aren't necessarily part of the "core" team but are important to the success of your project and to your team. Even though clients and management don't take part in the daily design and development work, you need to be aware of these two important roles in any project.

Client

Every project has a client, even if that client is your own team or company. The client plays a key role in your project because they will help determine your project's success. It's important to recognize when the client should be involved in decisions and which decisions can be made without their involvement. The client's level of involvement will depend largely on your relationship with your client and your client's expectations.

Client communication is primarily the responsibility of the project manager. The project manager should be the main client contact to avoid overloading other team members with direct requests from the client that may not have been vetted by team leads or may cause scope creep or other project issues.

When you organize how your team will work and collaborate, always remember that the client has a role within this process. Be sure to stay appropriately transparent about the project status, updates, and other information, while using correct communication channels when collaborating with your client.

Management

Although not part of the project team, your department, organization, or company management will play a key role in your project. They are the decision makers who invest in the company infrastructure to help teams work better and more efficiently.

Management sometimes gets a bad reputation—they may be seen as "out of touch" or "ignorant" of the technology or tools that go into doing "actual work." But you need to remember what their role is: to ensure that the people under them are well equipped to do their jobs and to ensure that the company is profitable.

Management doesn't need to understand the technology that their teams are using, but they do need to know what it will take to make their team more efficient and productive. This can take many forms, for example, helping to remove obstacles in the company or process; making purchasing decisions about software, hardware, and services technology; and providing leadership and a plan for how the team can grow and overcome larger project challenges, allowing them to tackle bigger and more exciting projects. Finally, as the decision makers for budgets and resources, management should understand the amount of effort required to successfully complete projects and maintain a healthy and profitable business.

So, don't discredit your management team; just remember that they don't need to focus on the details of the project. If they did, they wouldn't be doing their jobs.

DESIGN AND DEVELOPMENT

The design and development roles on a project can take many different forms, and they can be very difficult to tease out. The roles of people who do design and development work can vary greatly based on their individual disciplines and other experience.

The following sections will introduce various design and development disciplines that are common in many projects for the Flash Platform. To assist in understanding the very multidisciplinary world of design and development, refer to the discipline map shown in **Figure 3-1**.

The discipline map is a circular grid of eight sections. Each section represents a discipline: four for design and four for development. Within each discipline, there are three levels of experience: low, medium, and high. We'll review each of the disciplines and then explain how the sections relate to one another.

Design

There are many types of design roles in a project, and they vary based on the type of project being made.

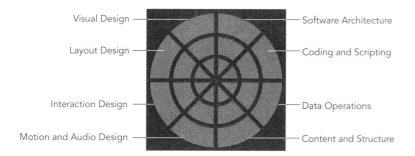

Figure 3-1 The discipline map

Visual design

For many projects, visual design is the most important design role on the project (**Figure 3-2**). The visual design creates the project's overall feel and look. One of the unique advantages of the Flash Platform is the amount of creative expression you can put into your project. Products such as Photoshop and Illustrator are primary tools for this discipline, giving visual designers the ability transform their creative visions into reality using tools for photography, illustration, painting, sketching, drawing, and compositing from numerous mixed media sources.

Figure 3-2 Visual design in the discipline map

Design elicits an emotional response. Finding and harnessing that emotion is done through visual design. Certain aspects of design, including color theory and typography, have psychological and sociological connections. Only through training and experience can a visual designer successfully connect what is being communicated to the desired emotional response.

Visual designers typically use a wide variety of tools. Products like Photoshop, Illustrator, Fireworks, and InDesign support specific design needs. Based on the visual designer's experience, his or her understanding of various design tools may vary. Some visual designers are extremely knowledgeable about Illustrator but not necessarily about Photoshop. For this reason, visual design is a very personal skill.

Layout design

Many people enter into the interactive world from the print side of design. For a variety of projects such as newspapers, annual reports, brochures, magazines, or books, the layout designer creates the flow in which the story unfolds (**Figure 3-3**). Good layout design is a learned skill that takes time to fully understand and get right. As the eyes of the consumer move from the printed page to the digital screen, the same principles of layout and story flow need to be present, but the method of execution changes.

Figure 3-3 Layout design in the discipline map

When telling a story or communicating an idea, the words, photographs, and illustrations are the heart of the idea. The story is enhanced by correct flow and positioning of illustrations and photography, and creative use of language.

The art of combining all of these together, and crafting your message in the tone or voice of your audience, is a difficult skill to master. To be successful, the design team needs to work closely and collaboratively with the visual designer.

Interaction design

With printed works, the reader's interaction with the product is with the physical page. An extreme example of this is a child's "pop-up" book, which is controlled through tabs, wheels, and inventive panels. When moving to the digital screen, the same story needs to be told. But the user interacts with the story much differently, and the software and technologies used to create the product need to rise to the challenge.

The emerging discipline of interaction design (**Figure 3-4**) is focused on the ways in which the user accesses and interacts with content. Some see this as the extension of layout design into the interactive world, in which the interface of the digital screen needs to have specific design considerations.

A consistent and predictable interface in a digital application will make it easier for the users to understand how the application is expected to behave.

Let's take, for example, Cover Flow, which is the animated, three-dimensional user interface in a number of software products. When Cover Flow was first introduced as an interactive element, it was new to many people. By making references to the physical world—showing items in a three-dimensional space and offering a scrollbar to move through that horizontal "shelf" of material—the user had a basis to successfully understand how to use Cover Flow. Cover Flow is now a known interactive behavior that your audience can understand. It shows us that user experience and interaction design can expand how people interface with content and applications.

Motion and audio design

With digital work, the user experiences more than just a still image. Motion, video, and sound all help tell a story and build two-way communication with the user. The production and creation of motion graphics, video, and audio are unique and valuable skills that can be added to the mix of design and development disciplines (**Figure 3-5**).

Styles of video can range from journalistic realism to artistic expression using a designer's combination of various skills and talents.

In almost any situation, audio can add significant value to an application. For example, a game that uses small sounds for button clicks and user interactions helps draw users into the experience. Choosing just the right audio for a project is both an art and a science.

Figure 3-4 Interaction design in the discipline map

Figure 3-5 Motion and audio design in the discipline map

Figure 3-6 Software architecture in the discipline map

Development

The other half of the creation process is the development of the behaviors, code, testing, and data.

Software architecture

The role of the architect (**Figure 3-6**) is to understand the project's various moving pieces and how they fit together. Just like an architect who designs a house, the software architect creates a bird's-eye view of the project, maps out each of the project's individual modules, and decides how the modules will work together.

In larger projects, the architect is especially crucial because the developers need to focus on their module (or specific section of the project) with assurance that someone is thinking of how their work will successfully integrate into the whole.

Development: Coding and scripting

When coding and scripting a project (**Figure 3-7**), the development resposibilities are typically separated into client-side and server-side tasks.

The client-side of development includes the publically exposed side of the project. The client developers typically build all of the things that the end user will see and do. These developers work with the project designers to transform the designers' ideas into real working interfaces.

The server-side of development consists of the non-consumer-facing pieces of the project. This includes how the application or project works with a database of dynamic content, works with other dependent technologies, or performs heavy-lifting processing and other plumbing of the project.

The client and server developers communicate with each other through the application program interface (API). This is an agreed-upon contract and model in which the server-side developers will provide hooks for the client-side developers to use in their project.

Data operations

Server-side developers typically work with someone who is a database administrator (DBA). DBAs are experts in working with, organizing, and structuring extensive amounts of data for fast and meaningful access (**Figure 3-8**).

Working with data involves more than setting up a database. It is a rigorous process of designing data structures for maximum speed and scalability for large projects. In addition, DBAs define how the server-side programmers will access the database contents through queries or by providing them information at regular intervals in a batch process.

Content and structure

The final discipline provides the structure and integration of the code (**Figure 3-9**). Integrating content into the code—whether it's text, images, audio, or interactive material—requires varying levels of sophistication based on the scope of the project.

For smaller-sized projects, this involves importing content and ensuring that it is in the proper form and file format, and of the appropriate size. For more

Figure 3-7 Coding and scripting in the discipline map

Figure 3-8 Data operations in the discipline map

Figure 3-9 Content and structure in the discipline map

advanced projects, sophisticated content management systems may be required to provide easier editing or content management without requiring additional development time.

Integrating content and providing structure to all of the content in your project is an important and sometimes overlooked role.

Putting the disciplines together

When looking at the various disciplines individually, as we have done here, it's easy to think that each discipline is independent of the other disciplines. In fact, the opposite is true. Every designer or developer has skills in some combination of all eight disciplines within and across design and development.

It is the unique combination of these disciplines—at various levels of sophistication and experience—that make each of us uniquely qualified to complete certain tasks and projects. To successfully complete your project, you must understand your own unique talents and those of each of your team members.

A single discipline map can visually demonstrate an individual's abilities in the eight disciplines. For example, **Figure 3-10** shows a discipline map for Doug Winnie, one of the authors of this book. In this map, the level of skill in each discipline is ranked as low, medium, high, or blank (meaning that he has no skill in that area). A lower level of skill is indicated on the inner circle, and a higher level of skill is indicated on the outer circle.

Looking at Doug's sample discipline map, we see that his strengths are interaction design and working with content and structure. While he has some experience working with data, we clearly wouldn't put him in charge of designing a large-scale database.

You can also apply discipline maps to tasks or aspects of a project, defining the roles that are required for successful completion. To make this easier, Adobe WorkflowLab lets you assign a discipline map to a workflow item or task to help keep track of the skills that are required to complete the project (**Figure 3-11**).

SUPPORT

In addition to the roles already discussed, other special roles help in creating a project and releasing it to the world. These are the quality assurance and build and release teams.

Quality assurance

No one is perfect, but your client and users will expect your project to be. To help meet this high expectation, a quality assurance or quality engineering team will ensure that any issues or problems with your application are reported to the designers or developers to fix and resolve.

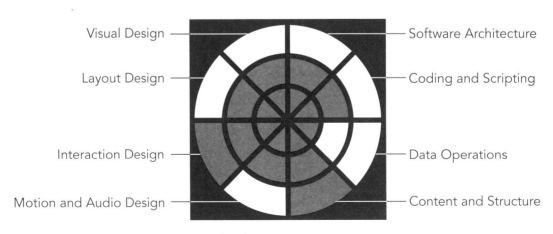

Figure 3-10 Sample combination of skills in a discipline map

Figure 3-11 Editing a discipline map in WorkflowLab

Quality engineers build a series of steps—based on collaboration with your team members and client—that define how the application should behave. If the results don't match the expectations, then that use case is logged as a *bug*. The bug is sent to the appropriate engineer or designer to resolve. Once fixed, the bug is reissued to the quality engineer for retesting.

Build and release

This specialized group of engineers work to combine code, design, and technology for testing by quality engineers or when the project is finished. Build and release deploys the project to the web server or as an application that can be installed on the user's computer.

Build and release engineers connect the potentially dozens or hundreds of modules, code, designs, and other technologies and integrate them into the final project. This work is often very complex. To be successful, it requires clear communication among all project contributors.

GETTING ROLES TO WORK TOGETHER

With any project, the number of different roles can make it difficult to know who is doing what. This is why clear communication among the team members and with the client is so important. When you need to resolve issues and successfully complete major project milestones, having clarity on ownership makes the process easier, collaborative, and streamlined.

Defining a method for collaboration

There are many different methods to definine how your team will work together to complete a project and solve critical problems. One of the methods used at some companies, including Adobe, is a model called a DACI.

DACI stands for "Driver, Approver, Contributor, and Informed." When a large milestone or outstanding question exists in a project, the DACI is used to identify roles for completing or resolving it. The following sections describe the roles of the DACI.

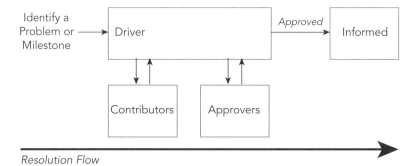

Figure 3-12
The flow of the DACI

Driver

The driver is usually a single person who is responsible for the ultimate resolution of the milestone or problem that needs to be completed. This person breaks down any communication barriers or problems that may prevent the completion of the project phase or issue resolution. This person also communicates the results of the resolution or completion of the project milestone.

Contributors

The contributors work with the driver to solve the problem or complete the milestone. These subject-matter experts come from the various areas of the project and work together to submit single or multiple proposals to a problem or to create the deliverable that is needed to complete the next stage of the project.

Approvers

The approvers are the stakeholders who have the authority to approve the proposed resolution or milestone. These can be managers or senior stakeholders who manage the teams and who make decisions that could change a team's process or approach to working together or completing certain tasks of a project.

Informed

The informed includes everyone who needs to know about the successful completion of a milestone or the resolution of a problem. When the DACI is complete, the result is sent to everyone who is in the informed category.

Using the DACI

The flow of the DACI (**Figure 3-12**) starts at the beginning of the next phase of a project or when someone identifies an issue. The driver is nominated to resolve the issue or complete the phase of the project. The driver then gathers the contributors to work on the situation and provides the approvers with a set of options or the completed milestone for approval. With the approvers' satisfaction, everyone who needs to be informed is contacted, and then the team moves on.

If the original proposal or milestone isn't approved, the flow goes back to the contributors to come up with a different resolution or to address any issues raised by the approvers. It is then resubmitted to the approvers to get their sign-off and wrap up the process.

When communicating the completion or resolution to the informed, it is also important to note who filled each role in the DACI, so everyone knows who was responsible for the resolution and who approved it. If there are issues later, you can look back at this and see whether additional or different people are required to better handle situations in the future.

CHAPTER 4

Defining Project Phases

Not every project is the same, but from a bird's-eye view, every project will consist of the same five phases: planning, design, development, build and release, and maintenance. This chapter will review the overall process at a high level. In subsequent parts of the book, we'll discuss each phase in more depth, including best practices for using Adobe software and technologies to facilitate the process.

Figure 4-1 shows the general workflow that we recommend for all your Flash Platform projects. Of course, the details and tasks that take place in each of these phases will vary based on the complexity and scope of your project, and we will cover those details in future chapters.

Figure 4-1
The overall workflow

As you can see, this process is fairly linear. The workflow covered in this book isn't focused on the methodology of the development process; instead, it's important to understand that each phase has a start and end, but certain ones take place concurrently with others. You may have heard people in the industry talk about iterative development models that aren't linear, such as Extreme Programming (XP), Agile, and others. The approach in this book consists of aspects of each of these methodologies and tells you how to facilitate them using Adobe tools, services, and technologies.

Now we'll discuss each section of the workflow in more detail and explore the goals that are associated with each of them.

PLANNING

During the planning phase of your project (**Figure 4-2**), you are defining what your project will require in order to be successful. This phase consists of several tasks, including constructing your project's high-level vision, determining the overall scope of your project, and, after analyzing the details of this scope, figuring out what type of resources you'll need in order to successfully complete the project based on a defined schedule.

Based on the scope of your project, the opinion of external stakeholders, or the requests of the client or customer, you may need to define specifically what the deliverables are going to be for the project.

Good planning goes beyond the initial scope of the project to help facilitate long-term vision. However, it's important to keep deadlines and budgets in mind when drafting the project's scope. During the planning process, it's a good idea to keep your client involved and allow them to become as much of an expert on the feature details as you and your team.

Ultimately, you need to ensure that your client, customer, team, and stakeholders know exactly what will define success for the project. There should be no doubt at the end of the planning process on what success means or the steps that will be taken to ensure that the project is successful.

As you may recall from earlier chapters, the workflow covered in this book involves planning throughout the entire workflow, as indicated in Figure 4-2. Consistently reevaluating your execution on the project and making planning adjustments are a core part of the methodology.

WHO'S WHO IN THE PLANNING PHASE

Generally, this phase involves the business development team, project managers, and design and development leads, who help provide implementation and resource details.

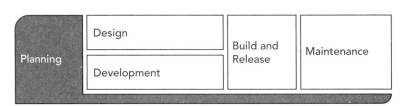

Figure 4-2
The planning phase

The chapters in Part II, "Planning," discuss this phase in more detail. We will discuss how a project can be taken from a simple idea and turned into a well-organized plan that can start your project on the road to success.

DESIGN

Most of the work that designers do involves putting their creative vision into words and attempting to communicate that vision as effectively as possible. Communicating something in words that is meant to stimulate all of the senses can be extremely difficult and time-consuming, but it's is also critical to the overall success of your project, especially when working with external development teams or vendors.

Each step of the design phase (see **Figure 4-3**) involves a creative process that evolves into a more detailed and granular expression of the overall project. This first starts with the creative brief that details the overall creative vision, theme, and objective of the visual design. Many times, the creative brief includes some user research to help back up the decision made on the vision, and it references other projects, clients, or competitors to help build a better understanding of what the project is going to do and, sometimes, what the project is meant to avoid.

Subsequent milestones for the design process can vary based on the complexity of your project and what

your overall role is. If you are doing a lot of the creative work yourself, you want to carefully guide your creative process so you can get valuable feedback from your client, without a significant amount of throwaway work. Developing wireframes and prototypes can improve the collaborative design process with your client and designer. These valuable steps give you the ability to experiment and interpret your project design requirements while in an isolated environment.

When in these collaborative and experimental phases, it is important to note that two types of design can be in play at the same time. The first is the overall visual design of the project. This is the overall creative expression using a surface as the stage. The other complementary design discipline is user experience (UX) design, which defines how the user can interact with that surface to get a deeper level of immersion with the creative experience. Many people see these two disciplines at odds, but they must be seen as complementary design requirements for your project—one to design the surface and the other to make that surface personal.

After you define the design requirements of the project, you then need to communicate this as thoroughly as possible to ensure that the production and development teams can implement and honor the approved design as seamlessly as possible. Creating style guides, design comps, and assets can take the question out of how to apply design to the project. It's almost impossible to accommodate all situations or use cases, but with experience, this process becomes more efficient and streamlined.

The chapters in Part III, "Design," cover this phase in more detail. We will discuss the Flash Platform tools that can make this design process easier and how to create detailed wireframes and design comps.

WHO'S WHO IN THE DESIGN PHASE

Generally, this phase involves the creative side of the team with oversight from design and project management, who also keep the development team informed.

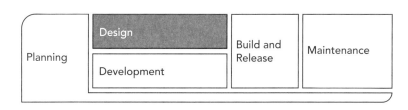

Figure 4-3
The design phase

DEVELOPMENT

Development starts with planning activities that give architects or lead developers the opportunity to examine and design a solid architecture that takes into account the feature set that was defined during the initial planning phase. This includes researching frameworks the project can leverage, syncing up with the server-side developers, and constructing the data schemas needed to communicate between the front-end and back-end applications. The outcome of this planning is to help provide feedback and detailed development estimates to the project management team so that they can construct a more precise project plan. Once you've planned the development, you can start the actual development of the product.

However, as you can see in **Figure 4-4**, development and design are parallel activities. This is because they continue to feed and consume each other in a symbiotic relationship. It is important as you continue through the development process that you are continually checking in with your design counterparts. This book refers to this as *syncing with your team* and the *designer and developer contract*.

Team sync includes regular meetings during the design and development phases to coordinate the parallel tasks at hand and to discuss the developer and designer contract. This contract is an informal guide on how to break up elements of an application or feature into small parts that can be defined by both design and code. This agreed-upon definition allows for a more seamless handoff when designs need to be integrated into the application code base.

The chapters in Part IV, "Development," cover this phase in more detail. We will discuss now to properly plan your development effort and how to successfully execute the construction of your application.

BUILD AND RELEASE

The build and release process (**Figure 4-5**) is broken down into four core aspects: development, testing, integrating, and distribution. The *development* aspect of the process is making sure that your development teams have a unified process for creating, managing, and verifying their content.

Testing is the process of making sure that the application your team is making behaves as intended and that no errors occur during normal (and ideally abnormal) use of the application.

WHO'S WHO IN THE DEVELOPMENT PHASE
Generally, this phase involves the programmers, database administrators, and software engineers of the team, with oversight from development leads and project management, who also keep the design team informed.

WHO'S WHO IN THE BUILD AND RELEASE PHASE
Generally, the build and release phase consists of team members responsible for testing and publishing versions of the project application for review and final release to the users.

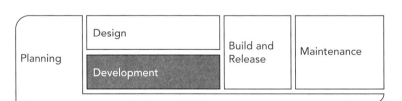

Figure 4-4
The development phase

Figure 4-5
The build and release phase

Integration is the process of bringing together different team members' (or roles') work into a unified application. This can include bringing the final design into the application, merging different developers' code, or integrating live data feeds from the back-end server team into the final application.

The final aspect of build and release is *distribution*, which is the process of making the final application available to the end user. This could be posting the application on your Web site or having the IT team push the desktop application across the network.

Trying to determine who exactly should be involved in build and release and what roles they take on depends on the size of the project, the structure of your team, the organization of your company, what other companies are involved (if there are any), and of course your client.

For larger projects, a dedicated staff, either internal or a third party, may handle all of the build and release roles. For smaller teams and projects, build and release roles may be assigned to your developers, designers, management, and even the client depending on your needs and requirements.

The chapters in Part V, "Build and Release," cover this phase in more detail. We will discuss what the build and release process entails and how your team can manage this process.

MAINTENANCE

Many projects, especially the medium-size to large ones, have long life spans that extend well beyond the first release of the application. Other projects, usually smaller ones, may not require any maintenance post-release. The maintenance phase (**Figure 4-6**) encompasses this post-release process and can include adding functionality, fixing newly discovered issues, or making changes to existing features to meet client, technology, and user needs.

Understanding what your client's and team's involvement will be after the initial release of your project is important so you can manage and prepare for this during the initial phases. Knowing that your client expects regular maintenance after launch will help guide your team in making critical design and development decisions up front so that you can enable faster and more reliable updates later.

WHO'S WHO IN THE MAINTENANCE PHASE

Generally, the maintenance phase can require your entire team or a subset of your team for new feature development, bug fixing, or other issues that may arise during the life span of the application.

Figure 4-6
The maintenance phase

Depending on the maintenance requirements and needs, you may need to dedicate your entire team for multiple release iterations. Each release may require its own planning, design, development, and build and release phases depending on the scope and needs of the update. Underestimating or not planning the maintenance process can easily make a previously successful project an unsuccessful one.

The chapter in Part VI, "Maintenance," covers this phase in more detail. We will discuss the maintenance process and how to plan for and manage the continued success of your project application until it is no longer required.

PART II.

PLANNING

CHAPTER 5

High-Level Vision and Team Organization

How many times have you been in the middle of the design or development of your project and wanted to slap yourself on the head and ask, "Why didn't we catch that already?" or "Why did we do it *this* way?"

Getting your Flash Platform project started on the right foot can be the most important part of ensuring a successful project. If you don't take the time to define your project goals in the beginning, then unexpected issues may crop up later. In this chapter, you'll learn the steps of successful high-level planning, how to define the boundaries of your project, how to get information about your end users, and how to set the stage for more detailed planning and feature definition for your design and development teams.

HIGH-LEVEL VISION

The beginning of any sized project should always start with defining the *high-level vision*—a brief synopsis of the project that defines the basic questions of who, what, how, why, and when. The high-level vision is the starting point for all planning, design, development, deployment, and maintenance phases of the project. It frames the project's bounds, starts the process of asking important questions, and allows you and your team to start defining goals that will lead to a successful project. It is also a building block for the project, one that you can use to verify that the project is on track and that it remains focused on its original goals.

If a client hires you or your team to develop a project, they may define the high-level vision for you, or defining the high-level may be you or your team's responsibility. Even if the high-level vision is already defined by the time you join in the process, it's important for you and everyone on the project to understand what a high-level vision is and why it can influence later phases of the process.

Who is the project targeting?

The first question that should be asked when defining a high-level vision is, "Who is this project for?" In other words, who is the client for the project? Is the client the end user, or does the client have its own set of users? Are you building an application for your company's internal team or business management? Or, are *you* the target audience of the final application?

If you or your team is building an application for a client, does the client know who their user base is yet? If not, then this is the time to start defining who the intended audience will be.

If the project is for your company, then it's critical to understand who exactly is going to use the final application because the intended users will become stakeholders later in the process.

If you are the end user, take a few minutes to write down why this is the right project for you. You may realize that the project benefits more people than you initially thought. For example, if you are creating a data visualization dashboard for your team, you may discover that other departments (or even other

clients) may need the same application because they are experiencing the same issues you are.

Many of the choices that are made later—such as the user interface layout, feature sets, deployment, and technology needs—are driven by the people who will end up using the project's deliverable. During this phase, it can be easy to assume that the intended audience is obvious, and it may be to you (or your client), but take the time to identify and write down the audience so that it is clearly defined up front. Later in the process, you can use user research (covered in more detail later in the chapter) to further define the project's target users.

What is the business problem?

The next question to ask is, "What is the business problem that the project is trying to solve?" A *business problem* is an issue that needs to be resolved. We use the term *business* loosely here, because what is trying to be resolved doesn't necessarily translate directly into a money or revenue source. A project always tries to solve one or more business problems; if not, then why should the time, money, and effort be spent on the project?

Even in projects that are not strictly business related, it's still important to define the problem being solved. For example, you may want to develop a free game that will be hosted on a Web site, yet there is an objective: to entertain. In this case, the business problem you are trying to solve is that there are bored people and your game will entertain them.

How should the problem be solved?

Now that you've defined what the business problem is, it's time to ask yourself (or the client), "How should the problem be solved, or how does the end user need to have the business problem solved?" You are not trying to define in detail how the problem should be solved at this point; the goal is to roughly sketch out what you (or the client) believe is the best way to solve it.

For example, if one of your business problems is that client orders are not being properly tracked, a possible solution is to build a custom tracking system using a Flash front end with a ColdFusion back end. From this starting point, you can define more business problems that arise from the current process and how you would like them solved via technology.

Coming up with proposed solutions to the problem is merely a starting point to inspire more thought and drive research to verify that the proposed solutions solve the defined business problem. Don't worry about being too specific, if you try to lock down the specific solutions at this stage, you will likely have too many open issues and assumptions.

Why should it be solved this way?

With the proposed solutions outlined, it's important to ask, "Why should the problems be solved this way?" Understanding why the proposed solution is the right one is just as important as understanding what the problem is. If the solution solves one problem but creates new issues, it's not really the best solution.

During this process, you should also look at whether the competition is solving the same problem and, if so, how they are solving it. If they're not solving it, then that is great validation to support why you need to solve the problem. If the competition is solving the issue, how can you improve on their solution? Has their solution created more problems than it has

solved? If so, how can you use this information to your advantage in your project planning and development processes?

When should it be solved?

Knowing when the project has to be done is critical to defining the project process. So ask yourself, "When should the problem be solved?" Is this a quick-turn-around, small-budget affair? Is this project locked to a set delivery date to meet marketing or business needs? Is this a mission-critical system that has to be right no matter how long it takes?

As with everything in the high-level vision, you don't need to have a set end date to complete the vision, but having a time range is important to structuring the overall process.

One thing to consider during this process is having *too* much time. Some of the most over-budget and problem-ridden projects have no time limit. Having some kind of timeframe for the project—even if it is an artificial deadline—can help structure a project and enable everyone to be in agreement as the project moves forward.

WHAT *ISN'T* A HIGH-LEVEL VISION?

When trying to define something, it can be helpful to discuss what a thing is not. Here are a few things that are definitely not a high-level vision:

- **Business plan:** A business plan is too broad to be used as a high-level vision. It can lead to a high-level vision, but it does not replace one.

- **Technical requirements:** Technical requirements that define technology/features should always follow a high-level vision, not the other way around.

- **Use cases:** Use cases are too detail oriented to be considered a high-level vision. These evolve from the high-level vision (and are covered later in this chapter).

- **Project plan/timeline:** Having a project plan is important, but a plan should never replace a high-level vision and should be developed later in the process.

- **User requests:** If a client comes to you with a bunch of requests from their user base, this does not mean they have a high-level vision.

- **A cocktail napkin:** A napkin is a great starting point for a high-level vision, but you need more information than late-night scribbles probably provide.

TEAM DEFINITION

Project discovery begins by reviewing the high-level vision—or what has been defined so far—and filling in the blanks as required. It is important to understand what the vision is for the project and how it is going to be applied across the rest of the project.

Defining stakeholders

During project discovery, you should define the initial stakeholders for the entire project by looking at the current vision and determining who needs to be involved. *Stakeholders* are the people, teams, departments, or companies that have a vested interest in the project's success. Some stakeholders may have only limited involvement, such as a legal department that needs to perform a review before the project is launched. Other stakeholders, such as the main client, may be involved with nearly every step of the project.

The following are a few common questions that should be asked to help define stakeholders:

- Who needs to be involved with the project, why and when?
- Who is developing the project?
- Who needs to review the project and why?
- When working with teams, who are the representatives of the teams?

Keep in mind that as projects move forward, the teams can change to involve other people, departments, divisions, or companies. When this kind of change occurs, you need to know who the new stakeholders are and how they are involved with the project.

Defining stakeholders doesn't have to be a long or formal process. The amount of time and effort spent on this step depends on the size of the project. For a small project, the stakeholders may be blatantly obvious, but as projects grow in scale, so does the number of people involved.

Once the stakeholders are defined for the project, it's time to bring them together for a kick-off meeting.

Determining team roles in the kick-off meeting

To start engaging stakeholders early in the project, hold a kick-off meeting with all members of the team. The goal of this meeting is to review the project's high-level vision and determine the roles and responsibilities of each of the stakeholders.

As reviewed in Chapter 3, you can break down the roles of a team into a number of categories including: Management, Project Management, Designer, Developer, and Quality Assurance. Each category is broken down into detailed roles depending on the project.

Depending on the size of your project, team members might be required to take on multiple roles. For example, if you are working independently on a small portfolio site for a photography client, then chances are you will be responsible for the project management, design (unless your client is handy with Photoshop), and development. In such a scenario, it might not be a bad idea to discuss the possibility of the client taking on the role of Quality Assurance. Since the client is the expert of the project's vision, they can fill this role quite well. Without a kick-off meeting, the client might not know that such a role exists or that they could fill the role.

For larger projects, team members typically have only one or two roles on the project. In the kick-off meeting, as the high-level vision is reviewed, a team member might make suggestions relating to roles and responsibilities. Based on the high-level vision's defined timeline (see "When should it be solved?" above), one team member might suggest that another member of the team could take on both the information architecture and user experience roles for the project.

Identifying gaps in roles within your team

One of the most important conclusions that can arise out of the kick-off meeting is that not all roles can be filled by the current set of team members. If this is the case, now is the perfect time to start the search for talent who can fulfill the newly defined roles.

Defining roles throughout the project

The roles and team members you have identified in the kick-off meeting are not set in stone. As you work through the rest of the planning phase, you will discover additional resources that will need to be added to the team, both internal and external. It is important to involve these new resources as soon as possible and give them the same high-level overview of the project that you gave the initial set of team members during the kick-off meeting.

SCOPE REVIEW AND DEFINITION

Before you go any further with your project, you need to have a better understanding of what exactly is the project requires. The size, sophistication, and magnitude of your project is called your project's *scope*. Defining scope will help you in multiple ways.

To start, you will need to know whether you are adequately staffed to deliver on the project and will rely on the definition of your scope to assist in finding the right people to build out your team.

To define your project's scope, involve the individuals on your team who have the broadest understanding of what is needed to complete a project. For larger teams, this usually translates to the project lead, technical architect, art director, or other designated leader in a discipline. For individuals working alone, it is often helpful to enlist the assistance of peers or the community either directly or indirectly to get important information necessary to build your project's scope.

When identifying the scope of your project, there are a number of scope categories to consider. Planning your project requires some level of comfort with unanswered questions and ambiguity. Over the course of the planning process, you'll be able to address these questions and gaps to the best of your ability, and then you can begin the creation of the project.

Understanding constraints

Every project has constraints that individually and collectively determine the overall scope and sophistication of the project.

Sometimes the word *constraints* has a negative connotation. Although constraints do put limits on projects, overcoming them has led to innovations that have inspired completely new product lines or industries. Constraints may be limitations by definition but aren't limitations on the opportunities that can come out of the project. Working successfully within the constraints and respecting them is the best way to enter into a project.

Some basic constraints are common for almost every project. This section will review each of them and how they are applied to your project.

Budget

All projects have a finite amount of money that can be spent on resources and equipment, but budgets come in different forms. Sometimes you have one lump sum of money that is available for an entire project, and how it's spent over the course of the project isn't important. Other times your budget will be tied to specific phases or milestones, and you won't have the entire sum of money available throughout the project. Or you may find that you can't spend tons of money on new artwork or on tons of people to help out, so you need to find ways to make do with less in certain areas or phases.

How ever your budget is structured, your budgetary limitations will need to be considered in determining the scope of your project.

Time

The next most common project constraint is time. Most projects have an end date. But schedules can take different forms, and sometimes aren't determined by the project at all.

The schedule and budget are often linked, meaning that the budget is calculated based on the duration of time the project will take, or vice versa. In project management terms, these two constraints have a symbiotic relationship. If you have a specific project or scope, when you constrict budget you'll often need to adjust the schedule accordingly.

For many projects, the schedule can be determined by another project in the company. For example, if you are creating a Web site for a restaurant, the project may be linked to the opening of the restaurant and can't be delayed. As we mentioned in the "Budget" section, the funds that are available may be linked to specific points in the fiscal year that can be applied to the schedule or due date for the project.

You may also find that a project will have multiple due dates or milestones. As projects get larger and have more phases or moving pieces, each of these phases may have specific dates associated with them. For example, your contract with your client or customer might require that specific milestones be met by certain dates. This reduces the perceived risk to the client, because the client knows that they'll have the opportunity to review the work at each milestone and make adjustments if necessary.

Building these milestones or checkpoints into your project schedule can help you build a relationship with your client. It puts the client at ease and makes it easier to complete sections of the project in a logical order. It helps to avoid an "all-or-nothing" approach when you embark on larger or more sophisticated projects. And having defined sections of a project helps with estimating because you can separate the project into each section or phase to identify costs.

Sometimes projects can have too *much* time. These projects may have a release date to submit for consideration on getting venture capital or other similar processes. For projects of this type, getting it right is more important than getting it done on time. At times, though, projects can enter into what is known as the *perpetual beta*, meaning that they never seem to get released and are plagued with growing levels of features without a set limit. Although new projects might not want to have a forced date set on them, there should be some well understood level of "release status" that can signify when the project is done and serve as a goal for the team.

Team and experience

At times, your team's experience (or lack thereof) can create constraints for your project. Each of us has a level of experience that allows us to tackle projects of a certain scale. Your team may not be up to the challenge of a very large-scale project or a project using certain technologies or frameworks. For example, if your team is unfamiliar with a particular technology that's required for a project, your ability to deliver will be limited unless your budget permits you to acquire additional people with the required skills. It's important to understand what each person on your team can do. Otherwise, you may need to find new individuals to help out at an increased cost that might not have been originally included in the budget.

Other client needs

Finally, clients will have their own needs and constraints that they will apply to the project. These can include limitations based on their target customer, their ability to deliver materials of a certain type, or their own sophistication as a company or team.

Conducting user research

When creating any type of interactive content or application, you must understand what the user wants or needs the software to do. More often than not, the client for whom you are building the software will not be the actual end user of the application. Accepting a client's assessment of what the user wants can sometimes lead to disastrous results. Does the client really know what the customer wants, or are they working based on an assumption?

The best way to ensure that your application is well-suited to your users is to simply ask them. Gathering user feedback is not a difficult task; you just need to know how to get honest feedback that you can use in your project. When gathering feedback, you need to think about how your users use similar applications or technologies.

The type of feedback you should solicit depends upon the size of your user group. If you are working with a small group of people, it's important to get qualitative feedback that will give you more detailed information. If, however, you are working with a larger group of people, it is better to get quantitative feedback that can make it easier to compare different groups of people. This is especially true if you don't have the time to sort through hundreds (or even thousands) of free-form responses.

The most important aspect of gathering feedback is to keep your questions neutral and not to slant your questions toward a desired answer. If you ask a question that prompts for an implementation to a specific user interface, you aren't asking the user for honest feedback. Instead, your question prompts the user to validate a decision that was based on an assumption and not on direct information.

Gathering user feedback is critical to every project. You should continue to solicit feedback at different stages throughout the development process. In the early planning stages, it is important to get a sense of what type of customer your user is. In later stages, you may ask your customer for more specific feedback on your application's design or other features, or ask for feedback based on the user's level of understanding of how to use an interface for an application.

Finally, if you have money available or have some time to mine the Internet, you can find tons of data and user research reports that are available for purchase or download to help jump start your project. These can give you details on industry-wide customer trends or behaviors that can be valuable to initial planning. Also, some companies specialize in user research and can be contracted to find objective customer feedback that you can use for your planning.

Creating use cases

What is the most basic activity of any project? A user will use your application to do something. Beginning with this concept, you can start to define the features of your project by defining items such as the user interface, design, content, technology, data, and so on.

Defining what the user can do in your application—or more specifically, what they can accomplish—is how you define the *use cases* of your project. Use cases describe a system from the user's point of view. In their simplest form, use cases outline the steps a user will take to accomplish his or her goal. For example, even a simple action—such as filling the gas tank of a car—requires that certain exact steps be followed: open the gas cap, remove the gas hose, push the lever to get gas flowing, and so on. The same idea applies to building a complex application or website.

You need to define exactly what the user will do to complete seemingly simple tasks. These are use cases.

1. When you create use cases, assume that you know nothing about the process or system you are creating, and try to find where you made assumptions about the intended users' knowledge. We all assume things when we initially give instructions. Sometimes we think that certain steps are common sense, and other times we lump them in with other steps or completely forget them altogether. Use cases can fail when we assume that all users will make the same assumptions that we did.

2. When you are building your project, you may have dozens of use cases or actions that the user can perform. The process of creating use cases can help you identify the priorities of your project and give you added perspective for your planning. In addition, as you continue to build your application, you will encounter use cases that haven't been identified and need to be added into the mix with the others.

3. Use cases give your project added context and details around what the users will actually accomplish, and give your team the ability to prioritize and embark on development with a greater understanding of what you are making. These use cases will be the first step in determining the feature set of the application, which is discussed in the next section.

FEATURE SET DEFINITION

A *feature set* is a breakdown of all of the "moving pieces" that will make up your product. The goal is to deconstruct the use cases and high-level vision into individual actionable items that together will achieve an end goal. By breaking down a larger problem into manageable pieces, the project team and client can gain a more detailed vision of the how, what, and when of the product.

To achieve better transparency across the team, at least one representative from each role of the project should be involved in defining the product's features. For example, even if the Quality Assurance person is not directly involved in the project until the QA/build and release phase, his or her understanding and involvement during the features definition phase will allow QA to better understand what they are testing. Also, QA's input may help other roles—such as Project Management—to understand the magnitude of a feature from everyone's standpoint and to assist in developing a more accurate estimate for all of the features.

It's also valuable to engage your client in some critical phases of this process. Involving the client will give them a better understanding of the project's execution and will bring added context to your communications. As a result, your client will become an expert on the product's end goals.

Feature breakdown

When you're first exploring features for the final application, explore beyond existing constraints such as project scope or technology. Allow the project team to brainstorm and build a solid yet creative list of potential features. The list, when complete, should contain all required features and some that might not have been initially obvious to the team or to your client. Not all of the proposed features will make it into the final set, but some features that were not originally considered key may be included in the final list.

Let's take an online video game e-commerce site as an example. Starting from the top, the team identifies features such as login. From there, the team goes further and identifies password recovery as a feature that supports the login process. During the initial brainstorming session, one team member who had recently issued a password recovery on another Web site noticed the site used a CAPTCHA to help keep bots from attempting to steal passwords. A CAPTCHA is a technique for providing a hand-shake between the user and the system to prevent bots from stealing or spamming the system. This team member suggests that the login and password recovery features use a similar system. The team likes the idea and adds it as a subfeature of both login and sign up.

This process will continue until the feature list meets all the requirements of the product scope. If you find that a feature is broken down even further into technical features such as database tables, it is good to stop there; otherwise, the team could make this the focus during the specification process, which we cover in Chapter 6.

TIP ◾ Mind mapping is a great exercise to facilitate feature brainstorming. With mind mapping you start with the overall goal of the product and related key features. Each key feature can be broken down even further into smaller and smaller chunks. The process can be done on a whiteboard allowing for team interaction and collaboration.

Prioritization and dependencies

Once you feel comfortable with your feature set, it is time to identify each feature's importance in the overall product scope. Certain features are required to make the product meet the end goal, while others are simply "nice-to-have."

Working off the brainstorming session, the team can begin to rank each feature as related to overall importance. Organizing features into priority groups is a good way to categorize features based on their importance. The grouping can be as detailed as the project requires. In its simplest form, you can group features into three categories: "must-have," "opportunity," and "nice-to-have." Each feature should be grouped into one of these categories. For example, sign up and login would be ranked as a "must-have" features, while the CAPTCHA feature would fall into the "nice-to-have" category since it is not required to make the product meet the end goal.

During the prioritization process, dependencies between features should be identified and documented in the feature set. As dependencies are identified, you may want to reorder previously set priorities—a feature marked with higher importance should not depend on one with a lower priority. If you find such a case, you should reprioritize one of the features so that the required feature is in the same or higher priority group.

Initial estimates and next steps

Once you have a completed feature set, the team can provide an initial time and/or cost estimate for each identified feature. Because a lot of the technical details have not yet been defined, the estimate can be a range instead of a single value. The estimation is only a starting point for a true evaluation of the project's scope, but once complete, it can provide a reality check to make sure the project is on track to meet the high-level vision's time and resource constraints.

Based on their individual roles, the team members should produce initial estimates for all of the features. For example, the design team will estimate the effort to produce items such as wireframes, style guides, and comps for each of the user interface features. Development will do the same, taking into account tasks such as technical architecture.

Once each estimate is complete, the project manger should combine the estimates. With a summation for each task, the team and client can gain a clearer vision of what features can be delivered to meet the constraints currently set for the project.

As the team moves forward in the planning phase and beyond, features will be adjusted based on new requirements. Some features will become more important and reprioritized, and others will be identified as new. Don't be afraid to revisit the feature set as your project scope and requirements mature.

BUZZWORD

Feature prioritization is a collaborative effort between the team and the client. You can use a tool, such as Acrobat.com's Buzzword, to create a sharable document that can be used to facilitate communication among the team. Once the team has prioritized the initial set of features, team members can add comments or rework features based on their understanding of the project. With version control, this tool can be helpful for team collaboration. Using Buzzword will make team integration more seamless as the team moves into discovery and commitment, discussed in Chapter 6, and the design and development phases discussed in Chapters 8, 9, 10, and 11.

SUMMARY CHECKLIST

At the end of this stage of the project, you should be able to answer the following questions:

- ✔ Do you have a high-level vision for your project, and does it answer the questions of who, what, how, why, and when?
- ✔ Do you know who your project stakeholders are, and have they been involved in your kick-off meeting?
- ✔ Who are your team members, and what are their roles? Do your team members know what their roles are?
- ✔ Are there role gaps in your team? If so, have you begun to fill those gaps through recruiting or other means?
- ✔ Can you articulate the scope of your project?
- ✔ What are the constraints of your project, including schedule, budget, team, and client limitations?
- ✔ Can you clearly define who your users are, what their challenges are, and how they would want those challenges to be solved?
- ✔ Do you have use cases defined that outline the steps to complete the solution that your project is delivering?
- ✔ Has your initial project feature set been defined and prioritized and shared with your client?
- ✔ Based on the feature set, have initial estimates been defined for each feature and for each role involved and shared with your client?

CHAPTER 6

Setting Expectations for Your Project

In Chapter 5, we discussed a project's initial planning stages and the importance of having a high-level vision, which leads to creating an initial feature set. The next step is to identify what exactly you are going to build.

This chapter covers the development of a feature specification, which expands your initial feature set by breaking down each feature into its requirements. You will learn about team discovery and why establishing a contract between the design and development teams is important to your project's success. And we'll discuss creating a project plan to schedule key aspects of the project, including individual tasks, dependencies, milestones, and the project's completion. Throughout the chapter we will illustrate Adobe Flash Platform tools and services that can facilitate team collaboration and discipline workflows.

BUILDING A PROJECT'S SPECIFICATION

A project's specification starts with the process of breaking down desired features into smaller behavioral chunks that explain exactly how each feature should operate, based on a set of use cases.

Developing a specification is an important step in your project planning, which will lead your team to a more efficient development and design process. A specification gives your team a model to which they can add other information as needed—for example, when gaps or other issues are discovered through the iterative design and development process. Having a strong specification helps reduce the risk of having to significantly redesign the user interface or refactor the code and functionality later in the process.

As you break down your desired features into functional units, you will discover where your features intersect. Understanding these dependencies up front helps you identify how each feature will behave related to other features in the overall application.

Getting your team involved

Developing a specification is not a task for a single role on your project team. At the very least, a member of each project role should contribute to the specification. The project manager is likely going to lead the process, but input from the lead developer, designer, and QA is ideal. Each contributor provides input from a unique disciplinary standpoint and with unique knowledge and experience. For example, a developer may catch missed functionality, such as a login

---

MEDIUM AND LARGE PROJECTS: THINK OF THE FUTURE

If your project contains multiple phases, it's a good idea to create a specification that covers as far into the future as possible, even if all of the features are not required for a particular phase of the project. A long-range specification helps developers create an application architecture that will make it easier to integrate future features.

---

needing to provide error messaging when a user fails to log in or when an account has expired. A project manager may overlook this kind of detail because he or she may not be familiar with the underlying process required for logging into the system (unless you are a one-person shop).

When the specification is complete, give all team members adequate time to review the document. Each member will benefit from seeing the detailed explanations of each feature to better understand how it may impact their specific responsibility in the project. Going forward, the document will be used as a guideline for team members as they complete their tasks. For a development team that practices test-driven development (TDD), the specification will be an invaluable resource when developers create unit tests for each of a feature's behaviors.

Exploring the types of specifications

The size of the project, the size of your project team, and the complexity of the problems you are trying to solve are all factors that can help determine which form your specification will take. A team does not have to choose only one of the following types. On some projects you may need to provide multiple documents to explain the project features.

- **Simple feature overview.** For smaller projects, a simple feature overview will most likely be sufficient. The goal of the simple feature overview is to build a list of features and their behaviors. The team first breaks the project down into features and then provides a single paragraph describing each feature functionality in a little more detail. Although this approach provides a detailed summary of each feature, for more complex features it might be too restrictive to accurately capture the essence of the behavior.

- **Multipage in-depth feature overview.** With complex and large projects that require a large project team, a multipage in-depth feature document not only provides a detailed summary of each feature (like the simple feature overview) but also breaks down each feature into detailed use cases and the resulting behavior. The result is a document that covers all of the possible behaviors of a feature. With this approach, developers and designers have all of the information they need to develop a feature without guessing how the feature should behave in a particular use case.

- **Visual sketches.** With rich user interface projects, specifications can also be presented or enhanced using sketches. For each feature, one or more quick sketches can be made for each of the feature's behaviors. The sketches can be done using a pencil and some paper (a technique that is popular in agile design) or using a visual tool such as Adobe Fireworks or Flash Catalyst. Both of those tools provide quick ways to sketch designs, and even add quick behavioral functionality to turn your sketches into basic prototypes.

- **Annotated wireframes.** Wireframes are a way to visually represent a skeleton layout of an application's user interface, as well as the presentation, flow, and orientation of content. Wireframes are usually created after a specification has been completed. In some situations, however, wireframes can act as the detailed specification of the project.

  When information architects or user experience designers create wireframes, they can provide annotations that mark a specific feature behavior in the right or left gutter of the wireframe. This visual and textual representation gives designers and developers a visual way to explore how a feature behaves.

  In many larger projects, annotated wireframes are a second stage of the specification process, based on a large document such as the multipage in-depth feature overview specification. We will explore wireframes in Chapter 8, "Planning Design."

Creating a specification using Adobe Buzzword

A variety of tools are available to help create your specification. If you are creating a simple feature overview or multipage in-depth feature overview, a document tool such as Adobe Buzzword can be a great asset

> ### TEST-DRIVEN DEVELOPMENT: FLASH BUILDER AND FLEX UNIT
>
> *Test-driven development* is a process of writing unit tests prior to actual development. A *unit test* is an automated test that verifies a specification of a feature. Flash Builder 4 Premium comes with FlexUnit 4, a testing suite that allows developer and QA engineers to develop automated tests cases and run those tests for verification as the application code base matures all from within Flash Builder. See Part V of this book, "Build and Release," for more information.

to allow for collaboration across the project team and with the client. Adobe Buzzword is a web-based word processing application that is part of the CS Live services bundle that comes with every edition of Creative Suite 5 (see **Figure 6-1**).

On larger project teams, feature specifications are often constructed by multiple team members. Using Buzzword, team members can coauthor a document and work on it simultaneously. In addition, you can assign unique editing roles that can restrict access to the document—to allow only commenting or to disable contributions entirely, for example. These roles can be adjusted, granted, or removed at any time.

With CS Live, feature specifications created in Buzzword can be integrated into other phases of the project. Within InDesign, designers can gain access to any Buzzword documents available with their Acrobat.com account and place and link that content into their design files. This can become extremely valuable when a designer is creating annotated wireframes that reference the specification.

When a Buzzword document is linked into an InDesign file, users are notified via the Links panel when the original document has been updated (see **Figure 6-2**). Documents can be re-synchronized and updated into the wireframes. After updating, the new text from the Buzzword document will repopulate the area designated for the document. This CS Live workflow is an easy way to keep wireframes in sync with the latest specifications.

Figure 6-1 Feature specification built using Adobe Buzzword.

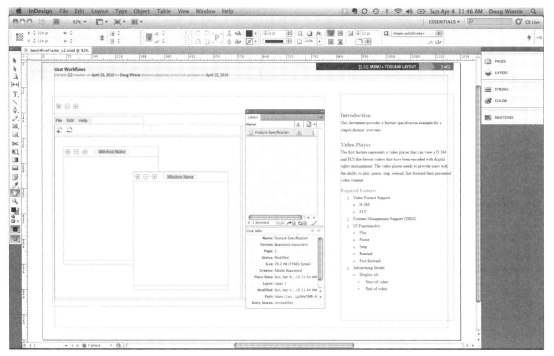

Figure 6-2 InDesign wireframe with Links panel showing updates available for placed Buzzword document.

DISCOVERING TEAM ROLES

When a specification is complete, it will act as a guide for each project role. The designer or design team will refer to the specification to help ensure that all feature functionality and behavior is covered when building the user interface, information architecture, or wireframes. Developers will use the specification to help construct the technical requirements of the application and determine the appropriate application architecture, code libraries, and existing frameworks. Quality Assurance, when developing test plans, will reference the specification as a checklist to ensure that each feature detail is verified in a test case.

The steps that each project role will follow in planning for the design, development, and build and release phases of the project will be discussed in detail in Chapters 8, 10, and 12.

Creating a contract between design and development

As the design and development teams create their materials and deliverables, it's important to establish a common touch point between the two disciplines. When building an application using the Flash Platform, designers and developers have the opportunity to break the old paradigm of "throw it over the fence" and establish a direct correlation between each group's work.

Specifically with Flex 4, developers or designers no longer have to break down creative assets such as Adobe Photoshop or Adobe Illustrator files into sliced

> ### THROW IT OVER THE FENCE
>
> This phrase is often used to describe a disconnected handoff process in which designs are delivered to the development team. In most projects, design assets will be converted into other types of assets in order to integrate them into the application code base. At this point, the original creative source files are no longer connected to the project. This disconnect results in a more complex process of updating graphics, layout, or other look-and-feel aspects of the application.

bitmap assets such as JPEGs, GIFs, or PNGs. With Flash Catalyst, a designer's creative assets can now be directly translated into Flex code converting layers, groups, and assets into MXML.

When wireframes have been completed (see Chapter 8 for more information on wireframing), the information architecture and layout of the application's interface is near completion. This means all assets of the elements have been designed to meet the project's functional specification. At this point, to ensure a cohesive integration of designs into the application, developers and designers should establish a component contract.

The contract isn't a formal document, but is an important agreement between both disciplines. The contract breaks down a user interface (via the

> ### FLEX 4: COMPONENT ARCHITECTURE
>
> Flex 4 has reengineered its component architecture to externalize the view from the logic of a component. Each component consists of two files: a skin file and a logic file. The skin file is linked to the logic file via a Cascade Style Sheets (CSS) property called skinClass. The skin contains the component's look and feel—border colors, font styles, and backgrounds, for example—and defines behaviors such as transitions and effects. Now that skin files are decoupled from the logic and linked via CSS, multiple designs can be created per component by creating additional linked skins.
>
> A component's logic file consists of the business logic necessary to fulfill the full requirements defined by the functional specification. The logic file will contain the code necessary to communicate with other components or the application as a whole.

wireframe) into individual distinct pieces. Each piece, which in Flex is called a *component*, will consist of parts and states. Parts are the various entities that make up a component. For example, in a video player, parts would include the play, pause, and stop buttons; the progress bar; and the display area that actually shows the video. In some cases a part can be another component with its own unique parts. In the video player example, a button is a built-in component available in Flex.

The states of a component are the various views a component can display based on each functional use case. In the case of a video player, the possible states would include a view that shows the video player when a video is paused and another when a video is not available.

NOTE ■ In Flash Catalyst, when you select a prebuilt component (such as a Horizontal Scrollbar), Flash Catalyst will show you the various states and parts available for that component (see **Figure 6-3**). When artwork is converted into a multipart component like the scrollbar, you will be prompted to identify which pieces of artwork will make up each component part.

When the contract has been established, design and development can begin constructing the component in parallel. The developer can begin to code the logic of the component, paying close attention to the component contract as they build out the component's business logic. Designers will begin their creative

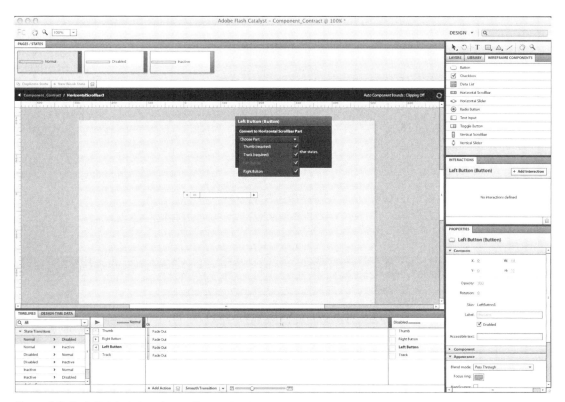

Figure 6-3 Flash Catalyst view of a scrollbar contract.

development of the component skin inside their favorite Creative Suite 5 application. As a component is designed, a designer needs to adhere to the component contract creating layers and assets that meet the needs of each of the component parts and states. In Chapters 8 and 10 we will focus in greater detail on the component contract in terms of each discipline (design and development).

For projects that are created using Flash Professional CS5, there isn't the Flex 4 component structure to work with. Instead, you will need to define more organically the elements and functionality of each functional part of the project. In place of components such as buttons, scrollbars, or data lists, you will have movie clips and graphical objects. In this case, your contract between design and development will carefully define the application's major functional pieces based on the technology and then define how designs will be created and imported to fulfill the start of the project and to help facilitate changes in both logic and design later in the project's cycle.

DEVELOPING A PROJECT PLAN

No matter the size of your project, it's always a good idea to construct a project plan to detail tasks, milestones, deliverables, and resources needed to execute your project. A project plan helps teams map project tasks across a given time period. Some tasks will be dependent on others, causing the dependent task to be delayed until the initial task has been completed. It's important to mark those dependencies so that a team can schedule appropriately. The project plan will tell your project manager and team what can feasibly be finished by a certain date, and it can determine when a project can be complete based on estimates on each task. If your project has a hard delivery date (such as meeting a marketing campaign launch), a project plan can help illustrate how far the project has been overscoped.

Overview of project plans

Project plans are very visual and easy to interpret, making them a good piece of data to share with clients.

When you illustrate on a calendar or in a spreadsheet how much work needs to be done to meet the project's feature list, your client can better understand the intricacies of the project, and may be willing to cut features if a deadline is in jeopardy.

Project plans can be developed in various ways and in phases. An initial project plan can be created once each team gives their estimates based on the initial feature set we discussed in Chapter 5, "High-Level Vision and Team Organization." This high-level project plan can cover both the initial estimate for each feature per phase (design, development, and build and release) and also cover planning tasks needed by each team role, such as developing the feature specification, wireframes, necessary prototypes, application architecture, reviews, test plans, and test cases.

When laying out the project plan, dependencies should be noted and illustrated. Wireframing, prototypes, application architecture, test plans, and test cases all cannot begin until the specification has been finalized. Therefore, the project plan should create start dates for these tasks dependent on the end date of the specification. By staggering tasks based on dependencies, a project's timeline will be established.

Project plan formats and tools

Project plans can be constructed in many different ways and with a variety of tools. The two formats we will discuss are *project timelines* and *task breakdowns*. Each format covers the same amount of information and provides the flexibility to adjust your project plan's details based on your needs.

Project timelines

Project timelines are a visual tool that allows project teams to lay out individual tasks or task groups across a horizontal timeline. Each task can be placed on the timeline showing its start and end time based on task dependencies and resource availability.

For example, although Adobe WorkflowLab was created to help illustrate workflows that utilized Adobe technologies to solve a common technical challenge, it has many features that allow it to be used as a basic project planning tool (see **Figure 6-4**). This

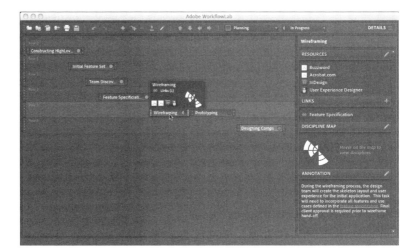

Figure 6-4 Project plan built using WorkflowLab.

free tool gives project teams an easy-to-use solution to build visual and detailed project plans. Specifically, you can create and group project tasks into categories denoting project phases or based on team roles such as design, development, quality assurance, project management, and others. With up to ten categories, all of your project roles should be covered.

In Chapter 3, "Understanding Roles in a Project," we described a designer and developer discipline map that helped illustrate what roles were involved in a particular task. WorkflowLab provides a similar discipline map that allows you to define a set of disciplines required to complete a given task. As the project matures, tasks can be marked with status updates to show progress and to highlight whether a task is "at risk" or has "failed."

Tasks can also link to internal or external assets such as PDFs, Photoshop, Illustrator, or Acrobat. com files. Team members can easily identify material necessary to complete a given task or can easily gain access to deliverables from a previous task. Using WorkflowLab, a team's project plan can mature as the project matures.

Task breakdowns

Another approach that can complement a timeline is to construct a vertical list of tasks grouped by categories or project phases. For each task, list a name, a description, a start and end date, a phase, and the resources dedicated to the completing the task.

Acrobat.com provides an online collaborative spreadsheet application called Tables that can be used to create your task breakdown project plan (see **Figure 6-5**). Tables provides all the functionality you would expect in a spreadsheet application, such as rows/columns (with sorting, filtering, and so on), formulas, and export options (to .pdf, .xls, or .cvs).

With online collaboration, your project plan can easily be shared with team members and the client. Tables allows multiple authors to work on the document simultaneously. When sharing, authors can assign various roles to individuals. "Co-author" or "Contributor" team members can modify the spreadsheet, provide comments, or view updates from other users in real time. As a "Reader," an individual can only view, sort, and filter the spreadsheet, which makes the role ideal for sharing with a client (see **Figure 6-6**).

Figure 6-5 Project plan built using Acrobat.com's Tables.

Figure 6-6 Project plan built using Acrobat.com's Tables shared with reviewer with "Reader" rights.

SUMMARY CHECKLIST

Understanding exactly what you are going to build and how you plan on building it is an important step toward a successful project. Before we move forward and review the overall project's scope and gain approval, let's review our checklist:

✔ Has the project team collaborated in the creation of a feature specification?

✔ Has the team been given adequate time to review the project's feature specification and provide feedback?

✔ Has the feature specification been shared with and approved by the client?

✔ Can the project team easily access the feature specification as a guide to accomplish their individual tasks going forward?

✔ Has adequate time been given to each of your project roles to accomplish their individual planning tasks?

✔ Have the design and development teams collaborated on a component contract?

✔ Have you formulated a project plan that provides a good estimate of the project schedule?

✔ Have you established a set of project milestones and a possible end date?

CHAPTER 7

Tuning and Adjusting for Success

B efore your team begins constructing your product or application, do a final review of your project plan to ensure that your team's goals are in line with the project's requirements.

At this point, your team has begun or completed their individual planning tasks based on the details of your project specification. As a result of each team's planning, team members will most likely have comments and concerns related to the project as a whole. In the preceeding chapters, we discussed what you are planning to build, not *how* you will build it. In this chapter, we will provide some guidance into what Flash Platform technologies you can leverage based on your project needs. Lastly, we will discuss the two types of workflows a project can follow during the design and development process.

CHOOSING THE RIGHT TECHNOLOGIES AND TOOLS

At this point in your project, your team probably has a good idea of what technologies you plan to use. Because this book focuses on the Adobe Flash Platform, we will assume you have decided to build your project for Flash Player or AIR for the browser, mobile device, or desktop. But deciding to go with Flash or AIR is only one of the many decisions you will need to make in choosing your tools.

In this section, we will help you answer four questions based on your project discovery thus far:

- Is your publishing size important?
- How video-rich is your product?
- How data-centric is your application?
- Which deployment environment is suitable for your application?

As you answer each question, your answers will affect the results of the remaining questions. It's a give-and-take exercise. After answering each question and prioritizing your answers based on their relative importance to your project, you will have a better sense of what tools and technologies within the Flash Platform are appropriate for your project.

Is your publishing size important?

For some projects, the final file size of your application may be an important factor in choosing how to build your Flash project. If your project is a banner ad, if you're creating marketing material that may need to be integrated on a third-party site, or if your application is for a mobile device, limiting the size of your compiled SWF is an important factor.

Figure 7-1 compares three tools, ActionScript, Flash Professional CS5, and Flex 4 SDK, based on your publishing size. As you can see, if a smaller file size is important to your project, you will probably want to consider building your application with only Action-Script or Flash Professional rather than using the Flex SDK for development.

Because the Flex 4 framework provides functionality that is commonly used in many applications, it can drastically reduce your development time. But Flex's memory and download footprint have the potential to be significantly larger than those of Flash Professional or plain old ActionScript. Flex 4 is working on decreasing subsequent downloads of the Flash SWF by externalizing the Flex library code into a Runtime Shared Library (RSL). Adobe creates RSLs for each version (including dot releases) of the Flex SDK. When a user downloads an application with a specific version of the SDK, that user will not need to download that version again, even if they visit a different site. This feature is not new to Flex 4 but is turned on by default in Flash Builder 4. Understanding how the file size impacts a Flex project versus an ActionScript-only project can help your team make the right technology choice for your client.

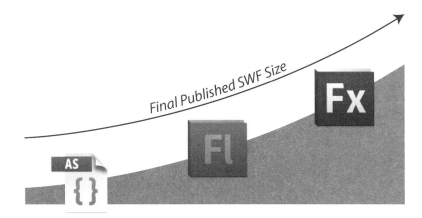

Figure 7-1 Flash Platform technology publishing size

ActionScript   Flash Professional CS5   Flex 4 SDK

How video-rich is your product?

If you're creating a media-rich product that delivers video content, you need to determine the best type of media technology to use. Adobe provides a suite of solutions (see **Figure** 7-2) that enhance and streamline the distribution, playback, and protection of your media content on top of the Flash Platform.

Your team first needs to evaluate the type of media encoding and playback your product will provide. Are you providing progressive or streaming media playback? For streaming, is your content streamed from a live broadcast? If your content is streamed from a live feed, you will most likely want to consider Adobe's Flash Media Interactive Streaming Server. If your project requires streaming but not from a live feed, Adobe offers a more cost-effective server called the Flash Media Streaming Server.

If you need to protect and encrypt your content, Flash Access can be used in conjunction with either of the streaming servers, can be used stand-alone for third-party implementations, or can be used with progressive downloads that rely on HTTP delivery.

No matter which distribution platform or encoding solution you choose, from the client's perspective your content will be viewed via the Flash Player. Because of this, if your content is video-rich, you should evaluate a client-side framework that gives users a robust video player interface to play, pause, toggle, rewind, and forward the video content they are viewing. Adobe has provided the Open Source Media Framework (OSMF) that can be used across all of the Adobe Flash Platform tools. Flash Catalyst allows users to create a video player with a single drop of a component on to the application stage. Flash Professional and Flash Builder can both integrate a video player built using OSMF.

Because OSMF is built entirely in ActionScript, if your project requires a smaller publishing size, OSMF can also be implemented in an ActionScript-only project.

How data-centric is your application?

You'll need to know how data-centric your application will be in order to choose your client-side and a server-side technology. **Figure** 7-3 shows a correlation between potential tools and the level of data in your application. If your application requires any type of server data, you will not be able to use *only* Flash Catalyst to construct your application. Catalyst only supports static data sets via its design-time data feature.

To use Flash Catalyst with live data, your team will need to open the finished Flash Catalyst FXP file in Flash Builder and add the data connection points. This workflow can be ideal since Flash Catalyst is a great tool to integrate designs from many of Creative Suite 5's products. You can then use Flash Builder to build out your project's application features, such as data connectivity.

Flash Catalyst allows users to add custom data to the DataList component. When a DataList is created on the project canvas, default data will be applied. Users have the ability to change this data into different types (such as an image) and can create as many or as few rows as needed in their application.

Flash Builder's data services feature allows you to easily connect your Flex application to a variety of server technologies—such as BlazeDS, ColdFusion, PHP, LifeCycle DS, and a few others—with an easy-to-use wizard. All of these features are built on top of Flex 4's enhanced server communication classes, which, in turn, are built atop ActionScript 3's base APIs. In Chapter 10, "Planning Development," we will

Flash Media Servers   Flash Access   Open Source Media Framework

Figure 7-2 Video distribution through Adobe available technology options

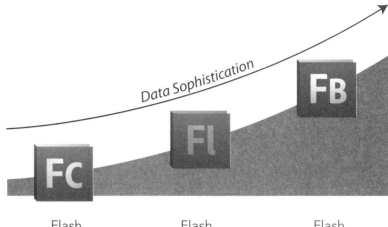

Figure 7-3 Comparing data-centric applications to available tools

Flash Catalyst CS5

Flash Professional CS5

Flash Builder 4

discuss the various communication classes available in ActionScript and Flex.

The integration into Flash Builder may help you choose your server technology; however, this isn't the only factor to consider. If your application requires large data sets or constant interaction with a server, you should consider using the AMF protocol. By design, HTTP communication is a one-way messaging system. For applications that require constant feedback, HTTP requires a client (such as your Flash application) to constantly request data (polling) from the server in order to be in sync. If your application is polling a server every few seconds, it could result in a drastic decrease of your user's bandwidth as well as degrade your application's performance.

AMF is a binary message format that allows for smaller, condensed data sets to flow back and forth

between client and server. In addition, the AMF protocol provides a push-and-pull message communication channel. This allows the server to push data to the client only when the data has been updated, thereby eliminating the need to continually poll the server to check for data updates. This alone will increase your application's overall performance. Most server technologies have third-party libraries that support the AMF protocol, and those supported by Flash Builder's data service features all provide an AMF option. More details will be discussed in Chapter 10.

Flash Professional also supports some features that assist in connecting with data sources. For applications that require Flash Lite or ActionScript 2, data components are available for server connections. This is not to say Flash Professional projects or ActionScript-only projects built in ActionScript 3 cannot connect to a data source, because they can. However, developers are required to code and develop a fair amount of the logic themselves or find third-party libraries to do so.

What deployment environment is suitable for your application?

Your specification should be leading you toward choosing your ideal deployment environment. Three options are available to any given Flash Platform project: web, desktop, and mobile (**Figure** 7-4).

FXP: FLEX PROJECT

The FXP format was introduced with Flash Catalyst CS5 and Flash Builder 4. A file of this type is simply a Flex project packaged into a single file. This file allows project teams to distribute Flash Catalyst files to development teams for further work in Flash Builder.

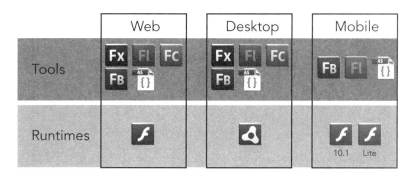

Figure 7-4 Flash Platform deployment options

Web. If you plan to distribute your application via the Web, the final asset will be a SWF file and most likely embedded inside an HTML web page or consumed by another SWF file. You can choose Flash Professional, Flash Builder, Flash Catalyst, Flex, ActionScript 3, or a combination of these tools to build your project. More than likely, your technology and tool decision will be made based on one or more of the previous questions discussed in this section.

Desktop. The second option is to deploy your project to the desktop. Adobe provides the Adobe Integrated Runtime (AIR)—a cross-platform desktop solution that allows a Flash Platform project to be deployed to Linux, Windows, and Mac OS computers all from the same code base and file format (.air). Both Flash Professional and Flash Builder take advantage of the AIR application programming interface (API) and provide publishing options to produce AIR application files for distribution. Because you are deploying to the desktop, the size of your application will probably not be a factor because installing the application will be a one-time event. Therefore, in Flash Builder, you can take advantage of the Flex framework without worrying about your file-size footprint.

Mobile. To deploy your application on a mobile device, your deployment options will be based on your target device.

If you are targeting smartphones or devices that support Flash Player 10.1, you can leverage your favorite tools to create your Flash application. But you'll need to consider your target device's processor and available memory.

With Flash-enabled devices that support the Flash Lite player, your development team can take advantage of Flash Professional to build your product. Flash

---

PROTOTYPING AIR APPLICATIONS

When developing an AIR application, you might need to create and demonstrate desktop functionality in a quick prototype. Creative Suite 5, Fireworks, Dreamweaver, and Flash Catalyst all have the ability to deploy to the AIR runtime. Dreamweaver and Fireworks both create AIR applications in HTML, JavaScript, and CSS by leveraging the API's available within the embedded WebKit engine. In Fireworks, users have access to AIR's interaction API, such as dragging, closing, or minimizing a desktop window. Flash Catalyst builds applications with the Flex 4 framework and is packaged as a web application inside the AIR container, but interaction controls (such as dragging) are not available.

FLEX AND MOBILE

Flex 4 will probably not be the ideal solution because the framework will most likely increase your memory and processor footprint beyond what the device can support, nor does Flex 4 currently support multitouch devices. However, Flash Builder 4 can be leveraged to create ActionScript-only projects that target mobile devices.

Lite 4 was introduced with Flash Professional CS5. This version includes the ability to build applications in ActionScript 3. With Flash Lite, developers can build mobile applications with a minimal set of the Flash Player API, resulting in a smaller memory and performance footprint.

The last mobile deployment option is to Apple's iPhone or iPod touch. With the release of Flash Professional CS5, applications can be targeted for the iPhone OS. Flash Professional will allow applications built in ActionScript 3 to be cross-compiled and packaged for developers to test on a device and deployed through Apple's existing distribution channel, which will make the application available for purchase from the iTunes Store.

ADJUSTING YOUR PROJECT

Each project team has a set of planning tasks that must be completed prior to the project's execution. At this point, your design, development, and build and release teams will be wrapping up their planning tasks outlined in Chapters 8, 10, and 12.

The design team will have constructed a set of wireframes and any necessary prototypes. The development team should have designed the application architecture required to build a solid, scalable, and maintainable application based on the set of defined features. And finally, the build and release team will have constructed their test plans and test cases based on the provided feature specification.

With input from your planning sessions, as well as from your client, you should conduct a final review of your project feature set and specification to ensure that there are no gaps or over-arching features that may have increased the size of the project and created substantial scope creep. Taking this final look will further refine your project, which will ultimately lead to a more seamless and efficient project life cycle.

Refining the feature set

The project's feature set is a living document that will change as your project progresses. Don't be afraid to update it at any time.

Based on your team's feedback, you can add or remove features and use cases, or modify the feature set to reflect any feature priorities that might have shifted. Your development team may have identified feature dependencies that might move one feature above another in the priority queue. Keep this document in a shared environment so that all team members and your client can access the most up-to-date version. If you are using Adobe Buzzword, designers will be notified inside InDesign when the document is updated. This notification allows InDesign to update its link as well as update to the latest document content.

Modifying project scope

After you review and refine the project's feature set and specification, the project's scope will most likely need to be adjusted. It's a good idea to note any changes to the feature set to help the client review the changes more easily. If your team is using Buzzword, the team members can add comments to areas of your project's specification that have changed and can detail why a feature or estimate has been modified. If your client has review access, they will be able to see changes to the document along with your comments, and they will be able to add their own comments in response.

After agreeing to a new priorities feature set, you'll need to review and update the project plan and adjust duration times for task changes, update milestones, and confirm or change the project's release date. Again, these adjustments will need to be shared with your client to ensure that they agree with the timeline changes.

Adapting team roles

With a better overall picture of the project landscape, you may need to adjust the roles within your team. In some cases, you might realize you'll need more developers as it becomes apparent your project has increased in size. Based on your technology choices, you might need to hire or contract an expert in a particular arena. For example, if you are deploying on a mobile platform for Flash Lite 4, you might want to hire a Flash Professional expert who has experience with mobile development. For server-side considerations, you might need an expert in the Flash Media Server suite of products.

If you have identified staffing gaps that require a particular expertise, see if any of your existing team members can take on those roles. If you can fill the role internally, be sure to adjust your project plan accordingly. Tasks related to the role should be expanded to account for extra time necessary for the team member to become familiar with their new role. Team members will need additional time to research the required technologies as well as gain a better grasp of industry best practices for implementing those technologies.

ASSIGNING THE ORDER OF TASKS: WATERFALL VS. ITERATIVE

As project construction begins, each team will be working hard to complete their portion of the project. Based on your project's needs and your team's work style, you will need to decide on the appropriate project workflow to accomplish features, tasks, and the project as a whole. Deciding on an approach, and understanding the need for continuous planning, will help you create a seamless handoff between team members.

There are two broad categories of software development processes: waterfall and iterative. Each has many variations based on different principles and techniques.

Waterfall

Waterfall provides project teams with a linear and synchronized process of completing one phase of a project prior to starting the next phase. As shown in **Figure 7-5**, planning is completed before design and design completes all assets and obtains client approval before development kickoff.

On small and medium-size projects with short timelines and budget, the waterfall approach is often ideal. Project scopes are small and initial planning can most likely cover most business requirements.

With a waterfall approach, there is little opportunity to change the feature set and the project scope because the entire project is released at once. Although this helps these projects to stay within budget and have little scope creep, there is also little opportunity for collaboration between the project team and client because the client is engaged only at the end of each phase.

Collaboration between team members can also be difficult. The design team often works in isolation without the development team's input. Features and technical feasibility requirements can be missed and only caught at design handoff or, even worse, late in the development phase. When gaps are discovered at handoff, your team will need to do more work to update designs to meet development pushback. This extra work will result in delays since development can't start until design is complete. From a build and release team perspective, testing can begin only when the project's development has been completed

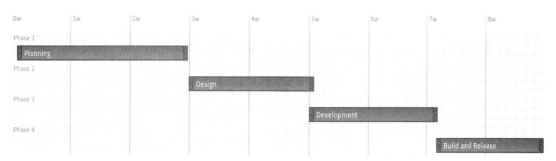

Figure 7-5 Waterfall workflow printed from Adobe WorkflowLab

rather than when features are released. By doing so, quality assurance (QA) will most likely be overloaded with testing.

If a waterfall approach is the best workflow for your team, pay close attention to up-front planning and establish a designer/developer contract like we discussed in Chapter 6, "Setting Expectations for Your Project." To avoid designing without team input, have regular (daily or weekly) design meetings in which the project management, development, and build and release teams can discuss the current progress of the design.

As development starts, it's wise to convert the regular design meetings into development meetings to show progress to the project team. These meetings allow the design team to provide feedback on how the development team is implementing the design. This is important when developing a Flash-based application because animations, effects, and transitions are a large part of the user interface experience. And since static designs do not describe such behaviors, it's essential for design to have an opportunity to comment on those portions of the user experience.

The design and development team meetings will also help QA prepare to test the application.

Iterative

An iterative, or *agile*, process allows your team to complete parts of an application in stages instead of all at once.

Figure 7-6 illustrates a sample project plan created with Adobe WorkflowLab that shows two iterations.

Each iteration consists of planning, design, development, and build and release. This process allows for more collaboration between team members and the client. Features are broken up into sets and designed, developed, and tested during a designated time period. Upon completion, the features are released to the client for review and feedback. At the start of the next iteration, features are planned and organized based on their priority and the feedback from the prior set of features.

On larger projects, your feature set may change as you develop your project. No matter how much up-front planning you do, features and their priorities will change as time passes and features are developed and integrated into your application. It's a good idea to break up your development into key iterations (milestones and sprints) that meet certain project goals.

At the beginning of each iteration, you'll need to adjust feature priorities, update existing features, and add new ones. And you'll need to adjust your specification—which is your common touch point for your team and your client—to reflect these changes, additions, and deletions. Based on those changes, your project plan and your team roles will need to be updated.

For each iteration, your project team will work together on a set of features. Because of the close cooperation required among the teams, an iterative kick-off meeting should take place to define the next set of features and discuss how to complete them in the given time frame. Your design and development teams should create a designer and developer contract

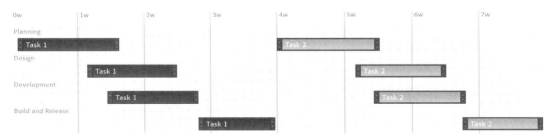

Figure 7-6 Iterative workflow printed from Adobe WorkflowLab

for each feature (see Chapter 6), which will create guidelines that will help the teams work in parallel and have a seamless handoff of designs. Iteration meetings will also provide QA with the information they need to create their testing strategies.

The chief advantage of the iterative approach is that it allows the client and your team to provide feedback on newly finished features. This flexibility, however, can lead to serious scope creep. When starting a project using the iterative workflow, you must explain to your client the potential consequences of constant revisions and changes to existing features. Iterative is a give and take approach to software development. If an existing feature needs to be modified, that task will take budget and time away from other features that have yet to be developed. If other features are not adjusted or removed from scope, the overall project time and cost will increase.

SUMMARY CHECKLIST

After proper planning and collaboration with your project team, you've decided what technologies are needed to complete your project. Based on these decisions and your team's feedback, you have updated your project' scope once again and have chosen the appropriate workflow for your project team.

Before going further, let's make sure you've answered all of these questions and are ready to begin the construction phases of your project.

- ✔ Have each of your teams provided feedback on the project's scope based on their initial planning efforts?
- ✔ Do the Flash Platform technologies you have chosen meet your project's requirements?
- ✔ Have you chosen the proper tools to build your application?
- ✔ Has your client approved your adjusted project plan and timeline?
- ✔ Have you agreed to a proper workflow that meets your project's needs?
- ✔ If you chose the iterative workflow, is your client aware of its potential for scope creep (which can increase project time and budget)?
- ✔ Have proper iterations been set to assist in project planning?

PART III

DESIGN

CHAPTER 8

Planning Design

When working with moderate- to large-sized projects that have multiple designers on a team who need to work together, it is increasingly important to get everyone on the "same page" so everyone's designs integrate well together.

Before you open Photoshop and start building your comp, you need to plan, starting at a very high level and later working your way down to the specifics. Defining specifics early on can add risk when broader concepts haven't been vetted or reviewed with your client or customer.

One approach to narrowing your design focus is to start with a broad-stroke discussion of the idea and capture the communication and collaboration at each step.

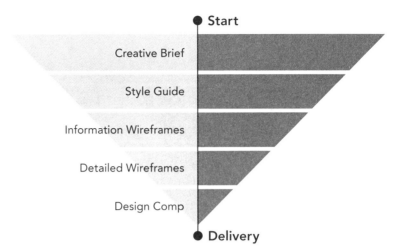

Start

Creative Brief

Style Guide

Information Wireframes

Detailed Wireframes

Design Comp

Delivery

Figure 8-1 Moving from broad to narrow focus through the design process

Start with discussions about the target customer, emotions, or themes that need to be considered by the design team and client. With each phase of the project, narrow the focus a bit more with the approach shown in **Figure 8-1**. If you find that your client has issues with a new direction you are moving in, go back to the previous level and make an adjustment. With a safe backward path at the ready, you will help prevent your team from having to start over from the beginning; plus, you can get client agreement or sign-off with each step.

This chapter will cover some ideas that can make this design process easier and more successful with larger teams and projects, starting from the very broad themes. In the next chapter, we'll discuss the lower two rungs of the process, which including creating detailed wireframes, creating design comps, and working efficiently with Creative Suite design tools.

DEFINING THE INTENT OF DESIGN

As we defined in Chapter 3, "Understanding Roles in a Project," design is meant to illicit an emotional response from the consumer. For example, when creating a piece of fine art, the artist wants to evoke a specific emotion or feeling within the person who is experiencing it. In the case of a project for a client, the designer needs to capture the emotion the client wants the viewer to have in order to drive the viewer to experience the intended emotion.

Identifying the emotion

When working with your client or customer, it is important that you first capture what they want the customer to do and how the customer should feel when they work with the material. Let's work through an example and demonstrate how this translates into what you design.

Imagine your client is a car company, and they need to sell a new car. Obviously the car company wants the user to buy the car; however, with a car, you can't just buy one over the Internet (or at least most people don't). In this case, the desired result, or *call to action*, is to drive the user to a Web application where they can build their own custom car with specific features, trims, colors, and interiors, and then contact a local dealer to purchase it. Everything about the Web site should guide or direct them to this call to action. The user should feel safe, comfortable, and connected to the car. The car should look new and inviting. Often you'll see cars on Web sites in silver; this helps make the car seem "blank" and open to the customer's own color choice.

The car-customizing application in this example is where customers take the good feelings they have about the car and personalize it to make it their own. They feel that this is their own unique vehicle that addresses their needs and desires. When they are satisfied, they can then quickly and easily contact a dealer to purchase it and send their exact specification.

Picturing the emotion

With this example, we have defined what the user should ultimately do based on their experience of the content or application. We also have mapped out how the user should feel on their way to the intended action.

Capturing this in written form is important to get confirmation from your client or customer on this very basic assessment of the early design and direction of the project. Your design team may be working on multiple projects, and it can be difficult to context-jump from one project to another, so having this guide can be helpful in the transition.

The common term for gathering this information is called the *creative brief*. This document is often the first design milestone and deliverable for a project that the client signs off on. You sit down with your client and talk through the ideas they already have in their mind and ask questions. You make design decisions based on assumptions or information that you and your client already have and know. In addition, identifying the reasons for these decisions can help you throughout the creative process.

Work with your client to identify who your target customer is, referring to the original high-level vision that started the entire project (see Chapter 5, "High-Level Vision and Team Organization," for more). This could be very broad or very narrow, but having an early sense of this will help focus your work. Based on this early information, designers often create *mood boards* where competitor concepts, similar customer targets, and industry examples are posted for the team to explore and exchange ideas.

Performing Internet searches on common search engines or on stock photography Web sites is a good starting place for your digital mood board. You can then bring your photos and videos into Photoshop.com to build your mood board (**Figure 8-2**).

Using Photoshop.com, you can post comments and ratings for the various items in your mood board. You can also invite others into group albums for the commenting and sharing of ideas and images. The Photoshop.com service lets you send e-mail invitations to your team to access the items in your group library. Depending on your client, they may also be a valuable contributor to the mood board to help find out more about their thoughts and feelings about the direction the design should take.

Documenting the emotion and action

With the mood board process finished, your design team should have a reasonably strong idea of what the client wants and what the intended audience needs. The next step is to start writing the creative brief.

Using the Acrobat.com service can make creating this document easier. Using Buzzword, which is part of Acrobat.com, you and your team can collaboratively write and compose the creative brief. In addition, Buzzword lets other stakeholders and the client review and comment on the document (**Figure 8-3**).

The creative brief should capture the following items and, at the end, be approved by your customer or client:

- Who is the target customer?
- What is already known about the target customer?
- What is the call to action for the customer?
- What are the emotions or feelings that the customer should have?
- Does the client or customer have existing designs or design requirements that need to be used?
- Provide examples of other work that is similar or has elements that can be used as examples.
- Provide examples that represent directions that you don't want to take.

As you can see, the creative brief gives a significant amount of direction to the design team to help guide their work in the future. Note that the creative brief can provide samples of example work or things that should be done, as well as examples of work or ideas that should be avoided. Sometimes it is easier to describe what you don't want than what you do.

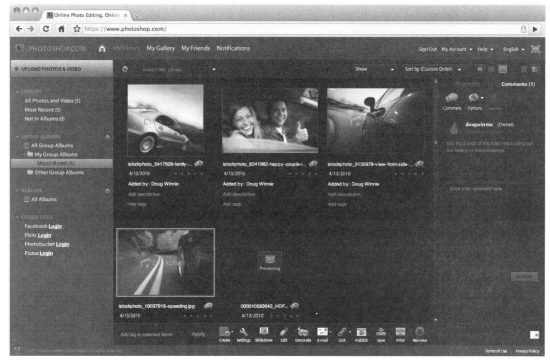

Figure 8-2 A digital mood board in Photoshop.com

Figure 8-3 Buzzword with a sample creative brief document with comments

Defining rules to design

Depending on your client, you may need to create an initial rule set for your design called a *style guide*. The style guide captures the various design requirements of a site. Larger clients may already have a style guide that you need to review to make sure that your designs meet within their style rules. Although this may seem limiting to the creative process, it will ensure that the client's materials have a similar look and feel across the various sites and applications in order to build a consistent brand.

Smaller clients may not have an existing style guide. One of the first elements you want to define is the use of color in your project.

Color is a very emotional element to any design. Extensive materials are available on the emotions that specific colors bring out in people: Blue is connected to calm and clean, orange to inexpensive, green to earthy or envy, and red to fire or danger. Your project's emotional requirements can play a significant impact on the color choices you use. In addition, based on various types of color theory, you can tie complementary colors into your base emotional color.

To help navigate through color exploration, Adobe provides a service called kuler (*http://kuler.adobe.com*). Kuler includes thousands of color themes constituting up to five colors that designers have submitted. Using Illustrator CS5 and other applications, you can find kuler integrated into the product with the kuler panel (**Figure 8-4**).

Using the kuler panel, you can search for keywords that have been associated with various color themes. Searching for *calm tree* will give you a number of themes that have been tagged with those keywords. From this point, you can select the themes to use in your project, or you can go directly into the kuler Web application and make adjustments.

When you go to the kuler Web application, you'll notice that you can create a new color theme from scratch, modify an existing theme, or sample colors from an image, such as from your digital mood board. From here, you can select a number of color theory rules such as analogous, monochromatic, and others to give you an aesthetically pleasing color combination that you can adjust and fine-tune with kuler.

Kuler offers other features such as geographically based color usage with its Pulse tool, which is linked to location and season to find pleasing color trends. Depending on your project, you may need to have multiple color values including RGB, CMYK, HSB, hexadecimal (for HTML and CSS), and others. Kuler is able to give you all of these color values to copy, or you can adjust them to match specific requirements from your client and see how that affects your theme.

When you are happy with your color palette, you can save it as an Adobe Swatch Exchange (ASE) file and load that into Illustrator CS5. You'll then have those same colors available for your project.

Another area that you can cover in your style guide is the use of type. Different combinations of type can add whimsy or sophistication to your site. Providing guidelines on type can help your designers create matching designs to support them.

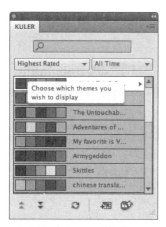

Figure 8-4 The kuler panel in Illustrator CS5

ACROBAT.COM WORKSPACES

Acrobat.com has a feature called *workspaces* that are regions that can be shared with individuals. All the contents within the workspace including Buzzword documents, Tables spreadsheets, Presentations slide shows, and uploaded PDFs are shared with the invitees. Workspaces are a great way to share multiple files automatically with key people on your team or with your client.

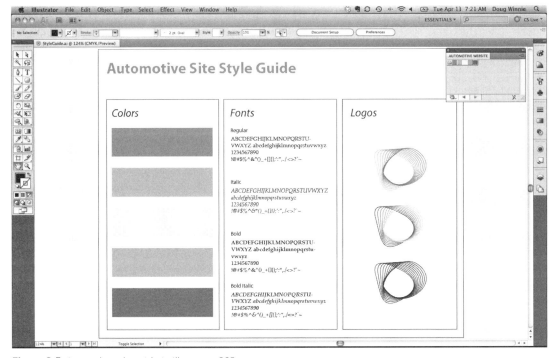

Figure 8-5 A sample style guide in Illustrator CS5

Finally, if your client has any existing logos, you should include them as well. Often, logo treatments come with a variety of formats depending on if they are used in a full-color, grayscale, or pure black-and-white format (**Figure 8-5**).

To help get client feedback and approval for your style guide, use the bundled CS Review service with Illustrator CS5 to post your style guide on the Web to an Acrobat.com workspace for your client to review, add comments, and collaborate with your designer.

CS Review lets you convert and upload Photoshop, Illustrator, and InDesign files to the Web for your client to review and comment on using a simple Web browser. To start a review, open the CS Review panel, and log in using your Adobe ID. You can then send the currently open document to the CS Review service (**Figure 8-6**).

When you do this, you can then notify your client about the review and get their feedback. They can then click areas they want to comment on and type their comment in the pop-up box. Comments that are made in CS Review are then saved in the service and appear in the source design application.

Figure 8-7 shows a style guide in Illustrator with a trail of comments for the designer to respond to and make adjustments based on the client or customer feedback.

SETTING UP CS REVIEW AND CS LIVE

When you install Creative Suite 5, you will be prompted to create an Adobe ID. Your Adobe ID is your login to the CS Live services, including CS Review. If you are unsure whether you are set up with CS Live, click the CS Live button in the application bar at the top of your Creative Suite 5 design application.

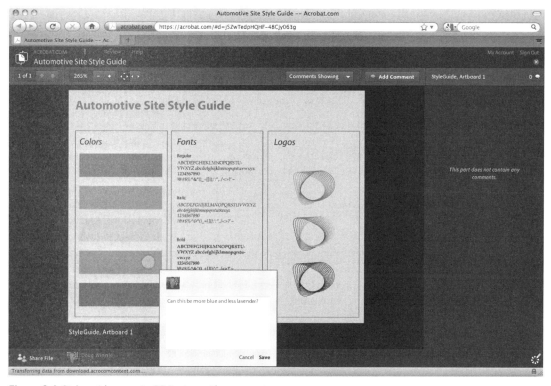

Figure 8-6 Style guide open in CS Review with comments

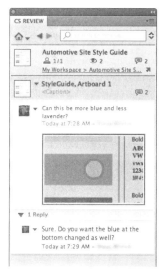

Figure 8-7 A comment trail in the Illustrator CS5 CS Review panel

Gathering client feedback early in the design process can save extensive amounts of rework later. Being crystal clear on your client's or customer's thoughts and feelings about various design directions and decisions will lead to a more successful project.

GIVING YOUR CREATIVITY STRUCTURE

With the up-front aspects of your early design planning complete, it is time to start putting some initial structure over what you are going to build in your project.

Depending on the scope of the project, you may find that you need to break up your structure planning process into two steps. For the sake of completeness, this book will walk through both levels of structure design; the first is called *information architecture*. (We'll cover more detailed wireframes, which is the second level, in the next chapter.)

When you have reached this point of the project, you have a strong indication of the theme, action, and feeling that the user should have when using the application or Web site. The next step is to start building an interface and flow that will help guide the user toward the call to action that was identified early on in the design process.

At this point, you can take several directions on how you want to lay out and organize your user interface or application content. Now is the time to put those ideas into *information wireframes* that you can then compare to each other and make educated decisions on which approach you should move forward with.

Architecting the interface

As a designer, you can use several Adobe products to complete this step, including Illustrator, InDesign, Fireworks, and Flash Catalyst. Each product has strengths and weaknesses when building wireframes. This section is an overview of what each product can do in Creative Suite 5.

Flash Catalyst CS5. Flash Catalyst CS5 has specific wireframe-drawing tools that make it easy to build blue-line wireframe shapes and objects. In addition, you can use prebuilt wireframe components and add basic interaction behaviors to each. This creates "live" wireframes and not just static artwork or pages.

Flash Catalyst doesn't support the CS Review commenting service export to PDF or other graphic formats that can be used for PDF reviews. So, getting client feedback would have to happen either in person, over e-mail, or through a Web conferencing service such as ConnectNOW, which is part of CS Live.

Fireworks CS5. Fireworks CS5 includes several vector and bitmap tools that accelerate the wireframe-drawing process. Fireworks also supports export to PDF for client review and comments using Acrobat Professional or Acrobat Reader.

Although Fireworks lets you create click through prototypes and wireframes, you can't build animated transitions or sophisticated component behaviors. In addition, Fireworks does not integrate with CS Review for simple client feedback. Also, if you use Fireworks and take your project to Flash Catalyst, you can't redesign the artwork with Fireworks very easily, as opposed to Illustrator.

InDesign CS5. The use of InDesign as a wireframing tool has been growing because of InDesign's existing ability to work easily with large documents containing potentially hundreds of pages. InDesign's large document management features take a lot of the pain out of managing large wireframe documents. InDesign also fully supports the CS Review service, and you can export to PDF for client review and feedback.

In addition, InDesign has a number of libraries that make it easier to work with wireframe designs including the EightShapes Unify kit. Using tool kits like this make it easy to drag and drop common user interface components to the document and then add annotations and other descriptive information.

InDesign also includes a number of Flash Professional–based animation presets. These can give your wireframes an added level of information at this wireframe stage on how the user would navigate through the application or Web site. For projects that are ultimately developed in Flash Professional, InDesign supports direct export to a native Flash Professional project using the FLA project format. This converts all the pages in InDesign to frames in Flash Professional and can help streamline your project when jumping into development.

One key advantage that InDesign has is the ability to link in external documents to populate text areas. This can work with external document files such as Microsoft Word or plain-text files but also works with the Buzzword online word processor that comes with

---

EIGHTSHAPES UNIFY

The Unify system consists of templates and symbols that can be used in Adobe InDesign to create components and pages for wireframes, prototypes, and other early design deliverables. You can download the tool kit at *http://unify.eightshapes.com*.

CS Live. This can make it much easier to integrate documentation with wireframes and give clients a clear picture of the overall information architecture. This can be beneficial if your development team is building a feature specification that should be linked to your wireframes at some point in the project.

InDesign CS5, however, doesn't support a streamlined export to Illustrator or Flash Catalyst. Also, the components that are in InDesign are not as sophisticated or customizable as the ones in Flash Catalyst, and not all of the animations or behaviors you define in InDesign will be preserved when you export to Flash Professional.

Illustrator CS5. For the example in this book, we will be using Illustrator for our wireframes. Illustrator doesn't support the large document features that InDesign does, but artwork that you create in Illustrator can be directly imported into Flash Catalyst and Flash Professional. In addition, if we wanted to make changes to the artwork when we bring it into Flash Catalyst, we would use Illustrator to do this as the designs or project changes and evolves.

Illustrator also supports the CS Review service, making it easy to get client feedback, or you can export to PDF and use the Acrobat products for review and comment. The multiple artboards allow a single Illustrator document to capture various wireframes, and each of these artboards is imported as a unique state or page in Flash Catalyst.

Unfortunately, Illustrator doesn't support the large document management features that are in InDesign and also lacks the Buzzword integration feature that can be very helpful when integrating written specifications with your wireframes.

In our example, we are going to continue with the automotive site example and show a few example information architecture wireframes created in Illustrator CS5.

The intent at this point is to sketch the various high-level user interface approaches you can take without going into significant details about the content or low-level structure of the various pieces. When you create these interface elements, you should refer to previous milestones and materials such as the high-level vision or any feature specifications that have already been developed to ensure that all the elements of the interface or project are accounted for in the wireframe design.

In Illustrator CS5, you can use the multiple artboards feature to create different wireframes in the same document. This is also helpful if you want to create symbols that are used multiple times in the Illustrator document to keep your wireframes looking consistent across different layouts (**Figure 8-8**).

Again, the intent of the wireframes at this point is not to get into the details of the design but to identify at a high level what the client or customer wants. What is equally valuable at this point is finding out what they *don't* want and to cross that off your list as possible options. Narrowing your options down is good to do early in the process. This will reduce the risk of going down a path that the client doesn't necessarily want.

You can get client feedback in multiple ways. In addition to CS Review, you can use Acrobat Professional 9 to submit a PDF for review. Using Illustrator, you can save your multiple artboard project as a PDF. Using Acrobat Professional 9, open the PDF, and set up an online shared review. When you submit the review, you can add e-mail addresses for people who need to review the document. Using Acrobat Reader, they can post comments and edits to the document. Those edits are then saved to the Acrobat.com server where all the reviewers can sync and see the group changes (**Figure 8-9**).

Some of the unique features of the Acrobat PDF review cycle are the ability to set up time restrictions for the review cycle and the ability to conduct the review with anything that can be converted to a PDF.

At this stage of the design process, you'll get some initial feedback from your client or customer on the overall user interface direction you could take the project next. When you have agreement from the client on the first level of detail with the information architecture wireframes, you can coordinate with your team and then drill down to the next level.

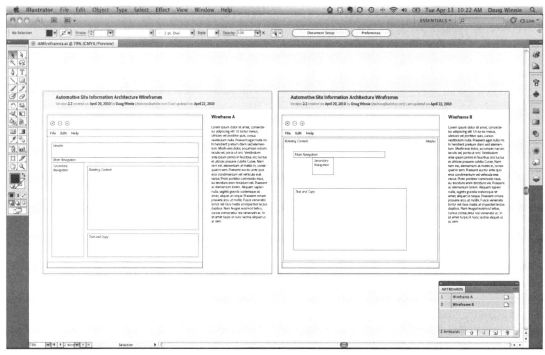

Figure 8-8 Wireframes in Illustrator CS5 artboards

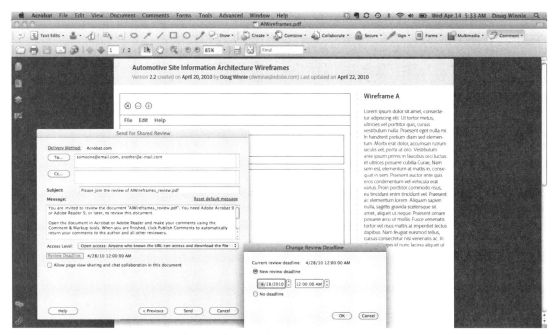

Figure 8-9 Wireframes in Acrobat Professional for shared review

Don't just take our word for it

We always want to please our clients; they are the ones with the checkbook who ultimately will pay for the project. However, sometimes the client isn't always right.

Let's admit it. Clients are smart, but they aren't always the actual customer of the product that is being built. When going through the initial design phases of the project, it is extremely valuable to get feedback from the intended customer of the project.

This is where user research and focus groups can become very helpful. Find individuals who are representative of the target customer, put the wireframes in front of them, and ask them their opinion. Try to determine whether the way you have organized the content is helpful for them. Are there requirements that the user has for a project that aren't captured yet?

If you find that a request coming from the potential customer is different from the client request, you can work on figuring out the right approach with the client. Generally, the client wants to make the project more successful for the customer; however, sometimes a client needs to make a change that is counter to what the customer wants. Having completed the due diligence of investigating and gathering customer feedback will help guide you and your client and will potentially protect you later.

SYNCING WITH YOUR TEAM

With the initial explorative creative steps finished, it is time to meet with the design, development, build and release, and management leads of the project in order to share the feedback provided by the client and the current status of the design work. Design decisions that visually or structurally seem minor can have vast differences in development or implementation scope.

Syncing with your team at this early stage will alert design, development, and management to any potential areas that should be avoided that could add significant scope to the project.

Sharing your information architecture wireframes with the development team may give them valuable information in how they architect the modules or application code for the developers to build.

The process of making wireframes and sharing these across the various roles of your team help build a contract between design and development. The high-level modules or pieces of the project are then clearly understood by team members, and just like with an architect's blueprint, each of the team members can visually understand the pieces of the project and start to drill down further into the details.

After you have communicated all this to your team, it is time to start more *detailed wireframes* and then begin the visual design with *design comps* for your project.

SUMMARY CHECKLIST

The early design steps for any project might not be visually compelling, but they are structurally important for any team to narrow their design focus and options to a manageable size. It is also helpful for the design team to help guide the client or customer down the design process. When you are finished with this part of the project, you should have the answers to the following questions:

✔ Do you know who the customer is?

✔ Do you know what the customer call to action is for the project?

✔ Have you defined the theme, emotion, or style of the project?

✔ Have you identified other examples that you can emulate or get inspiration from?

✔ Are there examples of ideas or concepts you want to avoid?

✔ Does the client have a style guide that you need to comply with?

✔ Do you have strong confidence that you are in sync with your client on the design direction and approach?

✔ Are the initial style rules of your project defined to your team's satisfaction?

✔ Have you explored various user interface concepts?

✔ Do you have validation from potential customers on how you have structured your information architecture?

✔ Do you have sign-off from your client with the high-level milestones of the project?

✔ Has your development and management team been briefed on the initial design aspects of the project?

CHAPTER 9

Iterative Design

In the previous chapter, you began the design process, focusing on the high-level aspects of the project and defining the call to action, the overall design direction, the specific design rules, and an overall architecture for the layout of the project. As you continue through the design process, you need to narrow your focus further, execute on specific design assets, and prepare your work for collaboration with developers.

Returning to the various layers of the design process (**Figure 9-1**), you have already moved through the topmost layers, so now you are ready for the more specific work of the detailed wireframes and design comps.

This chapter focuses on building more detailed wireframes for your project, building design comps, and working with Flash Catalyst and Flash Professional to update and manage those designs.

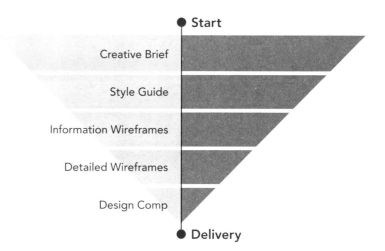

Figure 9-1 Moving from broad to narrow focus through the design process

ADDING DETAILS TO YOUR DESIGN

In the previous chapter, you built interactive architecture wireframes. These defined the various sections of the application and gave your client a first chance to give feedback on the visual design of the project. These wireframes are also valuable for the developers to get more insight into what the design team is planning on designing for the project. Giving your developers a view into the design of your project is a key part of building the contract between the design and development roles.

These wireframes are only the first step. Before jumping into the visual design process, you need to provide an additional layer of what the user will do in your application.

Mapping the user flow

In the early planning states of the project, the team created use cases, defining how the user will complete the major sections of the project; these then helped define the call to action that is part of the creative brief.

In this section of the project, you need more details on how the user will specifically use the major call to action and other features of the application or Web site. To do this, you will need to create a series of *user workflow diagrams.*

User workflows define the specific steps that a user needs to go through to complete a task. Although this may seem elementary to some, if you ignore this part of the process, you can easily build an inefficient and overly complex user interface. You've probably at some point been forced to work with a user interface that required five clicks to do something that should have taken only one. You don't want to create that type of bad user experience in your application, and developing some workflow diagrams will help.

A workflow diagram represents all the paths the user can take in an application and the steps, screens, and forms that are required to do it. Building a workflow diagram helps the future wireframe development because it defines what exactly needs to be wireframed to create a complete picture of the overall design of the project.

A workflow diagram has a few recommended pieces. **Figure 9-2** shows a workflow diagram that was created in Adobe Illustrator CS5.

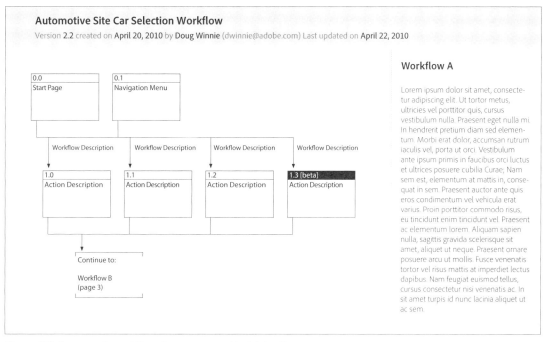

Figure 9-2 An example workflow diagram created in Adobe Illustrator

As you can see, the workflow diagram is divided into boxes. Each of these boxes represents a view or user interface element that the user needs to work with to complete part of the overall workflow. Each of these boxes uses a numbering system to help distinguish it from another. This serves two purposes:

- It gives people a specific reference point to refer people to in the workflow.
- It helps identify the various wireframe elements that you will need to create later in the design process.

Between the boxes are arrows to indicate the process that someone can take to complete a workflow step. As you can see, the user has four possible paths that can originate from two locations, or regions, of this example. These flows ultimately will take the user to the same location.

The middle row of boxes is numbered using the same number scheme: 1.0, 1.1, 1.2, and 1.3. This indicates that these steps of the process will take place in

the same location of the application and will be documented and wireframed in a single place, in this case, Wireframe 1. If you are building an application that will have additional features added in a later phase and know what some of those are now, you can add placeholders for them in your initial workflow diagrams, as we have here with item 1.3, which according to the workflow diagram is slated for the beta release.

As you can see, these four paths lead to the same location, in this case to another workflow diagram that is labeled for the reader to quickly identify where to go in the document.

When you need to represent a decision path, multiple possible actions can stem from the same step of the workflow. In this case, you need to identify the various paths you can take from that specific point.

In **Figure 9-3**, workflow item 2.13_d has a path coming out of it that breaks into two distinct directions. First, note that the item is marked as a dialog box. This description can be optional based on the

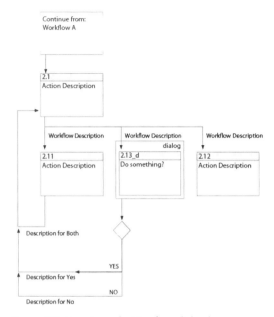

Figure 9-3 Mapping a decision for a dialog box

type of project you are working on, but this level of detail helps you know during the wireframe process whether a workflow item needs to be accommodated within an existing design or within an existing user interface construct such as a dialog box, alert window, or other item. In this case, it's a modal dialog box.

From the workflow item, the box links to a diamond icon. This represents a *decision*, or multiple-path breakpoint. Each of the breakpoints is represented by a unique line that branches out. Note that each line is clearly labeled to capture what path it is. In the case of this workflow, the paths converge to the same point, but you may have paths that diverge into unique workflow paths, into different sections of the application, or even out of the application entirely.

Be sure to also annotate and provide documentation for your workflow items in the document. This will help communicate to your client, customer, or team what happens at specific locations of the workflow and can provide important technical details for your development and design teams.

When you have all the workflows of your project mapped out in a workflow diagram, you can then review them with your client and with your team. Look to find inefficiencies with the workflow and make adjustments here before you go to the wireframe step. Often, you will find that you can consolidate workflow paths or even remove paths entirely that aren't required.

Make sure that your workflows are grouped, numbered, and named correctly, because you will be using the workflow steps in your diagram for the wireframes that you will make next. Similarly numbered workflow items usually are consolidated into a single wireframe.

Creating your linked wireframes

With the workflows of your project mapped out, you need to visually show the workflows in the product. To do this, you will create wireframes that are low-fidelity representations of your application design that show how the user interface will look and function after you apply the full-fidelity design.

Based on the steps we have suggested in this book, you can base your wireframes on two items:

- The information architecture wireframes that were covered in the previous chapter. These give you the high-level UI orientation that you will use for your wireframes at this step of the design process.
- The workflows covered earlier in this chapter. They represent all the use cases the user needs to perform in the application, which need to be fully wireframed to capture how the user interface will support the user workflows.

When you start your wireframe, you need to refer to your workflows first and capture the various screens or user interface elements that need to be built. The wireframe examples in this chapter (Figures 9-2 and 9-3) grouped common elements using a numbering system. Items 1.0, 1.1, and 1.2 in the workflows are all covered in a single screen or piece of the application. To match this workflow numbering system, you use the workflow item numbers in the wireframe.

Figure 9-4 shows the basic elements of a wireframe. In this case, the wireframe is for an AIR

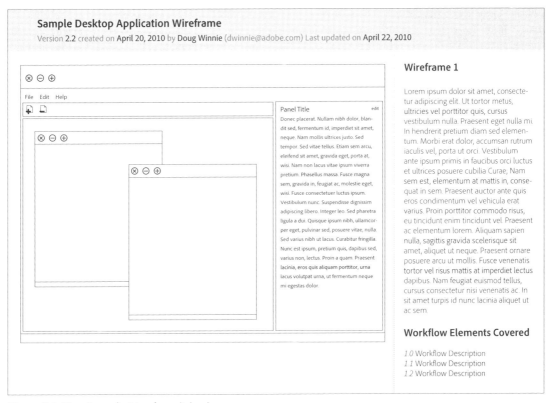

Figure 9-4 Mapping a decision for a dialog box

application. You'll notice that the application *chrome*, or window controls, is incorporated into the design. It is important to show the right context when building your wireframe. If you are building a browser-based application, for example, you should consider adding a browser interface around your application design to remind the reviewer that the application will appear in a browser window. This is something that is often overlooked but should be part of your wireframe at this stage.

You'll note that this wireframe is created in Illustrator, while in previous examples (specifically in Chapter 6, "Setting Expectations for Your Project") we used InDesign. You can use either tool for this task. One advantage we highlighted in Chapter 6 is that you can place into your InDesign document the feature

specification that was written separately in Buzzword to show both documents together.

In this Illustrator example, we have a region on the right side that can be used to capture notes regarding the wireframe. This is important in order to capture details that can easily be missed in a low-fidelity example as we have here. In addition, the bottom of the region highlights the workflows that are covered in this specific wireframe. This helps tie things back to the workflows that were created earlier in the project.

It may seem intimidating to have so much detail in your design process this early, even before you have cracked open Photoshop or have started introducing full-fidelity designs; however, this attention to detail is helpful for your developer peers, for preparing your testing strategy, and also for your client to get accurate information early in the design process so they can make educated decisions and communicate issues to the design team.

Using the CS Review feature of Illustrator and InDesign, you can send your wireframes to the client or customer for them to review and provide feedback on; when they sign off on them, you can then share with the development team and begin the visual design phase of the project.

When sharing your wireframes with the development team, they will begin to understand the visual architecture of the project and can divide the work into specific modules, components, or actions that need to be built. If working in an iterative development process, these modules can be spread out over the iterations of the project, and they will build the contract between what the designer creates later in the design process and what the developer builds based on the wireframes and user workflows.

DESIGNING THE VISUALS

With the early design process finished, you now have client and peer approval of your high-level design direction, you know the structure of the user interface, you have agreement on the workflows of the user, and you have wireframes that show how the user interface will support the workflows in a low-fidelity form.

Now is the time to crank up the pixels, prime the stylus, and put your visual design skills to work.

In this section, we'll review ways to work with your design project. First, you'll learn about wireframes and how to bring them into Flash Catalyst to design iteratively with Illustrator and Photoshop. Then, you'll learn how to create complete design comps in Illustrator, Photoshop, and Fireworks and how to import them into Flash Catalyst and Flash Professional. Finally, we'll also talk about how to work with other design stakeholders in your project and how to work with other files including audio and video assets.

Designing through wireframes and comps

Although you could start completely from a blank slate (or *artboard*, to use the correct term), it is easy to

miss something that was covered in the wireframe. To that end, updating the design from the wireframe to the full-fidelity design will ensure that all the elements of your project are in sync with what the client signed off on in the last phrase of the project.

Designing Flex applications using Flash Catalyst

You can use a number of workflows to design your Flex-based project using Flash Catalyst. This section will review each of these to help you understand the design requirements when working with Flash Catalyst.

Updating wireframe designs. When working with applications built using the Flex framework, you can bring your wireframes into Flash Catalyst and iteratively update the design of each element into full-fidelity designs; at the same time, you can convert artwork to interactive components and quickly assign behaviors to them.

When updating a wireframe design, you will bring each design element into Illustrator or Photoshop, change their designs, and then send the changes to Flash Catalyst. **Figure 9-5** shows an example of what a design looks like before and after performing this process.

With each of the elements you have in Flash Catalyst, you can select them and send them to Illustrator or Photoshop for redesign. Just select the graphics and then right-click them to select where you want to modify the design.

By selecting a design tool in Flash Catalyst (**Figure 9-6**), you will send the selected items to that tool. When you get to the requested design tool, you'll find that the graphic will be editable, and you'll have a screenshot of the overall application design that will be washed out and saved as a locked layer in the Layers panel. This will let you redesign the selected graphic in context with the rest of your application design.

NOTE ▪ When selecting objects to send to Creative Suite design tools, remember that vector objects can go only to Illustrator, not to Photoshop. To send vector objects to Photoshop, you need to rasterize them using the Flash Catalyst heads-up display or select Rasterize from the Modify menu.

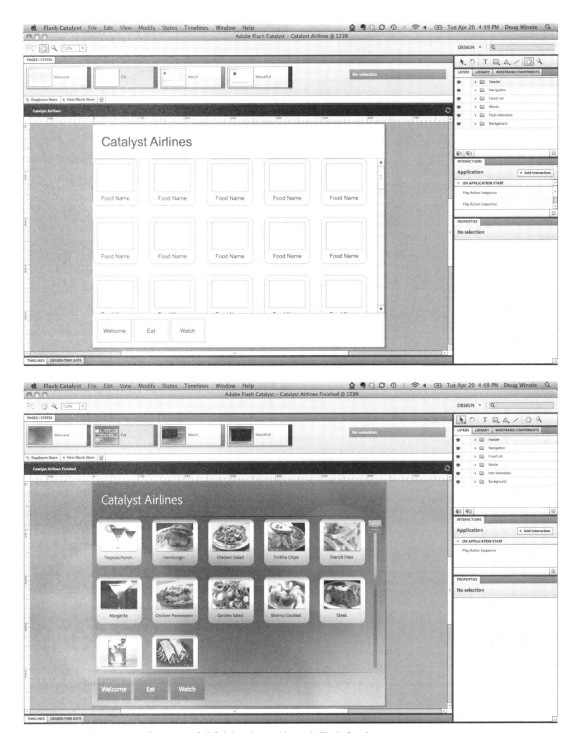

Figure 9-5 Updating a wireframe to a full-fidelity design through Flash Catalyst

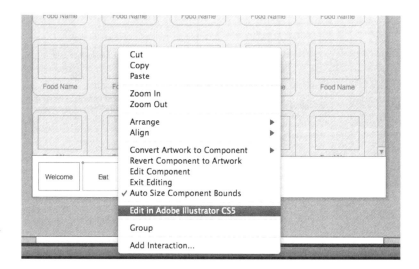

Figure 9-6 Selecting graphics in Flash Catalyst and using the Edit in… command

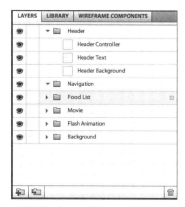

Figure 9-7 Working with layers in Flash Catalyst

From here, you can then use the Illustrator or Photoshop design tools to update the design to your desires.

Organizing your design structure. When working with designs in Flash Catalyst, it is critical that you keep your Layers panel organized and named (**Figure 9-7**). If you are new to interactive design, the Layers panel might have been something that wasn't extremely important for your daily workflow; however, when working with objects in Flash Catalyst, you'll find that proper naming will save you extensive amounts of frustration and time when you convert artwork into components and start building animated transitions for your project.

The Layers panel allows you to group objects into layer folders and give them unique names to help distinguish your designs from each other.

Creating components from artwork. When you have designs created in Flash Catalyst, you can convert artwork into interactive components. An example of this is when you need to make a button or other similar component. Using Flash Catalyst, you can select artwork and convert it to an interactive component using the heads-up display or the Modify menu (**Figure 9-8**).

When you create a component for one of the pre-built component types, the various states that are part of the component are created for you. This can help you complete other aspects of the design. For instance, when you create a button, there are commonly four unique states of a button (**Figure 9-9**): the up state (the normal state of the button), the over state (when the mouse cursor is over the button), the down state (when the mouse button is pressed while over the button), and the disabled state (when the button is disabled based on some configuration or situation in the application).

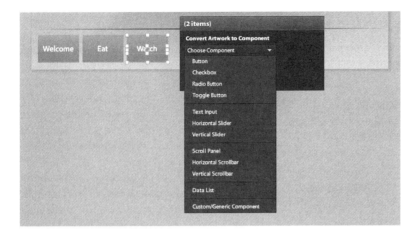

Figure 9-8 Converting artwork to a component in Flash Catalyst

Figure 9-9 Button states displayed in Flash Catalyst

ROUNDTRIP EXTENSIONS FOR PHOTOSHOP

When Creative Suite 5 shipped, the extensions required for sending designs from Flash Catalyst to Photoshop were not available. You can add them as Photoshop extensions by downloading and installing the extensions from this Web site: *http://www.adobe.com/go/photoshopfxg*.

When building custom components, the states are not predefined, and the designer needs to create them manually. Here is where the designer and developer contract plays an important role; it ensures that the way the designer is building the custom component will match what the developer is building and will support a relatively seamless integration of the design to the developer's code.

By converting the artwork to the component, you now have a more complete picture of the various design elements that need to be complete to fully design the application, even if those weren't captured in the initial design. This is an example of how you can iteratively design your components and designs using Flash Catalyst, Illustrator, and Photoshop.

TIP ■ You can use the Wireframe Components panel in Flash Catalyst to create your initial wireframe. These components already have the various component states and design elements that would need to be designed.

Building animated transitions and effects. One of the unique features of Flash Catalyst is in how you can add animated transitions to your project. Animated transitions are the changes that happen in your Flash Catalyst project when you move from one state or page of your project to another. Based on object visibility, position, rotation, and other properties, the transitions are created for you automatically; however, it is up to you as a designer to determine whether you want to choreograph or modify the style, speed, or ease of the transition effects.

WHAT IS AN ACTION SEQUENCE?

When you need to create an animated transition in Flash Catalyst but are not moving between states of the project, you need to create an *action sequence*. These are for when you build interactive behaviors but don't want to trigger a change in state in the application or component.

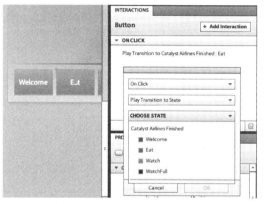

Figure 9-10 Creating an interaction on a button in Flash Catalyst

Adding interactions and behaviors. Flash Catalyst lets designers create interactive behaviors on components to execute specific actions such as playing transitions to states, playing action sequences, controlling video, and linking to URLs.

When working with the Interactions panel (**Figure 9-10**), the interactions are based on the capabilities of the individual component, so you will find that there are different behaviors for a button than there are for a data list.

Some component interactions give you control over when specific actions can happen. For example, when you create a button interaction, you can define a unique case for the interaction when you are in a specific state or page of your application or component.

Interactions built in Flash Catalyst are coded in ActionScript behind the scenes, which developers will then inherit when the project is handed off from design to development. What is so compelling about Flash Catalyst is that now the designer has the ability to build these interactive behaviors since they no longer need to be created through coding raw ActionScript.

Adding data. When building applications that will work with various pieces of data, it often becomes

WHEN A 1 ISN'T A 1

When building interactions based on the data list component, you can execute specific actions when a unique item is selected. To select the item, you choose a number from the list to attach the action to an item in the data list (**Figure 9-11**).

You'll notice that the default option is 0. This is using developer terminology for how items in the data list are numbered. Item 0 is the first item. Item 1 is the second item, and so forth. For guidance, you can refer to the Design Time Data panel, which uses the appropriate numbering in the row labels to help you match up your selections correctly.

Figure 9-11 Creating a unique interaction on data list item selection

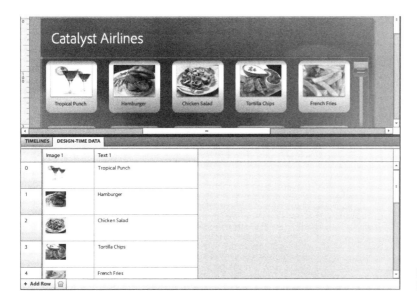

Figure 9-12 The Design-Time Data panel in Flash Catalyst

helpful to simulate actual data in the application to show a developer how the user interface would look and behave.

The Design-Time Data (DTD) panel (**Figure 9-12**) works with the data list component that you can create from a wireframe component or can build using various pieces of artwork. The DTD panel can include text and bitmaps that are part of the structure inside your data list component. Through the DTD panel, you can change the values of these properties, add new items to the data list, or remove items.

The data in the DTD panel is saved in a tag in the project that the developer can modify, or the developer can swap the design-time data with live data that they build a connection to in Flash Builder.

Working with component libraries. When working with multiple people on a team, you may want to spread the work of designing user interface elements or components across different people. When they design their components, they can export them using the Library panel in Flash Catalyst.

Using the Library panel (**Figure 9-13**), a designer can then import that external library into their project. However, currently in Flash Catalyst, when you export a library, you can't select specific items to export, so

Figure 9-13 Importing an external library into a project in Flash Catalyst

be sure that you have cleaned up your library and are handing off only those designs and components that are needed by the recipient.

Adding addition designs later in the project. You can add design assets at any time during the project, including importing Photoshop, Illustrator, FXG, or optimized graphics, as well as importing Flash Professional animations. When you work with Photoshop, Illustrator, or FXG files, you will have the same import options you had when you started your project and can then control the various layers of those files in Flash Catalyst.

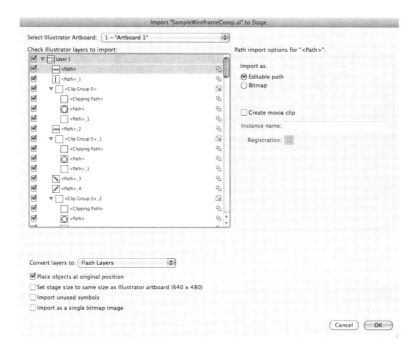

Designing using Flash Professional

When working with designs in Flash Professional, a number of similar workflows exist; we'll highlight the key differences to ensure greater success when working with Flash Professional.

Working with artwork. Flash Professional supports a large number of file types that you can import directly into your library or onto the stage of your already created project.

When importing Illustrator, Photoshop, or Fireworks documents into Flash Professional, you'll get a dialog box similar to **Figure 9-14**. In this dialog box, you have varying control over how you want each object or layer in your project converted when bringing designs to Flash Professional.

Two products support a direct export to a native Flash Professional project: InDesign and After Effects. Using InDesign and After Effects, you can export the document spread, wireframe document, motion graphic, or composite as a native Flash Professional project in order to preserve pages, layers, text, and

other attributes. This export process makes it faster to get started in Flash Professional.

In InDesign, you export your project as a Flash Professional FLA project. Using the dialog box shown in **Figure 9-15**, you can adjust your output settings including typographic quality, project size, and other information.

After exporting the project, you can open it directly in Flash Professional (**Figure 9-16**) and begin working with it. As you can imagine, this can be very helpful when working with wireframes that are in InDesign or when you need to repurpose assets that were used in a print spread in an interactive project.

Creating graphic symbols and MovieClips. When you work with designs in Flash Professional, they are grouped into a number of different types of categories. The first category is to keep them as simple graphics on the stage and not give them any structure. This is the simplest case for working with graphics, but it is also the most inflexible. Graphics that are on the stage of your project aren't saved or captured in the library,

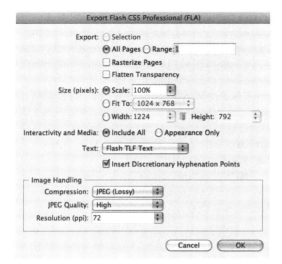

Figure 9-15 Exporting to a Flash Professional project from InDesign

and they can't be used more than once and keep a link to the same design.

The next level is to convert artwork into a graphic symbol using the Convert to Symbol dialog box (**Figure 9-17**). When you create a graphic symbol, you allow that object to be listed in the Library panel and can use it multiple times in your application design. You can then edit or modify the design of the library object inside the Library panel, and the changes will reflect across all instances of the symbol in the project. The limitation with graphic symbols is that they cannot easily be controlled using ActionScript, and they do not contain a timeline that you can use to build an animation.

The highest level in Flash Professional to convert artwork to is a MovieClip. Using the same workflow for creating a graphic symbol, you can build a MovieClip. This type of object can be easily controlled using ActionScript, and your developer can link it to an ActionScript class for even more flexibility. A MovieClip can have 9-slice scaling used to resize the

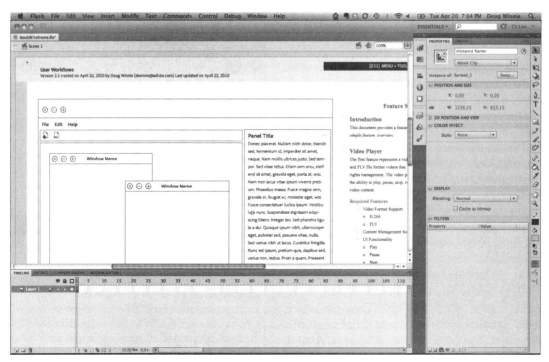

Figure 9-16 Flash Professional after opening an exported project from InDesign

Figure 9-17 Flash Professional Convert to Symbol dialog box

WHAT IS 9-SLICE SCALING?

When you create a MovieClip in Flash Professional, you have the option to create 9-slice scaling guides. These guides will allow you to virtually "slice" the object into nine sections. When you resize the object using various tools, settings, or ActionScript, the slices will use the guides to define which sections of the design can stretch horizontally, vertically, both horizontally and vertically, or not at all.

object, and it can contain a timeline to animate graphics and other items within the object.

Building animations. The core of Flash Professional is animation. Using Flash Professional, you can create extensive types of animations using the various graphic symbols and MovieClips you have built via the animation engine in Flash Professional.

The basic animation is the motion path. Motion path animations are built by creating a new animation on a graphic symbol or MovieClip and changing the animation at specific points along the adjustable duration of the animation. These points are converted into special frames called *keyframes* that capture what the object should look like on a specific frame. Flash Professional will automatically build the frames between the keyframes using its internal animation engine.

Shape and inverse kinematic animations. Using basic shapes in Flash Professional, you can create shape animations that morph the shape of objects between keyframes that you define. Shape animations are relatively simple and are not extremely flexible.

You can have greater control over the animation of shapes using the inverse kinematic engines in Flash Professional. Using the Bone tool, you can add structure to your shapes and then animate those "limbs" using the timeline engine.

In addition, you can connect individual objects with the Bone tool to then coordinate the animation of multiple objects together using settings you apply to each object, to each limb, and also through virtual inertia called *springs*.

"3D." Flash Professional supports the animation of objects in "3D." The quotation marks are intentional, because you can't import a 3D model into Flash Professional and animate it. Instead, you can take any object in Flash that is a 2D object and animate it in 3D space.

Animation in 3D involves two specific areas. The first is *rotation*. If you take an object and keep it in a fixed location, you can rotate it around the three axes. This is rotation in 3D. The second method is *translation*, where you can physically move the object along the three axes. By combining these axes, you can build more complex animations.

CLASSIC ANIMATION IN FLASH PROFESSIONAL

You may notice that Flash Professional has some options for creating tweens for "classic" animations. These features are based on the animation engine of Flash Professional from CS3 and older. They are still part of Flash Professional if you want to use the older animation model.

ACTIONSCRIPT ANIMATION

Some animators prefer to create their animations exclusively using ActionScript. Creating animations in ActionScript gives code-friendly designers the ability to define and extend the animation engine in Flash Professional beyond the limits of the product and include a number of external frameworks.

MOTION EDITOR

The Motion Editor panel (**Figure 9-18**) gives you much more extensive animation control over each animation property, including 3D axis control and filters. You can easily add per-property keyframes as well as customize eases and apply them to the various property timelines in the panel.

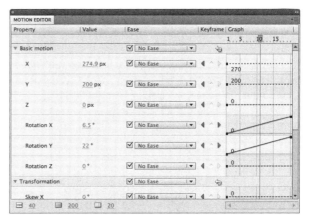

Figure 9-18 The Motion Editor panel in Flash Professional

When working in 3D, the perspective of the animation needs to be based on a point. This is called the *vanishing point*, and you can adjust the vanishing point to change the perspective that will be used for the animation.

Working with advanced text options. In addition to animation, Flash Professional has the most advanced typographic tools for designers to use when building interactive projects. Using the new Text Layout Framework (TLF), designers can build advanced type for their project, including international typographic support.

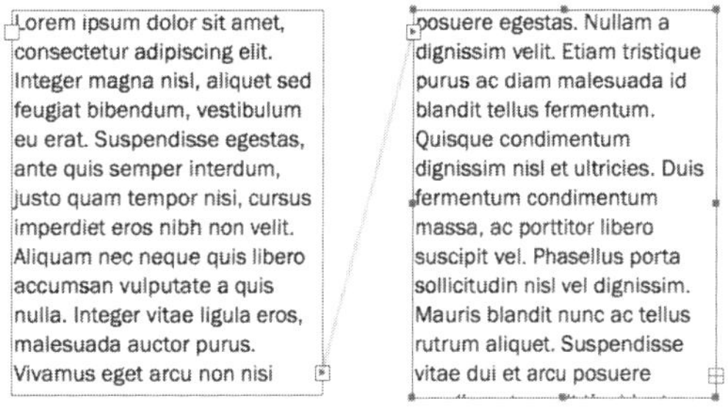

Other capabilities of the new text engine in Flash Professional are support for columns within text fields and the ability to link text boxes. When placing content that overflows the bounds of a text box, you will see an indicator that lets you create a new text box or link to another text box on the screen (**Figure 9-19**).

There are too many new text features to list here, but it is beneficial for designers to familiarize themselves with the numerous new text options that were previously not available.

Working with ActionScript as a designer. In the past as a designer, working with ActionScript was a

Figure 9-19 Text boxes linked together and text overflow indicator

painful but necessary activity to get your project to work correctly and to add any interactivity to your MovieClips and designs. In Flash Professional CS5, things have been made easier through the addition of *code snippets*.

Using the Code Snippets panel (**Figure 9-20**), you can create common ActionScript behaviors and apply them to objects in your project. When you use a snippet, you don't have to know by heart the ActionScript required to complete an action; instead, you can rely on the comments at the top of the snippet to help customize it to meet the behavior you want.

USING FLASH PROFESSIONAL TLF TEXT IN FLASH CATALYST

Flash Catalyst lets designers import Flash Professional and other SWFs into a project to display and play back animations or other interactive elements. When using TLF text, the publishing folder when you compile will contain a file with a name similar to textLayout_1.0.0.595.swz.

This is called a *runtime shared library* and contains the core elements of the new text framework. If you attempt to bring in the published SWF, you will find that it won't preserve your text. That is because the TLF library, by default, isn't baked into the SWF. To force Flash Professional to merge the text framework into the published FLA, you open the Publish Settings, and edit the Action-Script properties by selecting the TLF library from the Library tab and setting the default linkage to Merge into Code.

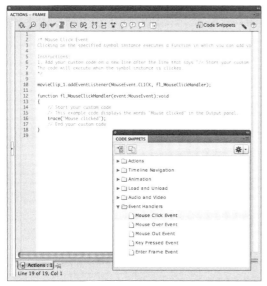

Figure 9-20 Actions panel showing an event handler added from the Code Snippets panel

Code snippets will give you enough to build basic interactivity into your project, but they can lead to broken code and issues if you aren't careful, so use code snippets sparingly and only if you have a basic understanding of ActionScript already.

Working efficiently with Creative Suite design tools

When working with designs in Flash Catalyst and Flash Professional, several features can make the overall process easier. Some of these are features that are new to Creative Suite 5, while others have been "hidden gems" for a couple of releases and are worth mentioning here.

Flash Catalyst document profile in Illustrator

When you start a new design in Adobe Illustrator, you can use a number of profiles to start your design. One of them is specifically for Flash Catalyst. Using this document profile (**Figure 9-21**), you can set common window resolutions for your design. The profile also configures Illustrator to work with pixels, sets the resolution that should be used for raster effects, and sets the proper color mode. It also sets up the new pixel grid that is part of CS5 to make it easier to position objects on the whole pixel for higher-fidelity import into Flash Catalyst.

In addition to initial document settings, the document profile also prepopulates the swatches, graphic styles, and symbols in your Illustrator panels with items that are helpful for creating Web site or application user interface designs.

The Flash Catalyst document preset is also just as useful for creating designs for Flash Professional.

Illustrator Flash Professional Text panel

When designing your artwork in Illustrator, you can set a number of Flash Professional type settings (**Figure 9-22**) before you even get into Flash Professional. This can save some time when you bring your artwork into Flash Professional, and it will convert text into read-only, selectable, or editable using the Text Layout Framework upon import and also preserve

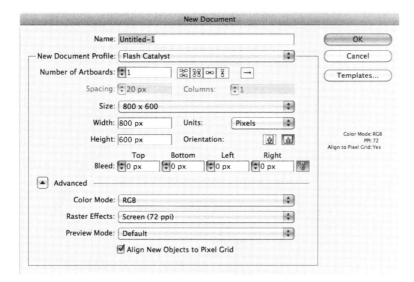

Figure 9-21 Creating a new document with a document profile in Illustrator

instance names that were set in Illustrator. (These settings are just for Flash Professional; the settings aren't preserved when the Illustrator comp is imported into Flash Catalyst.)

Artboards in Illustrator

When working with designs in Illustrator, you can break out the various pages or states of your application or component into artboards. You can create new artboards using the Artboard panel (**Figure 9-23**). These artboards are then imported into Flash Catalyst as unique pages or states in your project. When doing this, be sure to resolve any duplicated items that may exist in multiple states or pages.

In Flash Professional, you can import each unique artboard one at a time. This can help designers keep all the various designs for a Flash Professional project in a single file but allow them to group assets into logical groups using artboards.

Graphic styles in Illustrator

To help maintain design consistency between Illustrator users and documents, you can save design elements, gradients, symbols, and other objects as external graphic style libraries. By saving a library, you can define specific style rules that can be difficult to replicate manually each time, such as complex

Figure 9-22 Defining Flash Professional text properties in Illustrator

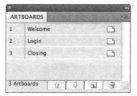

Figure 9-23 Artboards panel in Illustrator

WHAT IS PIXEL PREVIEW MODE?

You can set up *pixel preview mode* when starting a new document to display your objects based in pixels at the set resolution and dots per inch (DPI) settings (**Figure 9-24**). When you zoom in, you'll see the exact pixel representation instead of scaling up the stroke.

Setting this mode in Illustrator, when working with the Flash Platform, is important because Flash Player can support positions only up to a single pixel. Without this setting, Illustrator can create designs that have positions at subpixel positions, such as x = 3.879. When Flash Player tries to render this content, it will round off the decimal values, which can cause your design's layout to be rendered incorrectly.

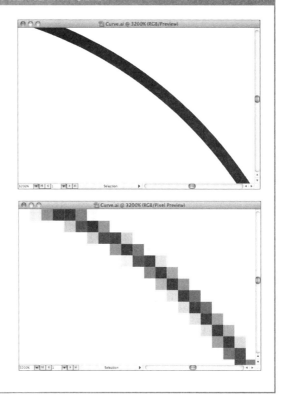

Figure 9-24 Viewing a curve with the normal view (top) or with pixel preview (bottom)

---

gradients with multiple stop points, specific colors, and other elements.

When you create these styles in Illustrator, you can save them as an external library. On another document, the library can be opened, and the styles will exist in their own custom panel (**Figure 9-25**) for use in the project.

Graphic styles can also be named to help identify each style in either an icon or list view.

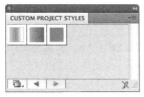

Figure 9-25 Panel showing a saved graphic style library in Illustrator

Adobe Swatch Exchange (ASE)

In the previous chapter, we discussed using kuler to help find aesthetically pleasing color combinations using common color best practices and community collaboration. When you import those color themes into Creative Suite, they are in a format called Adobe Swatch Exchange (ASE). ASE is a consistent format for exchanging color swatches between Creative Suite design tools. Using Photoshop, Illustrator, or Fireworks, you can exchange color themes consistently to ensure that the colors used for a project are always the same.

ASE isn't supported in Flash Professional or Flash Catalyst, but you can use ASE swatches when roundtripping your designs from Flash Catalyst with Illustrator and Photoshop.

Symbols in Illustrator

In Illustrator, if you are creating objects that are reused in multiple locations in your design, they can be saved as a symbol. Symbols in Illustrator let design objects be reused consistently in a project, and if the symbol is updated, the changes will cascade through all the objects.

When importing an Illustrator document with symbols into Flash Catalyst, symbols are converted to optimized graphics. When they're duplicated or when other instances are created by dragging them out from the Library panel, optimized graphics are linked to the same definition, which keeps the file size of your project small and optimizes your project better for your developer.

When working with Flash Professional, imported symbols are automatically converted to MovieClips in the library, making it easier to manage designs and keep a link to a single design definition.

Simplify layers for FXG in Photoshop

When working with Photoshop, there are so many filters, blend modes, and adjustment layers that you can add to your project that it can become very difficult to remember what is supported in Flash Player and what is not. To make this process easier, you can use the Simplify Layers for FXG script that is part of the Photoshop FXG Roundtrip Extensions (see the earlier "Roundtrip Extensions for Photoshop" sidebar for more information).

When using this script, Photoshop will analyze your layers and flatten or rasterize effects that aren't supported in Flash Player for maximum fidelity preservation when going to Flash Catalyst during a redesign round-trip workflow.

You can also use this script to process through your designs before importing your PSD into Flash Professional and Flash Catalyst for greater fidelity as well.

Layer comps and advanced Photoshop import options

When using the layer comp feature in Photoshop, you define the visibility of your layers as a "set" that can be quickly displayed to show various views into the project in a single Photoshop file. Layer comps are often used to show unique Web pages or states of an application design.

When importing Photoshop files into Flash Professional, you can select a specific layer comp to import using the Import dialog box. In Flash Catalyst, layer comp import is supported in the advanced options of the Photoshop Import Options dialog box. When importing layer comps into Flash Catalyst, make sure that you resolve any duplicated objects to ensure an efficient and optimized project when handed off to a developer.

WHY ARE DUPLICATES BAD?

When you have duplicates of items due to graphics being replicated in different artboards in Illustrator, pages in Fireworks, or layer comps in Photoshop, the redundancy can lead to significant size increase in your project and the application and can lead to inconsistencies when you adjust or make changes to objects in one state that aren't reflected in the other since it is a different discrete object.

In **Figure 9-26**, you'll see that there are two graphics that were imported from different artboards in Illustrator. If a change is made to the header in one of objects, the change wouldn't map to the other object. Worse yet, these two objects are represented in code as completely separate items, so your developer can easily be confused and not know which object to work with.

Figure 9-26 Redundant objects in Flash Catalyst

Exporting graphics for redesign from Flash Professional

Flash Professional supports two specific workflows for updating graphics with either Photoshop or Illustrator. When working with vector artwork, you can select specific objects for redesign and export as FXG. Using this format, you can then open them in Illustrator, update the design, and reimport them into Flash Professional.

To help streamline bitmap editing, you can select any bitmap in your library or on the stage and edit in Photoshop CS5 by right-clicking it. When you save the file, it will update the bitmap in Flash Professional.

Using Fireworks with Flash Catalyst

Fireworks CS5 is an amazing design tool that combines vector and bitmap tools into an easy-to-use product that is very approachable for designers and developers. Using Fireworks, you can create designs for Flash Professional and import the native PNG file that is saved from Fireworks into Flash Professional, but what about with Flash Catalyst?

With Flash Catalyst, you can't import the PNG file directly; the workflow when moving from Fireworks to Flash Catalyst is to export your design from Fireworks into FXG. Using the Export option, select FXG and Images. Then export your existing document, the current page, or the selected objects on the artboard. When you export a Fireworks design that contains multiple pages, those pages will convert to states when you open the FXG file in Flash Catalyst.

One important note is that components that you create in Fireworks will not automatically convert to components. You will have to define those manually when you open your project in Fireworks.

Working with Adobe Media Encoder

When working with video and audio assets, you may need to convert them into a compatible format for use in Flash Professional or Flash Catalyst. A number of formats are supported, and to help with the conversion process, you can use Adobe Media Encoder.

When opening audio or video files in Adobe Media Encoder, you can export them to Web-optimized versions for use in your projects including MP3, FLV, F4V, and H.264. Using the queue window (**Figure 9-27**),

you can set the destination type using the Format selector and choose the appropriate format. The Preset options provide more granular quality and output settings that you can optionally select.

If you are processing a number of files, you can create a watch folder. When running, Adobe Media Encoder will continually poll the watch folder for new files and automatically encode them using the settings you apply to the watch folder.

Tricks with fonts

With Adobe design products, there are extensive ways to work with fonts and typography. When working with type in your interactive projects, there are a few caveats to help optimize and streamline the process of working with fonts.

With more complex fonts that have multiple symbols, international characters, and ligatures, embedding the entire font into your project can become problematic. To keep your file size small, you can select specific ranges of characters within the font to embed into the project. Flash Professional and Flash Catalyst have specific locations where you can select these character ranges.

In Flash Professional, you can add fonts to your project using the Font Embedding command within the Type menu. This opens the Font Embedding dialog box (**Figure 9-28**), where you can select fonts and add them to the project. The fonts will be displayed in the library as a font type. You can also optionally link fonts to ActionScript classes. The fonts that are specifically added to the project will appear at the top of the font selector to ensure that only embedded fonts are used in the project.

You can also create embedded fonts from existing text fields. By selecting a text field and clicking the Embed… button in the Properties panel, you can then embed the fonts that are used in the text field.

When using Flash Catalyst, you define font embedding during the publishing process. In the Publish to SWF and AIR dialog box, you can embed fonts and define advanced settings. Using the Font Embedding dialog box (**Figure 9-29**), you can select the specific fonts to embed and define the character sets that will be used for the embedded font.

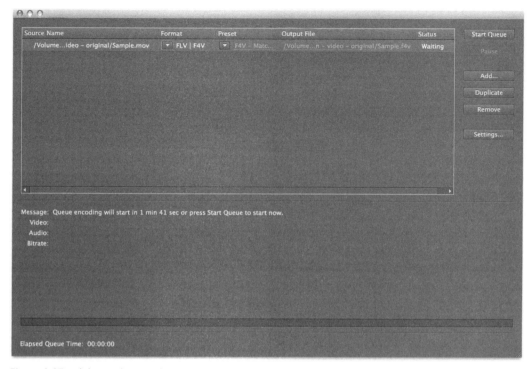

Figure 9-27 Adobe Media Encoder

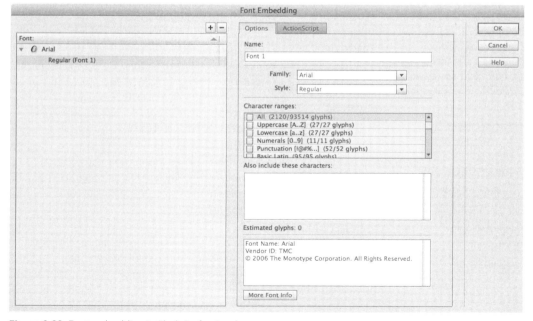

Figure 9-28 Font embedding in Flash Professional

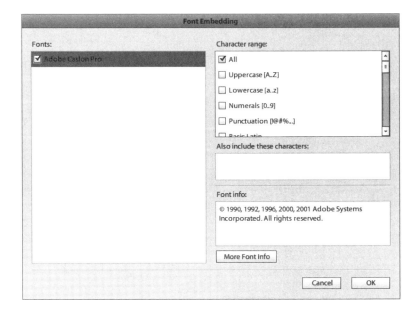

Figure 9-29 Font embedding in Flash Catalyst

TYPE 1 FONTS AND FLASH CATALYST

Flash Catalyst doesn't support Type 1 fonts when working with designs. When creating your designs in Illustrator, Fireworks, or Photoshop, make sure you are using TrueType or OpenType fonts for your projects. In addition, fonts that are common system fonts in Mac OS X are not supported in Flash Catalyst or in Flex.

PREPARING FOR THE HANDOFF

When you have completed your project in Flash Catalyst or Flash Professional, it is time to hand off your project to development to connect the project to live data or to do any heavy lifting with ActionScript that may be required with the project.

Ultimately, the contract you have between the designer and developer will determine how you want to transfer files between the people on your project. Be sure to agree on how you will transfer files with your developer ahead of time. The workflow and handoff process needs to be well communicated. Will you be transferring design files? Libraries of components? SWCs? Entire projects?

To help make that handoff as efficient as possible, there are a number of best practices, covered in the following sections, to help organize and ensure that the development team has a clean, high-quality product to start from when they do their work.

Keeping a tidy project

You don't want to have a messy closet, kitchen, or office, right? And you shouldn't have a messy library in your project. Having a clean and organized library will make it much easier for the recipient to find the various aspects of your project.

Organizing your Flash Professional project

In Flash Professional, the library contains all the graphic symbols, MovieClips, embedded fonts, video, components, and other reusable elements of your project. By default, Flash Professional doesn't force

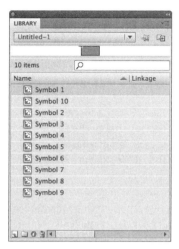

Figure 9-30 An unorganized library in Flash Professional

Figure 9-31 An organized library in Flash Professional

a structure on you when you start creating symbols, but the library can quickly get into an unorganized state after just creating a few objects, as shown in **Figure 9-30**.

The Library panel allows you to organize the various elements of the project into folders. By creating named folders, you can then sort and organize the various objects in your project. Also, when you create a new symbol, Flash Professional gives it a generic name by default, such as Symbol 1. If you didn't give your symbols unique names when they were created, you can adjust them in the Library panel. When you are done, you should have an organized library that will make you proud and your developer happy (**Figure 9-31**).

The work you do to organize your library also has other benefits. If you and your team are working with the new uncompressed XFL project format, you'll notice that your library structure will also flow to the XFL project folder (**Figure 9-32**). If you are working with a network share or with version control, you can then further organize your assets when working collaboratively.

In addition to the library, you need to ensure that you give your object instances clear, concise, identifiable names. Calling your object instances

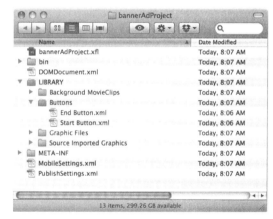

Figure 9-32 An XFL project folder, showing the organized folder structure of the library

movieClip_1, movieClip_2, movieClip_3, and so on, is not a clear and easy way to keep track of the various objects on the stage. Someone inheriting the project from you and looking exclusively at the code would have no idea which object was which.

Other key items to keep clean and organized are the timelines of your project. When working with the new animation engine in Flash Professional, it creates new timelines for each specific object you are animating. In addition, inverse kinematic animations and masks are also on separate layers, causing your timelines to quickly look messy (**Figure 9-33**).

Using folders and timeline names, you can organize the various timelines of your project. Flash Professional also allows you to create comments inside the timeline using keyframes. By selecting a keyframe, you can enter a label and select it to be a comment (or prefix the text with two forward slashes as a shortcut). It is also good to create comment timelines to put descriptions or author information that may be helpful for your team (**Figure 9-34**).

And remember, if you use the uncompressed XFL project, your timelines and comments within them are expressed in XFL and can be searched and used with your product team.

Keeping your objects named and organized in Flash Catalyst

When you create a design in Illustrator, Fireworks, or Photoshop and import the design into Flash Catalyst, the structure and names of your layers and layer folder or groups are preserved to help maintain context for you as a designer. When you create additional objects in Flash Catalyst, they are given generic names in the layer panel that can make it difficult to understand (**Figure 9-35**).

If you are handing off your Flash Catalyst project to another Flash Catalyst user or if you have components that have internal layer structure and are handing off libraries of components, an unorganized layer structure can make it difficult to maintain a solid context in your project.

What is more critical when working with Flash Catalyst is to keep your components clearly named in the Library panel. Components are the core building blocks of Flex and Flash Catalyst. If you keep the default names that Flash Catalyst gives your components, your developer can quickly get frustrated trying to keep track of what was CustomComponent1 versus CustomComponent2 (**Figure 9-36**).

When your developer opens this project in Flash Builder, they will find that all the component names in code use these generic names. In addition, all the

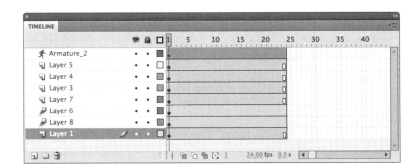

Figure 9-33 An XFL project folder, showing the organized folder structure of the library

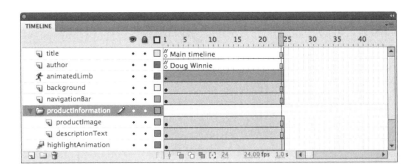

Figure 9-34 An XFL project folder, showing the organized folder structure of the library

Figure 9-35 An unorganized layer structure in Flash Catalyst

Figure 9-36 An unorganized component library in Flash Catalyst

Figure 9-37 A well-named component library in Flash Catalyst

components are saved as individual MXML files for the developer to open. These will also have the same matching names as the ones used in the library. So, you could have an entire project full of MXML files that have generic and useless filenames.

For this reason, it is critical that you keep your components clearly named for your developer to easily and efficiently work with the project when you hand it off to them (**Figure 9-37**).

HOW ARE LAYER NAMES HELPFUL FOR DEVELOPERS?

Layer names, when handed off to a developer, are saved as namespaced attributes called d:userLabel. So even if you hand off your project to a developer, using clear and concise layer names can help them see and understand the project when working with the generated code.

In addition, layer groups are saved in the code as MXML tags called <fx:DesignLayer> to help with code folding and organization in MXML.

You should consider organizing the vector objects in your project. By default, vector objects and the code that is part of them are placed inline with the rest of the code of the project. Often, the developer doesn't need to have this code in the project, and for projects that have complex vector information, the code can become intricate and be at risk for accidental modification by the developer, which can cause issues with the design.

When you are finished with the design of your project and are ready to hand off to developers, you can convert vector objects to optimized graphics (**Figure 9-38**). This will extract the vector code that is inline with the application code into an external file that the developer can safely ignore, allowing for much cleaner application code when opening the project.

If you are working with bitmaps, you can also set them to be externally linked bitmaps. When the project is published, you can then access the images outside of the project to make post-publish changes, and you can reduce the file size of the project.

Handing off to developers

You can hand off your project to the development team in multiple ways. Again, be sure to have an agreement or contract with your developer peers to determine how they want to get designs from you.

Figure 9-38 Converting vector artwork into an optimized graphic in Flash Catalyst

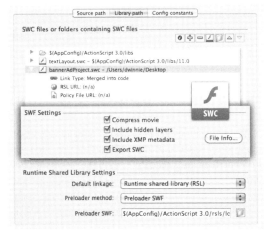

Figure 9-39 Publishing and library path settings for working with SWC files in Flash Professional

One of the simplest ways is to provide the native design files from Illustrator, Fireworks, or Photoshop and give them to the development team to work with. This obviously requires that the development team is using Creative Suite design tools, but for some teams this workflow can be highly efficient.

Developers may want to import designs into Flash Catalyst themselves, copy and paste code from Flash Catalyst's code workspace into their Flash Builder project, and then massage the code from there. Others prefer to slice and work with the graphics from the design tools.

If you are handing off design files—either alone or alongside your project files from Flash Professional and Flash Catalyst—you should make sure that all the assets are included. Often fonts, linked images, placed text, or other similar assets are missed when handing off to others. Missing fonts can especially cause issues when handing a project to developers.

Handing off libraries using Flash Professional

You can hand off project libraries from Flash Professional and Flash Catalyst in a number of ways. Using Flash Professional, if you have created classes for various MovieClips in your library, you can export these as SWC files to share with developers.

SWC files are compiled libraries that contain all the assets and code for the various components built in Flash Professional. You can set up Flash Professional to publish a SWC using the Flash publishing settings (**Figure 9-39**).

The developer then links to the SWC file in the library path settings for the project. When creating code, Flash Professional provides code hinting for the contents of the SWC to make coding easier. If the design or components change, the designer can export and updated SWC for the developer to replace in their project.

You can also open FLA files as external libraries for projects. When using this feature, a designer can create a library of assets that they save as a FLA file and then hand that project to another user. In Flash Professional, the library of that FLA can be opened as an external Library panel (**Figure 9-40**). Using this Library panel, the developer can import objects into the project by dragging and dropping from the external Library panel to the current project Library panel or to the stage.

Any folder organization, structure, naming, or other attributes are preserved when you copy the object into your project. If you have objects that have linked ActionScript classes, make sure they are accessible to the project; otherwise, you will get errors when you attempt to run or publish the project.

NOTE ▪ External libraries work with FLA files only. They cannot be used with uncompressed XFL projects.

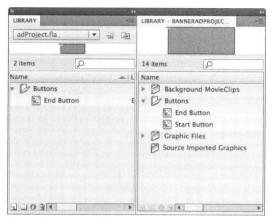

Figure 9-40 External library panel

Handing off projects and libraries from Flash Catalyst

When working with Flash Catalyst, there are two methods for handing off your project:

- Take the Flash Catalyst project file, or FXP, and send that to a developer. An FXP is a compressed Flex project that can be easily imported into Flash Builder to create a Flex project.
- Export the library of components as an FXPL file. This, when imported into Flash Builder, will be a Flex library project that the developer can then link to an existing Flex project and bring components that are part of the library into the main Flex project.

SYNCING WITH YOUR TEAM

When you started this chapter, you had some basic structure and ideas for the design of your project. Throughout the workflow and wireframe process, designers will craft and build the user experience of the project. Along the way, these designers share their work and intent for the designs with visual designers and developers on the team to ensure that everyone is in sync and is moving along on the same path.

When working as a designer in a team, building consistent designs can be a challenge. Luckily, Creative Suite has a number of tools and features that make it easier to create and share libraries, designers, colors, fonts, and other aspects of your project with each other to make the design workflow easier, less cumbersome, and more consistent across different designers on the team.

When you finish your designs using Illustrator, Fireworks, or Photoshop or complete your animations in Flash Professional or wrap up your application user interface designs in Flash Catalyst, you should sit down and sync with your team before handing off your work.

Make sure that the contract you built with your developer is honored with how you are building and structuring your project or designs to transfer to their new owner. Take the time to sit down with your developer or designer peers to review and answer questions, make adjustments, and provide supporting documentation that can help streamline the design process and handoff to developers.

Throughout this process, whether it is a complete handoff from design to development or whether you're using an iterative process where design and development are happening in parallel, the workflows, best practices, and other tips presented in this chapter will help your designers be as streamlined and efficient as possible and will help them design great work for the Flash Platform.

SUMMARY CHECKLIST

When working through the design process, you need to account for several aspects of the user workflow and visual design before you hand off the project to development. In addition, there are some pre-handoff steps that should be taken to ensure that your developer is getting work and projects that they can quickly start working from.

✔ Have you defined the workflow that your user will take to complete the use cases of your project?

✔ Have the user workflows been reviewed to find redundant steps that should be consolidated, or perhaps even eliminated, from the project?

✔ Do you have client approval on the user workflows of the project?

✔ Have you reviewed the user workflows with your developer peers so they know the steps and business logic that they need to build to facilitate the workflow?

✔ Have you created detailed wireframes that map out the steps of each user workflow?

✔ Have you reviewed your wireframes with your client and developer peers to get their feedback and comments?

✔ Do your developers understand the modules or logical parts of the project's user interface that they need to build?

✔ If you are using Flash Catalyst, has your user interface been fully designed including state transitions and user interactions?

✔ Have you provided valuable design-time data for data list components in Flash Catalyst that your developer can use to help connect the project to live data services?

✔ If you are using Flash Professional, have you created reusable graphic symbols or MovieClips that can help reduce redesign time and contribute to an organized project?

✔ Have you embedded required fonts into your Flash Catalyst or Flash Professional project?

✔ Have you met with your developer prior to handoff to ensure that the setup and structure of the design is in alignment with the designer and developer contract?

✔ Have you organized your project in a way that will make it easier to understand and comprehend for your team or for future updates later in the project?

✔ Are your Flash Catalyst components and layer names clearly named for developers to easily find the correct context when working with code?

✔ Have you provided your developer with the appropriate project handoff type including FLA, SWC, FXP, or FXPL?

PART IV

DEVELOPMENT

CHAPTER 10

Planning Development

Projects are becoming ever more rich in content, media, visual effects, and other user behaviors. With this increase in rich features, projects are growing in scope and longevity. The life span of an application has increased from mere days or weeks to potentially existing for years online, either on the desktop or on mobile platforms. Applications may undergo many iterations intended to enhance and increase value for customers. Because of this longevity, you should thoroughly plan your development efforts so your application will be stable, maintainable, and scalable.

In this chapter, we will cover architecting your application's components, content, and data layer. And we'll discuss setting up team guidelines for coding standards, which will help your team to create a more consistent code base. This process is important because when development teams consider all of these areas, they have a greater chance of producing an application that will be successful short and long term.

ARCHITECTING YOUR APPLICATION

In most medium to large-scale projects, the feature set will most likely change from inception to final deployment. Because of this, your application's code base needs to be flexible enough to adjust as features and use cases shift. If your application's foundation does not adjust to slight or even medium-size changes, your project risks failure in terms of schedule and budget. By spending time up front to architect your application, you can help guarantee a solid foundation and set of rules on which to build your application.

Use design patterns to solve common business problems

The art of computer science is more than a half of a century old. Over those 50-plus years, many common approaches to solving problems have been defined and shared openly. Even with all of the advancements in technology and programming languages, many of the common patterns that were developed years ago are still relevant today. In Flash, developers can take advantage of many of these *design patterns* to help solve issues that arise on a daily basis during development. Common patterns include the command, factory, and mediator.

You or your developers should be sure that you understand some of the most widely used patterns and adopt them inside your application or framework. We suggest openly discussing patterns among your team as the project progresses. This open dialogue will benefit junior and midlevel developers as they learn from the seasoned veterans.

Your team—especially if it's a large one—should keep your code base as consistent as possible. One developer will most likely need to work inside another's code in order to add new features or fix a bug. If design patterns are shared and used among team members, developers will have a greater chance of finding their way around unfamiliar code.

Consider adopting a framework

When architecting a project from the ground up, an application framework is usually the first place to look after you have had time to examine the feature set for your project. Frameworks are a starting point to get your application off the ground with relative ease. A *framework* is a collection of utilities, base classes, and design pattern implementations that help organize and compartmentalize different aspects of your application.

ARCHITECTING YOUR APPLICATION THROUGH DIAGRAMS

Part of your application planning process might include creating architecture diagrams of your system. The diagrams can include basic logic showing how the various divisions of your application will interact with each other. Diagrams are an easy way to explain technical features to nontechnical team members. Keep these diagrams in mind as we walk through the large areas of your application that should be considered when planning your architecture.

THE MODEL VIEW CONTROLLER PATTERN

The most common type of design pattern used in application frameworks by Flash developers is the Model, View, Controller (MVC) pattern. The MVC pattern separates your application's data (model), from your business logic (controller), and your application's look and feel (view), by grouping each part into unique tiers. This separation allows developers to identify where code lives based on its functionality and to easily modify or add behaviors to each area with little effect on the other two tiers. Almost all of the popular third-party frameworks available today are, at the core, based on the MVC pattern.

Third-party vs. custom frameworks

When planning your project, you'll need to decide whether a third-party or custom framework will be more efficient over the long term. It might be wise to choose a well-adopted framework such as Cairngorm, Mate, RobotLegs, PureMVC, or even Development-Arc Core. Choosing a well-established framework will make it easier to find external resources—such as documentation, examples, tutorials, and other research material—and to hire developers who are experienced using the chosen framework. This can be helpful when developers on your team leave or when you simply need to hire more developers.

Third-party frameworks provide a lot of functionality out of the box. But in order to understand the chosen framework, developers will need to be given time to research and learn about it. For larger projects, ramp-up time on a third-party framework can decrease over all development time by producing a consistent best practice for each developer when creating features. In the long run, the up-front cost is generally offset by the efficiency your developers will gain when refactoring or creating new features later in the project.

Third-party frameworks may not always meet your requirements or may be simply too complex for your needs. In that case, you will need to either make adjustments to the third-party framework, build add-ons to address your needs, or consider a custom framework.

Developing a custom framework can be valuable—especially on larger projects—because your custom system will be tailored to address your needs. The downside is that the up-front development time will increase if you plan on creating a well defined API and set of reusable patterns. The initial framework must be created prior to developing the project itself, which will cause a larger up-front construction phase. As your project matures, your team will need to account for time required to adjust the custom framework as updates and new features are needed.

On smaller projects, it might not make sense to adopt a formal framework, but it does still make sense to organize your code into certain "buckets" depending on the code's functionality. This means that you can simply split your layout/view, business, and server connection logic into separate ActionScript classes and store them in different packages. By organizing your code this way, you are essentially starting to create a custom framework, which can ultimately create a foundation that meets 100 percent of your needs.

Remember that you can mix and match third-party and custom frameworks. The goal of a framework is to bring consistency to your development team and code base.

Why frameworks?

Frameworks provide the organization needed to keep your code consistent over time and with different developers, which is especially useful when projects require a large code or multiple developers. A framework requires your code to follow predefined design patterns and organizes the code into compartments based on functionality—helping developers keep code consistent, no matter the size of your team or when they joined the project.

Organizing your code in a framework helps teams consolidate and reuse code that might otherwise be unwittingly duplicated by different developers. Frameworks also facilitate collaboration among your team members. For example, if one developer needs to jump in and tackle a bug or enhance a feature, the framework will make it easier to locate the source code that needs to change.

> ### SPARK: VIEW AND CONTROLLER BUILT INTO FLEX
>
> Flex 4 introduced a new component skinning architecture called Spark. With this new architecture, the skin (view) and component (controller) have been decoupled and linked via a CSS style property called skinClass. This decoupling makes it easier for designs to be implemented on top of already defined business logic (controller), allowing for a parallel designer and developer workflow. See Chapter 11, "Iterative Development," for details on the designer/developer contract and parallel workflows.

Why not frameworks?

If you are building a banner ad or a small one-off Flash application, it might not make sense to adopt or create your own framework. Projects with a short turnaround time often do not justify the time necessary to learn a third-party framework or to create a custom framework. And all frameworks will require additional time to set up inside your application. This extra time might not be possible if your project is estimated to take only 40 hours to develop.

Frameworks also require a lot of compartmentalizing of code. This means when developing a feature, many parts will need to be created to get your project integrated into the framework. For example, a developer who is creating a new data service in the Adobe Cairngorm Framework (following the best practices) would need to create a command class, event class, and service class and configure each into the application.

For larger projects, frameworks make more sense because you will likely reuse parts as your application grows (such as the data service mechanism that the Cairngorm framework provides). But for small projects, this type of development might cost you valuable time and will provide little benefit.

ARCHITECTING YOUR COMPONENTS

When architecting the structure of your application's layout tier, it's a good idea to break the user interface (UI) into organized components. Each component will contain distinct logic and behavior and, combined with other components, will make up a specific feature or use case.

Separating portions of the UI into distinct entities allows your application to be pieced together with a loosely coupled architecture. Developers can create and modify each component independently of other components. Because of the decoupling of components, one developer can be working on, say, the login system while another works on registration—all within the same code base.

Views

At a high level, your application may consist of multiple views, and each view represents a particular user interface element such as login or registration. A view consists of a set of subpieces, which together make up a higher level of functionality.

In Flash Catalyst, views are defined as pages. **Figure 10-1** illustrates a sample application with four views: welcome, login, forgot password, and registration. Each view has a unique role in the application as a whole, but each is distinct and decoupled from the others. If one does not exist or one's functionality changes, the others are not impacted.

Components

A view can be further broken down into components. A *component* is a set of common UI functionality that is isolated into a single class. The purpose of a component is to compartmentalize a set of behaviors that have the potential to be reused inside a view or another component.

Looking at the login example in Figure 10-1, you can break the view down into a series of components. The components are a sign-up button, two text fields, and a couple of labels. The purpose of the login view is to take input from the user and provide feedback based on the information entered into the two text fields. For this functionality to work, each component must complete its individual role. The text fields must accept user input, and the sign-up button must be able to handle a mouse click. Combined together, the view can perform validation on the input fields and provide feedback to the user.

A component consists of parts that are usually other subcomponents. This concept is identical to a view, except a component is classified as reusable, while a view is most likely used for one purpose.

Each part has a distinct role in a component's functionality. Because parts can be thought of as components, they can be reused if architected correctly in other components or directly in views.

Figure 10-1 Page management inside Flash Catalyst

Each component can contain different appearances based on user or system interactions. These appearances are known as states in the Flex world. For example, when a user rolls over a Flex button, the button will change its state from "up" to "over." By changing states, the button can show a slight change in the display to acknowledge the user's behavior. **Figure 10-2** shows an example of a Flex button in Flash Catalyst. A button can be represented in four states (Up, Over, Down, and Disabled).

The ability to create states is built into the Flex component architecture. If you are building your project in Flash Professional, you should plan and define a process for creating states in a common pattern across the development team.

A best practice for Flash Professional developers is to create individual MovieClip classes that represent a component and target them through frame numbers

or labels. In ActionScript-only projects, developers can achieve this by creating individual classes based on the Sprite class. To define states, each class would hide and show elements based on the user interaction with the class.

Flex 4 skins

With Flex 4, components built on top of the Spark architecture will split the look and feel of a component into a separate class defined as a skin. This skin class is attached to a component's base class by a new CSS property called skinClass. By separating the component from the skin, developers can focus on the business logic behind the scenes that allows a component to process data or handle a user event—such as a mouse click—without focusing on the layout of the skin.

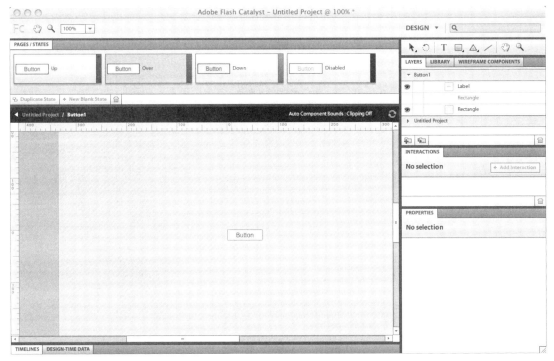

Figure 10-2 Flash Catalyst illustrating available states on a Flex button

In the new model, the skin class will contain all children of the component, such as a button, data group, or scrollbar. By keeping children inside the skin, your Flex components can provide dynamic layouts by allowing skin parts (children) to be optional. By adding such flexibility, users can create multiple skins for a component, some with a full set of features and some without.

NOTE ■ The Flex SDK contains a component life cycle that is important to Flex developers. Each component in the Flex ecosystem will move through this life cycle as it is born, grows, matures, and then dies. Understanding each phase of the life cycle is necessary to take advantage of various methods a component can override. Give your team time to research the life cycle and understand how each phase will affect their components. With a deeper understanding, your team will build a better-performing application.

ARCHITECTING APPLICATION CONTENT

A commonly overlooked architecture task is planning your content and how it will be implemented into your application. Content consists of text, images, audio, and videos that your application will consume and display. In many cases, externalizing (nonembedding) these types of resources is an afterthought. It's only when a client requests an update to a piece of content that it becomes apparent that this data should be external to the application.

For smaller projects, content can simply be externalized as a static XML file that is loaded into the application as it starts up. The XML file location could possibly be hard-coded into the application or provided dynamically as a Flash variable (flashvar). For a large application with large quantities of data, a content management system (CMS) or other server-side data stores might be required to allow for complex administration of application content.

The Flex SDK provides resource bundles to externalize strings, such as button labels, error messages, or company slogans. By default, resource bundles are compiled into the application. This does bind the content to the application requiring a recompile and deployment to users if content needs to be adjusted. However, an advantage to using resource bundles is localization. With your application's text completely externalized, your application can easily be compiled into a different locale—such as English to French—with a single change to the compile setting. By changing your locale, the mxmlc compiler will point your application at a new set of external files and compile those as the default resource bundle.

Images and videos can be embedded into your application at compile time for faster rendering. This means that when your application starts it will not have to request and download an asset required for display, such as a company logo. The disadvantage, however, is the same as with text content: If your client requests a change to an image, the entire application will have to be recompiled and distributed to your users.

There are several approaches to externalizing images and videos. One is to keep each item as an individual asset and store the items on the server for download. This allows developers to update single assets when a change is necessary. The disadvantage to this approach is that your application will have to download each asset separately, causing your application's response time to slow.

A more elegant solution is to create asset bundles in Flash Professional. Images can be packaged together inside a single Flash movie and loaded into your main Flash application at runtime. Inside the asset bundle, each image or asset (it could be vector/FXG) would be identified with a symbol. Within the main application, the symbol would be used to locate the asset within the asset bundle and render it to the display. This approach requires less download requests but can cause the same issue that we discussed earlier: If a single asset needs to be updated, the entire asset bundle will need to be recompiled and downloaded by the client. The good news is that only the asset bundle will need to be downloaded again (not the entire application). It's a good idea to break up asset bundles into logical groupings to minimize the effects of content changes across the rest of the application.

ARCHITECTING THE SERVER COMMUNICATION LAYER

Another aspect of most Flash applications is the communication flow between the client (your application) and a server. This layer is commonly referred to as the *services* or *data layer*. The services layer of your application should be planned in advanced and architected in a way that separates it from your application's layout.

The responsibility of your services layer is to send and receive data to and from an external source, such as a web server. Upon receiving a response from the server, your services layer will interpret raw data returned into a format that is understood by your application.

On larger teams, your server-side development team will manage server development. But on smaller

---

RESOURCE MODULES

Flex provides the ability to load resource bundles at runtime. Using the mxmlc compiler, resource bundles can be compiled into a resource module based on a single locale, such as en_US. Each resource module is compiled down to a unique SWF file. The resulting SWF can then be loaded into the application when needed at runtime.

If you are considering using resource modules, communicate this technical requirement to your build and release team. The compiler settings will need to be accounted for when build and deployment scripts are constructed.

teams, a single developer with expertise in Flash and server-side technology can handle this role. In either case, up-front planning will ensure both development efforts are in sync.

In Chapter 7, "Tuning and Adjusting for Success," we reviewed the importance of knowing how data-centric your application will be in order to choose your server-side technology. In the sections that follow, we will look at what communication methods and types of data formats are available for Flash Player. We will also examine server-side technology options available within Adobe's Flash Platform ecosystem.

What communication formats are available within the Flash Platform?

When architecting your Flash application, you need to understand what type of data your application will receive from the server-side system. Does your application require large volumes of data? Is your application connecting to an existing system? Will your application send hundreds of calls during a single user session? The answers to these questions will influence the data format you choose.

Basic formats. Most server implementations return data in a text format over HTTP. Flash Player and Flex 4 SDK can assist developers with translating well-formed text formats into different types of data. The Flash player out of the box will keep the result as text, but with some simple conversion techniques developers can quickly turn text into XML or generic objects.

If you plan on using the Flex SDK, you can take advantage of the HTTPService class for your server communication method. This class provides result data in XML, E4X, text, generic objects, or flashvars.

DON'T FORGET JSON

JavaScript Object Notation (JSON) is not supported natively by Flash Player or Flex; however, the open source library as3coreLib is available to enable JSON support in Flash. This library provides developers with the ability to serialize (create) and deserialize (read) JSON objects. Using JSON can help reduce the volume of data passed over the network by condensing data sets that would normally be formatted in XML into simple generic object notation that can be easily interpreted by most server- and client-side technologies. The following is an example of the same data set in XML and JSON.

XML
```
<employees>
  <employee firstName="James" lastName="Polanco" department="HR"/>
  <employee firstName="Aaron" lastName="Pedersen" department="IT"/>
  <employee firstName="Doug" lastName="Winnie" department="PM"/>
</employees>
```

JSON
```
{ employees:{
    employee:
    [
      {firstname:'"James"', lastname:'"Polanco"', department:'"HR"'},
      {firstname:'"Aaron"', lastname:'"Pedersen"', department:'"IT"'},
      {firstname:'"Doug"', lastname:'"Winnie"', department:'"PM"'}
    ]
  }
}
```

WHAT IS E4X?

E4X stands for ECMAScript for XML and is a new XML format introduced with Flash Player 9 and ActionScript 3. E4X allows developers to traverse the XML data set like you would a document model, such as HTML. With this ability, you can take advantage of dynamic querying of data to help speed up processing and assist the developer in targeting a specific piece of data without having to traverse the entire XML node tree.

For example, if you have a large set of XML nodes that represented all employees in your company and you want to retrieve only those who were part of human resources, you could query for those nodes that were marked in the "HR" department, as follows:

```
var hrEmployees:XMLList = xml.employee.(@department == "HR");
```

On medium and larger-scale projects, it's a good idea to create classes that represent an entity of data. In an MVC design pattern, this is referred to as the *model*. If your application has the concept of an employee, you would create an ActionScript class called `Employee`. This class in the Flash world is referred to as a *value object* (VO). If you are experienced with Java, it might be classified as a *data object* (DO). The class would contain a definition of each employee's attributes such as first name, last name, and department. Each attribute would be a public property on the `Employee` class, as shown in the following example:

```
package com.developmentarc.examples.dataobject {
    public class Employee {
        public var firstName:String;
        public var lastName:String;
        public var department:String;
    }
}
```

Because of this best practice, when you retrieve data from the server you will need to translate the raw data—no matter which format you use—into Action-Script value objects. If you retrieve a set of employees as XML, the data will need to be parsed and translated into an array of `Employee` objects. This task can be processor-intensive and time-consuming, for both development and during runtime.

Action Message Format. If your application needs to communicate large quantities of data, the action message format (AMF) is an ideal choice. AMF is simply ActionScript objects that have been serialized into a binary format and compressed. With a smaller footprint, your application's bandwidth will decrease compared to the text formats previously discussed. This alone can reduce server and cloud costs related to bandwidth. Because AMF is ActionScript, the serialization and deserialization process is incredibly fast and can out perform XML or JSON parsing.

For AMF to work, you will need to take advantage of a server-side technology that supports the serialization and deserialization of the binary ActionScript data. In most situations AMF is used in conjunction with Remote service calls, which allows for the Flash application to communicate directly with a service's methods on the server. We'll cover Remoting in the section that follows.

TIP ■ As we discussed above, when creating an application Model tier, it's good practice to create value object. Value objects are simple classes that describe a piece of data such as an Employee.

When using value objects with AMF, be sure to add the metatag [RemoteClass] to your class, this will instruct the compiler to include a description of the class to assist Flash Player in deserializing the object when it is being retrieved from storage.

YOU'RE USING AMF AND YOU NEVER KNEW IT

AMF is used under the hood throughout Flash Player for storage means such as Shared Objects and as a communication format for LocalConnection. These APIs abstract the serialization and deserialization of AMF for you.

Understanding Flash Platform communication methods

In the Flash Platform ecosystem there are three main methods by which Flash Player can communicate with a server-side API. In this section, we will explore HTTP, web services (SOAP), and remoting services and examine the benefits of each.

HTTP services. The most basic communication method available within Flash Player is a simple URL request that relies on the HTTP web protocol. Basic HTTP communication passes data back and forth between a server and a client application using simple parameters and plain text. For HTTP GET request, your application requests data by setting up a simple key/value pair used to submit data to the server. In the following HTTP get request, two parameters—the department and the first name—are passed to the server.

```
HTTP://www.example.com/employee?department=
➡HR&firstName=Aaron.
```

The result would be plain text formatted based on your application's needs (see "Basic formats," above).

For larger and more complex parameters, the HTTP POST method can be used. This method allows for more data characters and for data sets such as XML.

For basic communication in ActionScript, a combination of the URLRequest and URLLoader classes can be used to retrieve or send data to the server. The URL-Request class allows for data to be sent via HTTP. The resulting format is plain text, requiring code to parse the raw data into the format of choice.

A more robust option is to leverage the Flex SDK's HTTPService class. This class handles most scenarios when communication with simple HTTP requests. The class will handle input parameters and translate them into URL parameters similar to the URLRequest class. HTTPService also provides a good structure for handling results and failures based on HTTP status codes. URLLoader does not have this ability by default. As discussed, HTTPService provides a variety of result formats, requiring less code to translate the data into say, E4X.

HTTP communication requires very little infrastructure on either the client or the server. No special technology such as gateways, Java servlets, services, or remote proxies needs to be set up on the server side for communication to take place. But if more complex data needs to be passed back and forth between both sides, simple URL requests might not be the best method. Also, if large data sets are required, simple XML or JSON formats might not provide your application with the response time necessary when passing these data sets across the wire or when translating into native value objects.

Web services. Many of the publically available services provide Simple Object Access Protocol (SOAP) based APIs for requesting and submitting data. SOAP-based APIs provide a robust standardized structure used to pass XML formatted data back and forth between the client and server. The Flex SDK provides a WebService class to assist in communicating with a web service API over the SOAP protocol. This class will take care of formatting the input and response data as SOAP formatted XML for developers.

Remoting services. Remoting is technically classified as web services, but because AMF is at the core of Flash remoting, we have broken it out into its own category to help explain its benefits. The concept of remoting is to expose methods on the server side that can be directly accessed by the client-side code base. For example, with remoting, our Flash application would retrieve an individual employee by using a method call getEmployeeByName() on the server. This is done through a web service gateway setup on the server side.

The responsibility of the gateway is to serialize and deserialize AMF data passed from the client to the server into the native server technology such as Java. The gateway would then invoke the method call provided in the request. After retrieving the employee data from the database, the server would translate that data into AMF and send the response back to the client. On the client side, the remoting call would translate from AMF encoded employee object to either a generic object or to an Employee class.

With AMF at its core, remoting offers a lighter footprint for Flash applications. As explained above under formats, AMF is a compressed binary format that is native to Flash Player—data can be translated quickly allowing for less processing. Your application can provide large data sets, with less of a bandwidth and memory footprint.

In ActionScript or Flash Professional projects, developers can use the NetConnection class provided in the native Flash player API. This class allows you to target a method on the server by supplying a destination and allows for parameters to be passed to the server as AMF. See the following example for a basic implementation to a local AMF-based server:

```
protected function createEmployee(employee:
➡Employee):void {
  // create connection
  var connection:NetConnection =
➡new NetConnection();

  // set encoding type
  connection.objectEncoding = ObjectEncoding.
➡AMF3;

  // setup connection to message broker gateway
  connection.connect('HTTP://127.0.0.1:8400/
➡samples/messagebroker/amf');

  // create response handlers
  var responder:Responder = new Responder
➡(handleCreateEmployeeResult,
➡handleCreateEmployeeFault);
```

```
  // invoke create() method on server
  connection.call('employee.create', responder,
➡employee);
}
```

Flex provides a more robust solution with the RemoteObject class. The class allows for concurrent calls and a hook that ties into Flex's UI component architecture by showing a busy cursor. RemoteObject provides an ActionScript and MXML variant to execute remote calls. See the following example for a basic implementation in ActionScript to a local BlazeDS server:

```
protected function createEmployee(employee:
➡Employee):void {
  // create connection
  var remoteObject:RemoteObject =
➡new RemoteObject();

  // define main source
  remoteObject.source = "HTTP://127.0.0.1:8400/
➡samples/"

  // set service to invoice method on
  remoteObject.destination = "employee";

  // add event handlers
  remoteObject.create.
addEventListener(ResultEvent.RESULT,
➡handleCreateEmployeeResult);
  remoteObject.addEventListener(FaultEvent.FAULT,
➡handleCreateEmployeeFault);

  // invoke method on employee service
  remoteObject.create(employee);
}
```

Remoting does require an infrastructure on the server-side in order to expose methods and to interpret the AMF protocol. Be sure to budget an appropriate amount of time for the installation and testing of the proper server-side libraries.

Understanding server-side solutions

Adobe offers a variety of options for server based solutions, all of which provide multiple communication methods and formats options. These solutions allow you to communicate via raw HTTP, web services, or remoting. And most will support your desired format: XML, JSON, text, or AMF.

LiveCycle ES2. Adobe provides an enterprise level server solution called LiveCycle ES2. ES2 is a package of applications and tools that help businesses integrate legacy data and new data. With a suite of tools, developers can rapidly create rich user interfaces based on data sets and deploy them to their user base with little effort. The server solution allows for quick setup for remoting and web services for Flash application. The solution out of the box allows for AMF remoting and push communication.

Push communication allows the server to initiate a session with the client application and push data from the server. This type of communication allows for a lighter footprint when periodic messages need to be sent from the server to the client. Without push communication, a client-side application would have to periodically open a connection to the server and ask if there is any new data. With push, a connection will be opened only when data is ready.

BlazeDS. BlazeDS is a free alternative to some of LiveCycle's remoting features. With BlazeDS, you can tie AMF and remoting to your existing or new Java server application with a quick and easy configuration. BlazeDS offers basic remoting and communication via web services. Push technology is also available through the Messaging service, allowing your Flex application to subscribe and publish messages via push communication.

ColdFusion. ColdFusion is a widely popular server technology and language from Adobe. ColdFusion 9 provides easy setup of services that can be configured to communicate via a web service (SOAP), XML, JSON, or AMF remoting.

Developing a data contract

On many projects, both server and client side development work in parallel on the same features. The server developer creates the necessary APIs while the client side developer creates the user interface and the hooks to connect the Flash application to those APIs.

To facilitate a smooth parallel workflow between both disciplines, a data contract should be established for each API. The contract should describe what goes in and what comes out of each API. For an API such as getEmployeeByName, the contract should define that the method requires a parameter, "name," which should be a string. If your communication format is XML, the client and server architects should work together to develop an XML schema definition for the response from the getEmployeeByName API.

By agreeing to a contract, the client-side developer can develop against mock (fake or test) data until the real API has been created. The mock data will conform to the agreed-upon structure and will allow the Flash developer to invoke service calls, process data, and render that data into the UI without a fully operational API.

There are two approaches to creating mock data for client development. On the server-side, the developer can create stub APIs that simply return static data in the required format. If your required format is AMF, your server-side code could simply create an Employee object and send it back via the remoting channel. When the real API is ready, the server developer can simply switch the code base to the real API with no effort on the client-side (besides testing, of course!).

The second approach is to develop mock data inside the Flash application. This approach requires more development effort, but provides more control for the

---

NON-ADOBE REMOTING OPTIONS

Remoting and AMF communication does not necessary need to be based around an Adobe centric server-side solution. The AMF protocol has been openly published by Adobe to allow for more server side options. There are remoting solutions available for .NET, Rails/Ruby, PHP, Python, and many more.

FLASH BUILDER 4: DISCOVERING REMOTE SERVICES

Flash Builder 4 provides the Data Services panel to set up your application's communication layer with existing services. The panel supports PHP, Web Service, XML, LiveCycle Data Services (LCDS), BlazeDS, and ColdFusion.

To quickly discover remote services, you can tie your application to a PHP, LCDS, BlazeDS, or Cold-Fusion server, and Flash Builder 4 will discover all public methods available on the service and will autogenerate your application's service layer for you.

Even if you are not a fan of generated code, this tool can help with up front planning as you inspect and discover the available features of an existing service. See **Figure 10-3** for a look at the Data/Services panel.

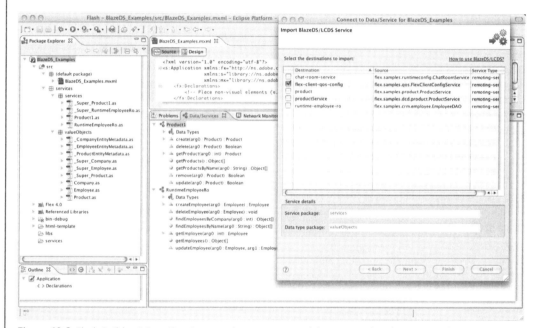

Figure 10-3 Flash Builder 4 Data/Services panel, connecting and discovering the BlazeDS sample services.

client-side developer. It also requires less involvement from the server-side developer, which allows that developer to stay focused on the tasks at hand. You can provide different data sets in order to test different use cases for a particular API. For the getEmployee-ByName example, a developer can create one data set that tests for no employees being found and another set that tests for two or more employees with the same name being found.

A few of the Flex application frameworks provide mock services to facilitate parallel development along with unit testing. DevelopmentArc's Core library provides an HTTPService framework called Service Request Dispatcher (SRD) that provides a hook for mock data calls. This framework currently works for Flex HTTPService calls and not web service or remoting. The Mate Framework also provides a Mock service layer that allows developers to fake any HTTPService, RemoteObject, or WebService calls.

Like all other aspects of planning, the data contract will change as the project and the application progress. As the project matures, APIs and their data sets will evolve. Don't be afraid to communicate necessary changes to the server and to accept those changes in your Flash application. Keep your mock services up to date even when your product goes live. This consistency will assist with future development iterations that require parallel client and server development.

Establishing coding standards

If you are a lone ranger and the single developer on a project, you have already established a standard way of coding, and it will usually be consistent across the entire application code base. It's your way or the highway! Most projects, however, require more than one developer.

Each developer will work on certain portions of the application based on the architecture and the feature set. Most of the time a developer will be required to touch source code that was developed by someone else—even if only during bug fixing. Diving into someone else's code can be a daunting endeavor. The developer never knows what to expect and will probably need to ask questions of the author of the code. But what happens if that developer has quit or, worse, been fired?

To help alleviate such madness, coding standards should be established during the planning stages of development to generalize various portions of the application code base. This does not mean that each developer's code syntax has to mimic the exact form used by the architect or lead developer. Everyone has an opinion on where a curly brace should be positioned and that level of detail can be left up to the individual developer. But at a higher level, you can set up a few simple guidelines to help code be more legible and identifiable by the entire team.

Naming conventions

An easy way to add consistency throughout your application code base is to create a set of naming conventions for various aspects of your source code.

Classes. Consistent class naming within your application can help developers quickly find what they are looking for. The lead developer should categorize various types of classes and provide a guide for class naming based on functionality. Some common types of classes are managers, utility, service, and value object. Each of these can have a certain structure that will help developers understand a class's functionality by its name. An example from the Flex SDK is utility classes; most are appended with `Util` postfix such as `StringUtil.as`. A developer can easily interpret this class as one that provides a set of utility methods used to manipulate strings.

Methods. Naming methods consistently throughout the source code can also help developers understand a method's purpose without having to dive in and reverse engineer the inner workings of the method. For example, naming your event handler methods with a consistent syntax will help developers quickly understand that a method is intended as a handler. This convention also helps organize the outline panel and code hinting in Flash Builder or your Flash IDE of choice.

The authors of this book pre-append all event handles with the "handle" prefix, such as `handleOkButtonClick`. At a quick glance, a developer can understand this method is intended to handle a mouse click on the a class's OK button. Using Flash Builder's code hinting a developer can type "handle" and be presented with all event handler methods available in the class.

Variables. For common types of variables, a convention should be defined and shared across your development team. A common practice for constants is to use uppercase and underscore between words, like the following:

```
public static const MAX_WIDTH:String = 400;
```

Some Flash developers prefer to pre-append an underscore (or two) to help identify that a variable is private. This practice dates back to ActionScript 1 and 2 when variables were not strictly types. Only some developers use this practice, so you should define a standard up front for consistency.

Package organization

Your project should be compartmentalized into various pieces based on their functionality. Each grouping should be organized into packages inside your project source. By organizing code in packages, developers can quickly identify classes and functionality required to complete a development task.

At a high level, pieces of your application should be grouped together in a common package and then broken down further into more distinct packages based on class functionality. High-level grouping could include user interface components, utility classes, and your data communication layer (service).

Each high-level package can be further dissected. With UI components in Flex 4, it's a good idea to separate the component and its skin file into separate packages. Another example is when Flash Builder 4 generates the service code within the Data/Services panel. The generated service classes will be organizes under the "services" package, and value objects will be placed in their own package called "valueObject"(see **Figure 10-4**).

Commenting

No matter how well you standardize your naming conventions or your package organization, all of the necessary information about a method will not be seen at a quick glance. A developer who is fixing a bug or refactoring another's code base may have detailed questions about how a specific piece of functionality works. By providing comments on a class, method, and even on a per-line basis, developers can read the plain English comments to better understand what's happening in a chunk of code. Not only does commenting help those who are given the unfortunate task of working inside someone else's code, it also provides a reminder for the author of the code base.

Figure 10-4 Flash Builder's Data Service Package organization

ASDOCING YOUR CODE

Adobe provides a command-line utility called ASDoc for source code document generation, which is similar to Java's JavaDoc. When a development team comments classes and methods in a specific way, the ASDoc utility can be used to generate HTML based API documentation for each class in the application's code base. This is a convenient tool for developers who are creating modules, utility classes, and other reusable components of a larger application. By providing HTML-based documentation, the development teams can share common code and promote transparency and code reuse between team members.

Flash Builder 4 also supports the ASDoc syntax and can provide code documentation hints within the IDE. This can be very helpful when you are creating large projects that interact with code that was handled by other developers on your team. If the code is ASDoc notated, then you can easily read and understand it without having to open the AS file.

How many times have you come back to code six months or even two weeks later and had no idea what you were thinking at the time? By adding a few words, you can prevent yourself from reverse engineering your own block of code.

SYNCING WITH YOUR TEAM

After the development planning phase is complete, the architect or lead developer should communicate all of the technical information to the project leads. This information is key in helping the project managers identify issues with the feature specification, project scope, and established milestones.

If your project requires technical documentation—such as a technical specification or architecture diagrams—this is a good time to deliver such documentation and share it with the team. Throughout the iterative development process (covered in Chapter 11), we will discuss how regular team syncs will help keep the communication lines open between design, development, QA, and the rest of the team.

SUMMARY CHECKLIST

With a sufficient amount of time, your development team should have a good sense of what they are going to build and how they are going to build it. Before moving forward with constructing the application, let's evaluate a few keys of planning for development.

✔ Have you evaluated the type of framework required for your project?

✔ If you have chosen a third-party framework, has your development team been given adequate time to learn the framework?

✔ Have you established an initial pattern to split up your application's components?

✔ Is your application content dynamic? Will it change over time? If so, do you have a strategy for externalizing the content?

✔ Has a format for your communication layer been reviewed with the server team?

✔ Are you aware of the required methods for invoking data from the server?

✔ Have you gathered all of the necessary information about the server technology that will be used in conjunction with your Flash application?

✔ Has your team established a server contract for each API that your application requires?

✔ Have you defined your project's coding standards?

✔ Have you distributed your coding standards to your development team and published the standards in a location that's accessible to all team members?

✔ Have you shared the results from your planning and architecture with your project lead?

✔ Have you made adjustments to your project scope and timeline based on your technical assessment thus far?

CHAPTER 11

Iterative
Development

After planning the project's development phase and after coordi-
nating with the design team, your development team is ready to
being construction. Development will most likely not take place in
one large effort. In most medium to large projects, tasks are divided
into iterations and milestones. Each iteration will consist of a set of
features that when complete will make up a milestone. Because the
development of rich applications in Flash is usually based on complex interactive designs, your development team will need to be in
sync with the design team during each iteration.

In this chapter, we will first discuss what it takes to initially get a project off the ground and how to start constructing your project's initial
code structure. Then we will examine how that structure changes
based on the Flash Platform technology of choice. We will also cover
how you can take advantage of automated testing to ensure the stability of your application as development continues throughout the
project.

After your initial project has been structured and shared with the development team, development iterations can begin. Each iteration at its core will be broken down into component development. Therefore, we will cover the ways to construct your components in order to separate the design and logic of them. This separation will lend itself to a seamless design integration based on the developer and designer contract.

Finally, we will again discuss the important aspects of syncing with your team and what development deliverables from the iteration should be shared with other project team members.

DEVELOPING YOUR INITIAL PROJECT

Imagine the start of a project where each developer begins building the application based on their feature requirements and not the application as a whole. Each developer would be left to make important decisions that would impact each of the other developers. For example, two developers might require a tweening library to complete their features for an iteration. If each developer chose a different version of the same library, it would have drastic effects once code is shared between team members.

For large projects with multiple developers, you should make these types of common decisions and construct the initial foundation of your project prior to the entire development team's involvement in the project's creation. The architect or lead developer on the project should be tasked with setting up the initial project structure. Part of the initial setup includes making architectural decisions about using external libraries, deciding whether a custom or third-party framework should be used, and deciding whether the development team should test the application code and, if so, where and when automated testing should be used.

Remember, your final application can contain multiple Flash projects. Your main project may be a Flex application that requires Flash Professional projects for some of its components or one that requires a Flex library containing common utility classes that are shared between projects. Keep this in mind as we discuss the important items to consider when setting up the main project.

Defining project structure based on your Flash Platform tool

Your initial project structure will be dictated based on the type of Flash Platform project you create. Flash Professional, Flash Builder, and Flash Catalyst each set up their projects with a similar, yet not identical, structure.

When creating a Flash Platform project, five unique elements are required: your source code, required libraries, third-party libraries, required assets for compilation, and a location for your compiled application. Each of these will vary based on the Flash Platform tool and project type. In the following sections, you will discover what each tool and their project types provide when you create a project and what additions you should make in order to bring consistency to the project.

Defining projects in Flash Professional CS5

When starting with Flash Professional, you can use one of many workflows to create projects and applications. In this section, we will focus on creating a project with the Flash Project option on the Flash Professional splash screen. Clicking the Flash Project option will display the Project panel (see **Figure 11-1**). In the Project panel, you can create a new project and specify a directory where all of the project's assets should be stored. By default when you create a project, nothing is created out of the box, not even a project directory. Because of this behavior, it's a good idea to manually create a unique directory when creating a project. This will ensure a location for project-specific assets. As you can see in the example in Figure 11-1, we have created a project directory called Initial_Flash_Pro_Project.

Once you've established a project, you need to create the actual Flash application. When creating a new Flash application in Flash Professional, developers have multiple application types, including ActionScript 3.0, ActionScript 2.0, Adobe AIR 2.0, and Flash Lite 4. Each of these types creates a similar application structure. The main difference with each

Figure 11-1 The Project panel in Flash Professional illustrating the project's initial structure

is the configuration of the ActionScript settings, the required libraries, and the deployment methods.

At the center of any Flash Professional application is a FLA file. A FLA is an application file that contains all of your application's internal assets and configuration such as the movie dimensions, ActionScript settings, library links, symbols, timelines, and frame scripts.

If your project requires ActionScript code, it's a best practice to define a Document class for your application. The Document class is an ActionScript file that links to your FLA as the root, or "main," class for your application. This text-based file will exist outside your FLA and will be located at the same level in the project structure as the FLA.

WHAT IS A DOCUMENT CLASS?

The Document class is an ActionScript file that is associated with your project FLA, and it incorporates all object-oriented functions of your project FLA. Using a Document class allows your Flash Professional FLA file to have class constructors, attributes, and methods. Using a Document class will allow your project to be instantiated as an object when compiled as a SWC and referenced in other projects.

Outside the Document class, other ActionScript classes can be associated with your application. ActionScript could include utility classes used by your Document class or others that are associated with symbols in your application's assets library. To keep consistent with Flash Builder, all the source code should live under a src directory, which will need to be created manually through the Project panel. Under the source directory, your project team will create all the required ActionScript classes in an organized package structure based on the application architecture and naming conventions you defined in Chapter 10, "Planning Development." In our example in Figure 11-1, we created an Employee utility class called `EmployeeUtil` and placed it under the src directory in the proper package structure.

One exception to storing ActionScript assets under the src directory is your Document class; by default, Flash Professional creates this file at the same directory level as the associated FLA.

NOTE ■ Flash Professional will not by default associate the src directory with source code. To set this up, users will need to adjust the FLA's ActionScript settings and point the source path at ./src instead of at the . path.

Your application will be linked to the available libraries that come with Flash Professional such as the Text Layout Framework. You can access and modify libraries by selecting the ActionScript settings for your application. Refer to **Figure 11-2** for a glimpse at the Settings panel. From this panel, developers can link to third-party libraries or source paths based on the needs of the application. For example, if your application plans on using a framework such as RobotLegs, which is an AS3 framework, you can link to the SWC and tie it into your project.

However, when you link to an asset that is outside your project folder through the panel, it does not copy the asset into your project folder. Therefore, when you share the initial project folder with others, the reference to the third-party library will be broken because the linked assets were not copied into the project.

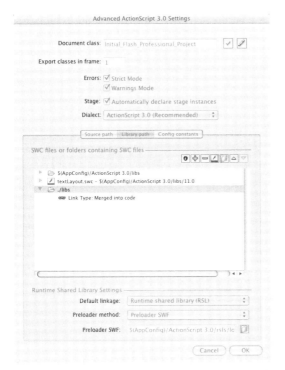

Figure 11-2 Flash Professional ActionScript settings and library path

To alleviate such gaps when sharing projects with team members, it's a best practice to create a libs directory in your project folder and copy all the necessary libraries there. Once a library is manually copied, you can link your application to the libs directory through the Settings panel. Once referenced, all libraries in libs will be picked up by your project.

NOTE ▪ When linking the libs directory to an application, use a relative path instead of an absolute path. Using absolute paths will create full paths based on the developer's operating system where the Flash project is stored, such as the C:\Documents And Settings\users\..\project\. path. Relative paths create paths that are based on the application's location as a start point, not the full path to the file. This enables other developers to check out the project and have

their application be configured correctly because the paths are looked up "relative" to the location of the application and not based on the system folders of the developer who linked the library.

Defining projects in Flash Builder 4

Flash Builder 4 gives developers four options when creating Flash-based projects: Flex, ActionScript, Flex Library, and Flash Professional. Each of these project types will create a slightly different package structure, but at the root, they have the same three main elements:

- Your initial project will be set up with a root source directory where all of your project's code will be stored. As new files are created, they will be stored in this directory by default. This is the start of your source package structure, and you should extend it to fit your project needs based on the project coding standards.

- Your initial setup will link any required libraries to your project. This pseudodirectory is not really created in your project folder structure; it's simply a link to all the libraries required by your project. You will be able to expand this list of requirements when you set up third-party libraries.

- The last item in your generated project structure is a compile target. Each project type in Flash Builder will contain a directory that will be used to store the project's compiled assets. When your project is compiled and previewed in Flash Builder, this directory will be targeted to run your compiled project.

Now that we have covered the commonalities, we'll talk about each project type in detail and discuss what sets each apart from the others.

Flex projects. These use the Flex framework including MXML, ActionScript, CSS, and the mxmlc compiler to build Flash applications. With a combination of Flash Builder and Flex, developers can take advantage of design view to control and adjust objects in a visual display.

TEXT LAYOUT FRAMEWORK (TLF)

The new TLF library provides enhanced text layout and formatting capabilities in your Flash applications. TLF is provided with Flash Professional CS5 and the Flex 4 SDK (Flash Builder and Flash Catalyst). Developers can take advantage of advanced layout settings such as left-to-right and vertical text flow. In addition, the framework provides advanced controls such as cut and paste and undo.

Figure 11-3 Flex project structure in Flash Builder 4

When creating a Flex project, you will be given the choice of whether you plan on deploying your project to the Web or to the desktop as an Adobe AIR application. For the most part, the two projects will contain a similar structure with a couple of additions for those deployed to the Web. See **Figure 11-3** for package details on a Web-deployed Flex project.

The root application MXML file of your project will be generated automatically when the project is created. This MXML file is your starting point for your application. For Web deployment, the root of your MXML file will extend the Spark `Application` class. For AIR, your project will be built upon the `WindowedApplication` class. The application MXML file will be stored under the src directory, which will be your starting point for all the source code required in the project.

When a project is set up, the default Flex SDK will be configured into the project. By default in Flash Builder, projects will be linked to the Flex 4 SDK.

NOTE ■ The Flex 3.5 SDK is also available in the Flash Builder installation.

In the Package Explorer shown earlier in Figure 11-3, when you expand the linked SDK, it will display all the required libraries such as spark.swc, sparkskins.swc, rpc.swc, and so on. Each of these is an independent library, and together they make up the Flex SDK. For AIR projects, a few different libraries will be linked to give developers the additional AIR features that are available only for desktop applications.

For Web deployment, Flex projects contain the html-template folder, which holds all the necessary files needed to deploy your project to the Web. This includes a basic HTML template file (index.template .html) that will be used to embed your compiled Flex application on a Web page. Upon compilation of your project, all files in the directory will be copied to the bin-debug directory where your project will run from. The index.template.html file will be configured based on your project's settings, copied to bin-debug, and renamed based on your project name. In the example in Figure 11-3, the HTML file has been copied and renamed to Initial_Flex_Project_Structure.html. All libraries that are loaded at runtime are also compiled and stored here.

The libs directory is used when you are linking compiled third-party libraries to your project. If you are using a framework such as RobotLegs, you would copy the compiled framework into your libs directory, and it would automatically be linked to your project.

When linked, your project has access to any of the classes within that library.

Flex Library projects. These are packages of code that provide common shared functionality that can be leveraged by multiple applications and projects. Libraries cannot be run on their own and must be used within an application. The goal of such a project is to decouple code, such as a framework, into its own entity. This enables the library to grow and mature outside of an application as a whole and be leveraged by multiple projects. A library when compiled will generate a SWC extension. **Figure 11-4** illustrates the various pieces of a Flex library.

Similar to a Flex project, a library will contain a src directory where all code for the library will reside. This directory will be empty when the project is first conceived. This is because there is no starting point for a library. It's up to the developer to create the structure of the code.

The library project will link to the Flex SDK in the same way as a standard Flex project. The difference is that by default no libs directory is created. If your library needs references to other libraries, it's a good idea to create a libs directory and store required libraries there.

Instead of a bin-debug, Flex libraries will contain a bin directory. This directory will store the compiled library SWC. By default the complied library will take the name of the project. In this chapter's example, the library file will be named Sample_Flex_Library.swc.

ActionScript projects. These are created with the intent of building your application with nothing more than ActionScript code, without requiring Flash Professional or the Flex SDK. When a new project is created, an initial ActionScript base class will be created with the same name as your project. This class will be marked by default as the entry point for the compilation of your application. The base class will be stored in a src directory similar to a Flex project. **Figure 11-5** shows the default structure generated by Flash Builder.

The project will link to the subset Flex 4 SDK that gives you access to the lower-level libraries such as the Text Layout Framework and the Open Source Media Framework (OSMF).

Figure 11-4 Flex Library project structure in Flash Builder 4

Figure 11-5 ActionScript project generated by Flash Builder

When creating an ActionScript project in Flash Builder, you can deploy the project only via the Web. The project structure will reflect this deployment configuration. Two directories, bin-debug and html-template, are created and used for the same purposes as Flex projects that are configured for Web deployment.

Flash Professional projects. These are a new project type introduced with Flash Builder 4. You can create these files in Flash Builder or initiate them in Flash

Professional when creating the application's Document class. Flash Professional projects in Flash Builder are those that are based on an application FLA. When creating a project via Flash Builder, you will be prompted to locate the main FLA of your project. This means you will need to open Flash Professional, create an initial application, and save the FLA, prior to creating a project in Flash Builder. Once the FLA is created and selected in Flash Builder, the project will be generated and configured in Flash Builder. **Figure 11-6** shows the Flash Builder's Project Explorer, and you can see that the project contains a slightly different structure than the Flex and ActionScript projects.

TIP ■ When saving your FLA from Flash Professional, be sure to save it to a directory with no other assets. If your FLA parent directory contains other assets that are not part of your project, they will show up when you create your Flash Builder project under the source directory reference.

The source directory of your project will be a reference to the directory that contains your FLA file. As you add ActionScript files to your project in Flash Builder, the files will be stored in this directory at the same level as your FLA. Your Document class will be your first ActionScript class and be positioned at the

default package. The Document class by default will share the same name with your FLA, so it should be easy to identify. In the example in Figure 11-6, the class is named Sample_Flash_Pro_Project.as.

NOTE ■ All ActionScript created in your Flash Builder project will be stored in the directory in which you created your FLA file. When the project is checked into a repository, be sure to include both the Flash Professional and Flex Builder project directories.

Your library references will hold all the available APIs in Flash Professional such as your player globals and TLF libraries. These libraries will be associated with your installation of Flash Professional.

Since Flash Professional applications are by default deployed to the Web, Flash Builder will create the initial project structure to include the bin-debug and html-template directories.

Note that Flash Professional projects will not include a libs directory. It's good practice to create one for all external libraries your project will use. With each library contained in your project structure, all team members can be assured they will have all the necessary assets when they check the project out of source control.

Defining projects in Flash Catalyst

When starting a project with Flash Catalyst, users will be shown the tool's design workspace, and the project structure will be hidden from the user's point of view. Behind the scenes, Flash Catalyst is organizing the project structure the same as a Flex project created in Flash Builder. To see the structure, you can switch to the code workspace with the Project Navigator, which looks very similar to Flash Builder's Project Explorer (see **Figure 11-7**).

The code workspace is read-only, meaning the project structure will be locked down to the conventions enforced by Flash Catalyst. All source will be stored in the src directory. At the root of the project is an MXML file called Main.mxml file, which acts as the starting point for the Flash Catalyst project. As you style out-of-the-box components and build custom

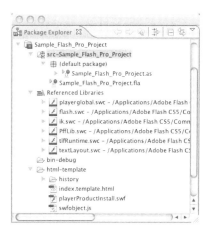

Figure 11-6 Flash Professional project structure in Flash Builder 4

Figure 11-7 Flash Catalyst project structure

components, the src directory will expand to include more component and Flex 4 skin files.

The project structure will contain the now familiar bin-debug and html-template directories used to configure and deploy your Flex project to the Web.

Since Flash Catalyst is built to leverage the Spark architecture, the Flex 4 SDK will be linked to the project. You can't configure third-party libraries in Flash Catalyst at this time; for this type of customization, you need to migrate your project to Flash Builder.

When a project is saved in Flash Catalyst, it is packaged into an FXP file. FXP is similar to the FLA file in Flash Professional, meaning it's really a compressed package structure. The FXP file when imported as an archive will contain the same structure shown in the Project Navigator in Figure 11-7.

With a single file, project teams can easily hand off the project to other team members. For further development, FXP files can be imported into Flash Builder.

NOTE ■ An FXP generated by Flash Builder cannot be opened in Flash Catalyst at this time.

Expanding your initial project structure

After your Flash Platform tool of choice has set up your project structure, it's a good idea to define all the common but custom pieces of your project. The initial project structure defines how your project assets will be compartmentalized. Assets include source code, third-party libraries, configuration files, externalized content, and visual assets such as images or videos.

Each of these content types should have their own distinct location in your project's structure. By defining your structure, you are implementing a coding standard as discussed in Chapter 10.

After defining the structure, it's important to check the project into your source control system and supply a set of instructions to your development team to help them set up their local development environments properly. (For more information about development environments, refer to Part V, "Build and Release.")

With this initial structure in place, developers will be able to answer questions like "Where does a new icon for the header go?" and "Are we externalizing all text content and, if so, where?" themselves.

Setting up frameworks and third-party libraries

With your structure set, it's a good idea to download and configure all the third-party libraries needed for the project. Libraries could include your favorite tween library such as gTween or your application framework of choice.

Third-party libraries are provided in two types, either as compiled SWCs or as source code. In both Flash Builder and Flash Professional, you can set up your project to link to either type.

SWC files provide a compiled version of the library you are using. A single file allows for quick and easy distribution of the code. And with the code being created by a third party, you will most likely not be modifying it. However, you can take SWCs and link source to them. This will provide developers with the ability to dive into the third-party code (not modify it) during debug sessions. With this ability, developers can add breakpoints and verify the data that has been supplied to the third-party class and method you are targeting.

With SWC files, you have the ability either to compile the library into your application SWF or to load the library at runtime via a runtime shared library (RSL).

When compiling libraries into the application, you are adding weight to your final project's download size. The good news is that the compile process will include only the code from the SWC library that is actually used in your application. For example, if a library is 45 KB and you use only one class, the size impact will be nowhere close to the entire 45 KB.

There are disadvantages to compiling libraries into your source. If you plan to have multiple applications that leverage the same libraries, you are causing your users to download the external library content multiple times. This is where RSLs come into play.

RSLs are libraries that are downloaded when the application first starts. During compilation, all libraries that have been marked as RSLs will be tracked, and a list will be generated. When the application starts, each library will be downloaded and loaded into the application for reference. Once downloaded, RSLs are stored in the browser cache based on their URLs. Once

in the cache, the libraries will not be downloaded again until the user's cache is cleared. By doing so, libraries can be reused across multiple applications that are referencing the same library at the same URL.

The downside of using RSLs is related to startup time. Because the entire library is downloaded (or retrieved from cache) and loaded into your application, the application will take longer to start. If you are using only one or two classes in a large library, loading the entire library at runtime doesn't make sense.

All libraries linked to your project as a SWC or as source can be configured as an RSL. To do so, you will need to configure each library's link type in the project's library path. In **Figure 11-8** we have begun to configure the RobotLegs framework to be linked as an RSL. Since each library is configured separately,

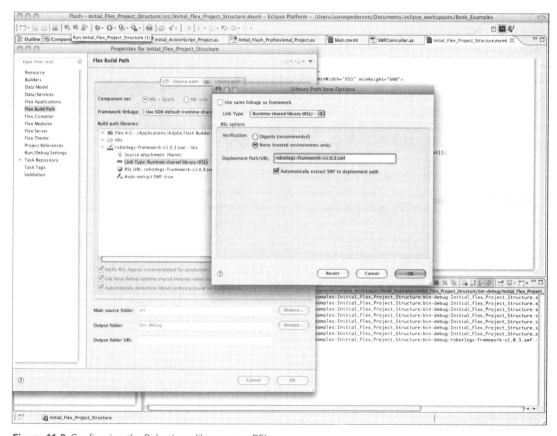

Figure 11-8 Configuring the RobotLegs library as an RSL

the lead developer can pick and choice which librar-ies to include during compilation and which to load at runtime.

There is also the option to link directly to the source of a library, which is a good idea for larger projects and teams that are creating multiple applications that need to leverage a common base. If such a scenario is neces-sary for your team, you can set up a separate project in Flash Professional or Flash Builder for your library. This library can be checked into source control as its own entity and then tied to your other application. In the library path settings of Flash Builder, you can directly link a library project in your workspace to your project.

Establishing an application testing harness

When setting up your initial project structure, you should start thinking about testing. A common mis-take is to think testing is simply related to quality assurance (QA) and the process of verifying a com-pleted feature.

Although QA testing is essential to the success of a project, testing while in development can save many hours over the course of your project and the life of your application.

During your project setup, it's wise to devise how much developer testing should take place and then set up the hooks in your project to allow developers to create tests as they work and automatically run them in the code environment. Part of the decision making will be to decide what type of tool you will use and where the tests your developer create will reside.

What is unit testing?

As features of your project are constructed, develop-ers have an opportunity to build automated tests that can be run against a particular feature's functionality. These types of tests are referred to as *unit tests* and are logical code that verifies use cases in a feature. For example, a developer might create a utility class to assist with common functions required for employees. This class would provide various methods such as one to filter an array of employees and find all those within

the human resource department. This method could be coded and verified manually by the developer, or a unit test could be created and automatically run to verify various scenarios. In this particular example, a developer would need to verify the following sce-narios: What happens when the array is empty? What happens when no human resource employees are found? What happens when more than one employee is found?

As you can see, this is a lot to manually test. With a set of unit tests, however, a developer, through code, can automatically test the feature and the various uses cases that revolve around it. If features change over time and the utility class is refactored, the unit tests are there to verify the functionality still produces the same results as before.

How much of your application should you unit test?

The amount of unit testing depends on a few factors and the methodology to which you subscribe. On smaller projects that have a short turnaround time, have a short life span, or have little to no code that is shared between features, it probably does not make sense to add unit testing to the development overhead of your team.

On larger projects that require multiple devel-opers and a good size project scope, it's a good idea to do some unit testing. At the very least, common code that is shared between features should be tested. This common code could be used internally in one project, such as in the earlier employee utility class example, or as a library that will be used on multiple projects or applications.

At the extreme end of the unit testing perspective is Test Driven Development (TDD). Under the TDD philosophy, developers create tests prior to developing the actual feature. The idea is to plan and architecture a feature prior to writing a single line of code. The developer writes unit tests that fail because no code has yet to be written, but as a developer codes the fea-ture, the tests begin to pass. In theory, when all tests pass, the feature has been completed.

Unit testing tools

Your development team can leverage multiple unit testing frameworks and tools to apply as much testing to your application as you see fit. The amount of testing that is covering your application code base is often referred to as *code coverage*. As you choose a tool, make sure you keep your build and release team up-to-date with your decision. They will need to integrate the unit tests and the tool of choice into their build and deploy system so that all functionality can be verified when the code is built and deployed to each environment.

Flash Builder 4 Premium comes outfitted with the newest version of FlexUnit (version 4). Flash Builder allows users to create test suites and test cases and to run them through the tool with a few simple clicks. FlexUnit can be downloaded outside Flash Builder and also utilized on both Flash Professional and ActionScript-only projects.

AsUnit is a popular community-driven testing framework that is on par with FlexUnit. This framework can be leveraged on any type of Flash project dating back to Flash Player 6. This means you can use AsUnit to test ActionScript 1, 2, and 3 projects; Flash Professional projects; Flex projects; and Flash Lite projects.

A new tool that many are leveraging for Flex and ActionScript projects outside of Flash Builder and Flash Professional is ProjectSprouts. ProjectSprouts has generators, similar to Ruby on Rails, that produce skeleton ActionScript classes for you based on templates. Part of the generation process will autogenerate test cases and suites with ASUnit. This means each new class you create will have an associated test case class. This type of generation lends itself well to the TDD philosophy.

Distributing the project to team members

On projects that include more than one developer or a separate build and release team, the team needs to discuss code distribution, or the process of sharing finished content with all members of the team. For smaller projects, this process could be as simple as packaging a Flex project as an archive in the format of an FXP. For Flash Professional projects, a simple ZIP file could be used to distribute code to other members.

This type of single-file exchange is successful if the handoff is one way and synchronized. A developer, when finished with their feature, would hand the code to another. The second developer would open the archive and expand on the work of the first developer. However, in most scenarios, developers will be working in parallel, and a one-way handoff is not feasible.

With more complex coding-sharing requirements, project teams should consider adopting a source control system such as Subversion, CVS, or Git. With a source control system, the project assets can be shared in a distributed fashion. One developer can be working on one set of features and, when complete, can check that code into the source control system for distribution to the rest of the team. Other members can sync up to the repository and download any changes to the project.

Flash Builder comes fitted with a CVS client that allows users to connect to a CVS repository and share assets all within the same tool. Since Flash Builder is built on top of the Eclipse integrated development environment (IDE), developers can install a variety of plug-ins that include other source control systems such as Subversion and Git.

If a source control system is required by your team, it's a good idea to coordinate the requirements with the build and release team so that they can create the appropriate processes to check out code during deployment.

DEVELOPING COMPONENTS AND INTEGRATING DESIGNS

The largest part of your development effort will be revolve around building the application's user interface of your application. As we discussed during planning development (Chapter 10), your user interface can be broken down into components based on features. At a high level, your interface will consist of views, and each view will represent a full interface in your application such as a login screen. Views can be further broken down into components. Each component will represent an isolated chunk of functionality that displays and accepts user input.

In this section, you will learn what it takes to develop and deliver a successful component based on a parallel communication workflow with the design team. Part of a successful component is building or leveraging its support tiers such as business logic and server communication. We will examine the effort of integrating the completed component into the application ecosystem after a component is complete. Lastly, we will strategize on how to approach refactoring and iterating on a finished component.

Executing the designer and developer contract

With most large applications, design will not be completed prior to the start of development. Most likely development will have to start building components in parallel with the design team. This can be a scary path to follow, and developers will ask, "What will the component layout look like? How is the component suppose to behave when a user clicks a button?" Developers have valid reasons to be concerned. The fear is that their initial work will all be thrown away once the design has been completed. However, via a little up-front communication with the design team, an informal contract, and a solid component architecture, these fears can be overcome.

Establishing parts and states

The easiest way to communicate components, in a language that both designers and developer understand, is through wireframes. As we discussed in Chapter 8, "Planning Design," wireframes are a visual

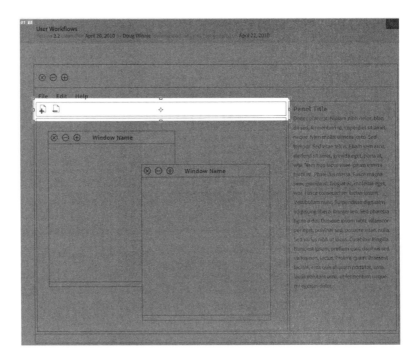

Figure 11-9 InDesign wireframe of control bar

representation of the feature specification defined during the planning phase of the project. They are also a great asset when defining the designer and developer contract.

When a new iteration begins, the designer and developer need to sit down and dissect the proposed features based on the wireframes. In **Figure 11-9**, both disciplines can interpret all the parts that make up the control bar of the application. In this simple example, there are two parts: the add and remove buttons.

Once each part is defined, each rendering state needs to be identified based on all use cases. For instance, our control bar will have one state when no item is selected and another when an item is selected. Based on these states, the designer and developer can determine what parts are affected based on the scenario. In the example, the remove button will be disabled when no item is selected.

With this vital information, the developer now has all the data necessary to architect and construct a component based on the designer and developer contract.

Architecting your components

The goal with any type of Flash development is to separate design from logic. This is especially true when developing a component. Your component's responsibility should be divided into two buckets. The first bucket is the logic, which handles the heavy lifting of the component, such as sending and receiving application data. The logic portion of your component is also responsible for handling behaviors from the user as they interact with the component's design. Based on those interactions, your component will decide what next to do such as enter a different state or dispatch an event from the component.

The other bucket in your component is the design. When you think design, you need to think not only about layout and graphics but also behaviors such as effects and transitions. Behaviors should have as minimal an impact as possible on the logic of your component.

On smaller projects where full design comps are in hand, it's still important to code with this separation

in mind. In many projects, the "look and feel" of your application is the only piece your client will ever see or understand. Therefore, it's the most likely area of your application that will change over the course of the project and the life of your application. By isolation design from logic, you can help build flexibility into your code base for user interface updates.

Creating wireframe components based on the contract

How you go about building your component depends on your Flash Platform project type.

Flex 4 provides a new skinning architecture called Spark, which has been the basis for the component model used throughout this book. The architecture splits the design UI of a component into a separate class called a *skin*, and Flex ties the skin to the component class at runtime.

The component is created as an ActionScript class, and the skin is created as an MXML file. The component class will define all of the component's parts by declaring public variables of the necessary type, such as Button or TextArea. Each part (such as our add and remove buttons) requires a special metadata tag declaration that allows the compiler to designate a class property as a *skin part*.

A skin part informs the component's associated skin that this is an element of the component that may be shown as part of the skin's UI. Each skin part can be marked as either required or optional. By marking a skin part as required, you are telling the skin that it has to display this part in the UI. By marking a skin part as optional, you let the skin decide if and when it shows the part in the UI.

By defining parts, you allow for the component class to utilize multiple skins, which also informs the skin what parts of the component are available to the skin. In our example of the control bar, we have two skin parts, both of which are required.

Next, each skin state must be configured in order to sync with the states in your soon-to-be-created skin class. Skin states are also marked with a metadata tag, but no property needs to be created with each declaration.

The following example illustrates the declarations for both the control bar's skin parts and the skin states:

```
package com.examples.wireframeComponents.
ui.components
{
    import spark.components.Button;
    import spark.components.supportClasses.
SkinnableComponent;

    public class ControlBar extends
SkinnableComponent {

        /* Skin Parts */
        [SkinPart(required="true")]
        public var add_button:Button;

        [SkinPart(required="true")]
        public var remove_button:Button;

        /* SKin States */
        [SkinState("itemSelected")]

        [SkinState("noItemSelected")]

        public function ControlBar() {
            super();
        }
    }
}
```

Your skin class will be based on the Flex *Skin* class. This class will define all the parts as user interface elements and lay them out as needed based on the wireframes. Each part will be declared as the same type we defined in the component class. In our example, both parts are of type Button.

TIP ■ When creating a new skin class, Flash Builder 4 provides a new creation type called MXML skin. By choosing this type, developers have the option to copy an existing skin. When an existing skin is chosen, the original skin's content will be copied directly to the new skin. Take

advantage of this feature when you are creating skins for out-of-the-box Flex components, such as the VideoPlayer.

Next in our skin class, the states of the component need to be created. Those states would be defined as itemSelected and noItemSelected. Each of these states will affect the example's add button by changing its disabled property based on the state. The following is an example of the control bar wireframe skin:

```
<?xml version="1.0" encoding="utf-8"?>
<s:Skin xmlns:fx="http://ns.adobe.com/mxml/2009"
    xmlns:s="library://ns.adobe.com/flex/spark"
    xmlns:mx="library://ns.adobe.com/flex/mx">
    <!-- host component -->
    <fx:Metadata>
        [HostComponent("com.examples.
wireframeComponents.ui.components.ControlBar")]
    </fx:Metadata>

    <!-- Skin States -->
    <s:states>
        <s:State name="itemSelected" />
        <s:State name="noItemSelected" />
    </s:states>

    <!-- SkinParts
    name=remove_button, type=spark.components.
Button;, required=true
    name=add_button, type=spark.components.
Button;, required=true
    -->
    <s:HGroup>
        <s:Button id="add_button" label="Add"/>
        <s:Button id="remove_button"
label="Remove" enabled="true" enabled.
noItemSelected="false"/>
    </s:HGroup>
</s:Skin>
```

Flash Professional does not provide an architecture out of the box that splits a component into parts and states. However, you can leverage a best practice to help split a component into its design and logic

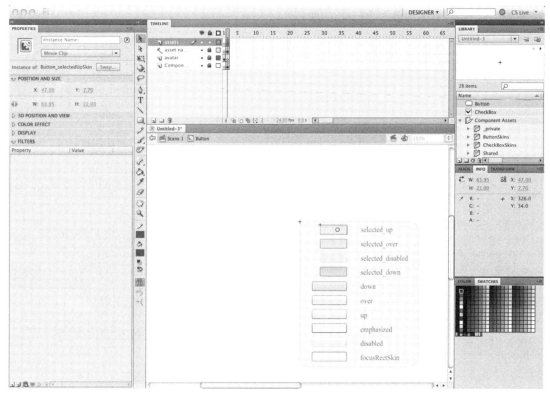

Figure 11-10 Flash Professional, view of a button's skin parts

compartments. Each part of the component can be set up as a MovieClip symbol and controlled by a backing ActionScript class of the component. Each state can be identified by timeline frames and controlled by the ActionScript class.

Looking at the most basic example, a Flash Button (**Figure 11-10**), you can see the parts are designated in the second frame. Each part is a MovieClip and provides a symbol instance name so it can be targeted. In the Button example, states are targeted and changed not by label frames but by the backing ActionScript class. This approach is adequate if transitions are not required. If transitions are required, it makes sense to create your states based on frames and provide transitions between those frames.

Once the designs are complete, the designer or developer can easily target the skin and integrate the design assets as needed, without having knowledge of the intricacies of the component's logic.

For Flex projects that require highly customized and animated components, Flash Professional can be leveraged by wrapping a Flash component in the Flex-BaseComponent. From Flash Builder, developers can quickly add a Flash component to the design view and begin to edit the file in Flash Professional. With Flash Professional, developers would create their components as if they were any other type of Flash content. When finished, Flash Professional will package the file in a SWC library, and the component will be added to the libs directory of your Flex project. Because under the hood the Flash component is really a Flex component, it will be treated as a first-class citizen and will expose all of its methods, properties, and events as if it were a component created in Flash Builder.

COMPONENTS VS. CONTAINERS

When building Flex assets, either in Flash Professional or in Flex Builder, you will notice the option of creating either a container or a component. The responsibility of a *container* is to lay out a variable number of children based on the layout rules of the container. An example would be the VGroup in Flex 4, which lays out its children in a vertical hierarchy based on the order children are added. A *component* provides a set number of parts that are technically children but are known prior to instantiation.

Component and containers in Flex can both be skinned via a skin class or through Flash Professional. In most situations, a container will consist of no skin parts or states. The main purpose of the skin class is to define the background, border, and any other visual design elements that are not related to each child. With Flash Professional, designers can create animations or other behaviors for the look and feel of a container.

Developing supporting tiers

In most situations, a component needs to interact with the application as a whole and distribute information about user and system interactions that have occurred within the component. In a component that requires data from a server, it seems easy enough to write the code necessary to connect to the server and handle the response directly in the component's logic class. After all, that's what the logic class is for, right? The problem with this approach is that if you have multiple components that need the same data, you will be repeating code in multiple places. And what if the server address or configuration changes a year after the application launches? Developers would have to track down and refactor each instance of the code.

The better solution is to decouple application logic, such as sending and receiving data, from the component into its own set of classes. The set of classes and their organization will be defined by the application framework your team has decided to build your application around.

When creating a component, the developer will need to also construct these application base classes. The first objective is to identify any classes that have already been created. If a service exists for retrieving employee data, there is no point in creating it a second time. If a new class is required, the developer should create it based on the framework structure and based on the coding standards created during planning. Once created, the application tiers should be well documented so other developers can understand quickly how to leverage the code.

Integrating design into components

Once wireframe components have been completed and the design assets have been approved by the client, it's time to integrate the real look and feel into each component. With Creative Suite 5, developers or designers can leverage a number of workflows to integrate real designs into already created components.

Flash Professional

Flash Professional applications and components allow developers to take design assets from Fireworks, Illustrator, or Photoshop and import and use them as assets for your component or project.

With assets imported into your Flash Professional library, the wireframe symbols of your component can be replaced with the correct artifacts from the imported design assets. Since you are changing only the look and feel, you will ideally not be required to touch the backing ActionScript. If symbols or assets are related to existing transitions, try to use the swap symbol feature as much as possible. By default when replacing symbols or assets, related transitions are removed. Using the swap feature will prevent this.

Flash Builder

Flex projects provide two options for integrating designs into components. The first is to create Flash libraries with a different symbol for each part and state of the component. For the simple control bar example, the library would contain an up, down, over, and disabled symbol for the add and remove buttons.

Flex 4 provides a new set of MXML tags that support the FXG specification. This new subset of MXML allows for a direct migration of FXG into MXML components. When users take assets from Photoshop, Fireworks, or Illustrator and open them via Flash Catalyst, they are converted to MXML based on FXG syntax.

Flash Catalyst

Flash Catalyst users can create skins for built-in wireframe components such as a Scrollbar. Also, users can create generic components, which can mimic custom components that might already be created in the Flex application.

For our example, the control bar wireframe component has already been created in Flash Builder. In Flash Catalyst, the design assets from the designer's favorite CS5 design tool can be converted into a generic component in Flash Catalyst, which mimics the control bar's look and feel. With this component, the designer or developer can set up the needed states and can style the add and remove buttons in Catalyst.

In the custom component, any transitions required between states can be defined via Flash Catalyst's timeline. Once complete, the Flash Catalyst assets can be saved as an FXP or exported as an FXPL file and imported into Flash Builder for integration into the control bar wireframe component.

Integrating components into the application

When a component has been created, it needs to be integrated into the application. In most situations, the component is identified as part of a view or another component and can be added via the timeline in Flash Professional, in ActionScript, or in Flex as MXML.

For Flex applications, the size of the compiled SWF can quickly become an issue. Each time a component embeds a visual asset such as an image or a Flash asset library, the artifact must be included in the compiled application SWF.

One way to help alleviate the initial download size of your application is to break up components into *modules*. If a component is not required when the app first loads, it might make sense to externalize

> ### FLEX PROJECT LIBRARY (FXPL)
>
> FXPL is a Flex project library file package introduced with Flash Catalyst. The purpose of the format is to allow custom components created in Flash Catalyst to be shared between users and for importing into Flash Builder. When imported into Flash Builder, the FXPL is unpackaged into a Flex Library project.

the content into a module and load the contents into the application when needed. The downside to modules, however, is the time necessary to download and load it into the application. If a module weighs 100KB and the user is on a slow connection, there might be a lag when the user clicks the area of the site that requires the module and before it loads. Keep this type of experience in mind as you decide how to break up your application's components.

Iterating on components

On larger projects and those that practice an iterative development workflow, components will most likely be iterated on over the course of the project. When a component needs to be modified, the first question is whether the required change is to the logic, to the design, or to both. If the logic is changing, a developer can target the component logic class and make the necessary changes without engaging other roles on the project.

For design changes, the developer and designer need to identify what needs to be changed and whether it will affect the logic of the component. If the required changes impact the component parts and states, updates to the logic will be necessary, and both parties should revisit the component contract to ensure everyone is on the same page.

For Flash Professional components, the backing ActionScript and timeline will need to be modified to handle the required changes. Design can be targeted to the identifiable symbols and supporting graphical assets.

For Flex, the developer can target the component class and add or remove parts and states where needed. The design will impact the skin class and will require an update to the MXMLG and the layout of the skin parts where necessary.

SYNCING WITH YOUR TEAM

When all components for an iteration are completed, the team should gather and share the iterative deliverables. With design integrated into the wireframe components, developers should demo the components to the project team and, in particular, the design team. Feedback is essential to ensure the design vision has been meet.

Any changes to the application or components that might impact quality assurance should be shared. If new features were added or removed, those will impact QA's testing plans. If new unit tests were developed to test portions of the application, the QA and build and release teams should be made aware so they can adjust their testing and deployment routine to include verification of those tests.

The build and release team should also be made aware if any new projects were created to support the main project. Was a new Flash Project created to generate visual assets? Was a new Flex Library project created to provide a new set of common utility classes? All of these questions will be important to the build and release process and their deployment scripts.

Part of the team sync process should include code reviews of the new components. The goal is for senior-level developers to review the code base created by other team members. By reviewing code, senior developers can ensure coding standards and identify memory leaks and possible performance bottlenecks. For the lower-level developers, the process will give them one-on-one time with the more experienced developers to allow them to ask questions and learn from the comments and suggestions made.

SUMMARY CHECKLIST

In this chapter, we identified a series of efforts required when setting up your initial project for team development. We looked at how each iteration can pinpoint components for development and how those components can be split to assist in a parallel design and development workflow. Before moving on to the build and release phase, you'll want to be able to answer the following questions:

✔ Has a lead developer been given time to set up the initial structure of the project?

✔ Has the initial project structure been expanded to define the location of valuable project assets?

✔ Based on the type of project created, have additional libraries been downloaded and configured into the project?

✔ Has your team considered configuring libraries as compiled libraries, source, or RSLs?

✔ Once complete, has the project been checked into a source control system?

✔ Has a development environment guide been created and shared with team members?

✔ Has your team discussed the need for testing during development?

✔ If testing is required, have you chosen the proper testing framework and shared this decision with the build and release and QA teams?

✔ For each component, has the developer and design met and defined the component's parts and states (contract)?

✔ Has the component's architecture separated the look and feel from the logic of the component?

✔ Has a wireframe component been developed that matches the designer and developer contract for the component?

✔ Have the supporting tiers been created to assist in the functionality required for a component?

✔ Have the supporting tiers been documented?

✔ Have final designs been integrated into the skin portion of the component?

✔ When the component is integrated into the application, is the size of the component taken into account?

✔ When iterating on a component, have the designer and developer identified what parts need to change?

✔ Has the final component been shared with the project team?

✔ Has design had time to verify the design vision?

✔ Has build and release and QA teams been made aware of any development environment changes that will affect those role?

✔ Have code reviews been given to new components by development peers?

PART V

BUILD AND RELEASE

CHAPTER 12

Planning Build and Release

The build and release process starts during the planning phase and runs throughout the life of the project. At the start of the project, if your team—be it you, your developers, or your dedicated team—is responsible for managing the build and release process, then you need to spend some time forecasting the requirements for the process.

When planning the build and release process, your goal is to determine what the overall roles, tasks, and requirements need to be to successfully implement a consistent build, testing, review, and deployment strategy. In this chapter, you'll learn how the build and release process is defined and how you and your team can establish a process that best suits your project.

DEFINING AN ENVIRONMENT

When first establishing the build and release process, your team needs to define the overall environment in which the project will be developed, integrated, tested, and distributed. Defining an environment consists of two distinct parts: deployment and environments.

Determining your deployment

Determining how the users will get the application starts with two series of important questions. The first group of questions is used to define what type of project you are building. This will help define your build requirements and the technologies required. The second group of questions covers how your team, client, and users will get the application for review, testing, and final distribution.

What type of project do you have?

The first question is, "Is the project viewed in a Web browser?" This means that an end user will use a browser to navigate to a URL address to view your application. This application could be an entire Flash-based Web site, banner ad, Flash game hosted online, or other similar type of application. Understanding that the application will be hosted on a Web server will help define what kind of environments need to be established for your project.

If the project is Web server based, then the next question is, "Will the application be Flex, Action-Script only, or Flash Professional based?" Depending on your answer, the build process will vary. If you are developing a Flex or ActionScript 3–only project that uses the Flex complier, your team has the ability to leverage this compiler using build tools such as Ant, Maven, or other build-oriented technologies. If you are using Flash Professional, the build process will require building the SWF from within the tool.

The next question to ask is, "Is your project going to be launched as a desktop application using AIR?" The process of deploying an AIR application has different challenges and considerations than an application in a Web browser. Some of the issues involve the process of certifying the publisher of the AIR application, using automated updates, versioning the application, and others. We will dive deeper into these issues later in this and the following chapters.

The next question is, "Will the application need server-provided data?" This question applies to both browser and AIR-based applications. Not all projects require live data from servers, but if they do, then this adds another dimension to the complexity of the environments required for the project.

How will your project be distributed?

At this point, when you have outlined what you are building, the next series of questions is focused around the build process and how the application will be distributed to various people during the project and beyond.

The first question is, "How will the client get builds?" As the project design and development proceed, the client will want the ability to review the progress. If the project is browser based and needs live data, you may need to configure testing servers that allow the client to log in and review changes.

If the project is a banner ad or other SWF-based application that does not require data, some clients prefer getting just the SWF and any associated HTML directly via e-mail or a shared folder. We don't recommend this for client review because it is better to have a testing or review server. By having a dedicated review location, you can control and guarantee the version of the application and content the client is reviewing.

With an AIR-based application, you can hand new builds directly to the client, or you can even integrate AIR's ability to auto-update the application once the user has installed a build. If you take the auto-update approach, a public server location will be required to host the update XML file that defines the current version. Using auto-update is a good idea when you have multiple client reviewers so that you can push new builds to them as required.

The second distribution question is, "How does the team get builds?" This only applies if you have more than one person on the project. Throughout the development iterations of the project, new builds of the application will be required for internal review and testing. This system should be separated from the client review system because rapid iterative development changes may cause the internal team's build to be unstable or even unusable until the issue is resolved in the next build.

Possible configurations include having a local (internal) server that hosts the builds for development review. There can be a shared location where files are posted for the team to access. If you have remote team members, you will need to make sure that the internal locations are accessible to all of your team members.

The final distribution question is, "How will the final project be deployed?" Many options are available. To determine which is best, you should consider some of the following questions: Is your client hosting the application? If so, does your team need to configure the server, or will the client handle this? Is your team responsible for setting up the application on the live servers? Does the client just expect the source to be delivered at the end of the project and they will handle the final build and release?

Knowing exactly how the project is being deployed to the end user will help you and your team to develop the final process.

Structuring your environments

Answering, or at least considering, the previous questions will help guide you and your team in defining the actual environments required for the project. We will cover three main environments: development, testing/integration, and deployment.

Development environment

The development environment's main goal is to provide an established and predefined set of systems and configurations to unify the design, development, and build and release processes among the teams. This step defines the overall development environment that best suits your project's needs.

HOW DOES YOUR TEAM USE BUILDS?

When considering how the team gets builds, it's important to consider which team members need the builds and why. Throughout the project, different team members need to access the current build for different reasons. Project managers may need to review the project's current state with the client. Designers will need to review the application for design fidelity before it's sent to the client for final review.

For each of your team members, their level of sophistication and technical ability may not be as high as other team members, meaning that ease of access and availability are important. For example, when the project manager or designer needs to review the build, they should not have to spend time configuring a system to access content; they should be able to easily navigate to a URL or install an AIR application. Make sure to keep these kinds of considerations in the back of your mind as you plan how your team members will access builds.

For most small projects, development environments and their sophistication level are not as critical as for larger projects. The main complexity around development environments occurs when multiple people are working on the project and they all need similar, if not exactly the same, work setup for the project's life cycle.

In this section, we'll explore several important considerations when planning development environments.

Servers. What servers are required for your development environment? If your application requires Web server data, you will need to define development servers both for your back-end server engineers and for your Flash/Flex developers to use when creating server and data based functionality. A common practice is to run a local web server on the developer's machine that has a copy of all the server logic and data used for development. If this is the case, then you will need to define a configuration guide that outlines what technology should be used, such as XMAPP, ColdFusion, virtual machines, or others, and how it should be installed on the developer's machine. Your team may also use developer lanes. *Lanes* are dedicated shared servers that provide a stable yet shared point of contact for each developer to use as data sources. These are often defined by the IT team and are configured the same way from project to project.

Machines. What development machines are required? Are you using OS X, Windows, or Linux? Does every person on the team have multiple machines or just one? If you are bringing in third-party consultants or contractors, are you responsible for providing them with computers? This information should be determined up front because it will help define the machine configurations and the amount of time required for adding new team members. This can get especially tricky as new people are brought onto the project midstream and they need to get their computer configured to work on the project.

Code repositories. As you consider the complexities of a project when working with multiple people and teams, a code repository or depot can help individuals work more efficiently when working on various components or sections of a project. They enable team sharing, code/asset management, and a revision history to track changes, and they help facilitate restoration for backups. This is the time to pick which technology should be used, such as Git, Subversion, or CVS (if you and your team have not already adopted one), as well as decide whether you are hosting the depot or whether you are going with a third-party hosting company. For larger firms, it may make sense to host your own depot, but with the strides of cloud computing, many third-party hosting sites provide a secure, stable, and affordable option.

Asset location and management. It is important to define and standardize where your assets such as documents, graphics, audio, video, and others are stored and organized. By creating consistency, your team can easily add, modify, and, most importantly, find the assets required for a task. We recommend leveraging a combination of code repositories and other backup-enabled locations to prevent accidental loss of content. It's too easy to delete or replace an important file on a shared folder, which can make the original asset unrecoverable.

Multiple team access. As teams grow in size and become spread across departments, locations, or companies, defining a set of shared locations becomes more and more critical. Your team will need to define common locations and processes around how these

ASSET MANAGEMENT

When managing assets—from documents to designs—multiple technologies make team collaboration much easier. Services such as Acrobat.com or Dropbox.com can help manage and secure documents and other assets. They provide shared access, file and folder controls, and revision histories.

For more complex projects with thousands of assets and documents, enterprise-level digital asset management systems (also known as DAMs) can help streamline creation, revision, and deployment of interdependent assets throughout your team, departments, and company.

locations will be configured and shared. It is also important to understand any limitations that may have to be overcome. For example, a commonly used location for your internal team may be inaccessible to other team members because of a firewall or other security systems. These kinds of issues typically arise in larger firms, and the IT team should be consulted when planning your development environment.

Flash Builder and Flash Professional configuration. Defining a standard configuration for Flash Builder and Flash Professional is an important process. Configuration includes Flex SDK versions, player versions, locales, libraries such as external SWCs and externally referenced projects, document classes, folder structure, repository location, and any other common settings that should be defined across the team. Having a unified configuration means that as your team modifies the application—or, more importantly, the overall structure—the process of building and testing the SWF or AIR file remains the same for all team members.

Issue and task tracking. Issue tracking is the process of logging, managing, and updating issues within the current project's application. Third-party tools, such as Jira, Bugzilla, Traq, Mantis, BaseCamp, and others, allow your team and client to report and manage issues within an application. In addition to issues, many of these tools can track tasks as well as allow team members to manage and comment on their assigned task progress. The team should determine how issues will be tracked for the project and where these tools will be located. Just like code repositories, issue-tracking software can be hosted locally or with a third-party hosting provider.

Environment setup documentation. Once your team has defined the different aspects of the development environment, it is a good idea to prepare a configuration and standards document. This document outlines how environments are configured, where assets are located, how development accesses data, configuration standards for Flash Builder and Flash Professional, and any other information that helps new and existing team members manage their environment.

Testing environment

Defining the testing environment is similar to creating the development environment. The goal of the testing environment is to create a separate area to integrate and test specific iterations of the application as it is being developed. Unlike the development environment, which is a one-to-one ratio for each member of the team, the testing environment should be designed as a many-to-one configuration to allow multiple members of the team, and even the client, to view regular releases of the application.

Servers. Just like with the development environment, testing servers should be established to provide a dedicated and stable location to integrate code and assets to verify that the application is working as intended.

Machines / virtualization. Having dedicated testing machines enables the team members to verify builds in a consistent environment. Depending on the complexity and configuration of the application, certain software applications allow you to snapshot the state of an operating system (OS) and then return to it at any time. This is ideal for testing the installs, updates, and any other configurations that may change the OS. By having a common starting point, the testing team members can restart with a clean slate every time. OS virtualization is also a great way to create test environments that can be shared among the team members to verify that each test pass is done on identical configurations.

Automated testing software. Automated testing is the process of creating a series of programmatic tests that can be executed on the current build of the application. An ever-growing number of testing tools are available for the Flash Platform such as ASUnit, FlexUnit, and Flex Monkey, just to name a few. Automated tools for testing can enable a more streamlined development process, but they do introduce another level of complexity that requires more time to develop and maintain during the life of the project.

Internal vs. client facing. As the project moves forward, it is important to demonstrate progress to the client. You and your team will need to determine whether the client requires an accessible testing environment so that they can perform their own review of the application. Client-facing test environments tend to be more important for browser-based applications because a Web server is often required to display the content. AIR applications are easier to distribute since you can simply provide the client with an AIR file.

Deployment environment

The deployment environment varies greatly depending on how the project and client relationships are defined. In some projects, the client will handle deployment of the final application on their environment, such as their Web site or intranet. In other cases, it may be you or your team's responsibility to create a deployment environment where the final application will exist.

Servers. Just like with the development and testing environments, dedicated deployment (or live) servers should be established to provide a dedicated and stable location for the end user to access when interacting with the final application. You can use preexisting servers, or, if this is a new project, setting up deployment servers may be part of the project scope.

Code delivery. When developing projects for a third-party client, deployment often includes delivering the final source code and assets to the client. This can also include generated documentation from tools such as ASDoc or other documentation such as user and developer guides that outline the structure of the project and the underlying code.

DEFINING THE BUILD PROCESS

Once you've discussed and defined the different environments, the next step is to define the overall build process that will be used throughout the project. The build process incorporates the integration, building, and testing of the release. This process will occur at regular weekly, daily, hourly, or even individual code check-in intervals during the project.

Who is building and deploying?

You need to know whether your team is responsible for handling the build and deploy process or whether it's being handled by the client or a third party. If the client is handling this process, there has to be an established way of delivering the code and assets to them so that they can build and deploy the application. You also have to establish when the delivery will occur. To ensure successful build and release, you should determine whether your delivery will be based on milestones, feature completion, or regular intervals throughout your project.

WHY DIFFERENT ENVIRONMENTS?

When planning a project, a common question that arises is, "Why do we need so many environments?" Separating development, testing, and production servers is an important process to consider because many changes occur during the development cycle that can impact the overall experience for those reviewing or using the existing builds.

For example, a client could be in the process of reviewing the beta 1 build of a browser-based application that requires a lot of server-side data when the development team realizes that the format of the data being sent from the server needs to be updated to fix a bug in the current build. If the review application shares the same server that the developers are using, then changing the data structure has the potential to cause the current beta build to break. The new build expects the new format, but the old build does not. By separating the systems, development can continue without interruption or being worried about their changes cascading down to other review or live versions of the application.

Do you need a dedicated process or team?

If your team is responsible for build and deploy, then a process should be outlined even if it is as simple as defining where and when the SWF gets built or created. For small projects, a dedicated and detailed process may not be required. It could be as simple as compiling a SWF, making sure it works as expected, and then giving it to the client.

For larger projects, a dedicated process becomes more important. As more developers and designers become involved in the project, managing the content and code becomes more complex and time-consuming. Many questions can arise: Which are the most up-to-date assets? When should a new build be distributed for testing? When should the builds be tested? This information should be defined up front so that your team knows how the day-to-day process should be executed.

For medium to large projects, one or more people may be responsible for building, testing, and deploying builds throughout the process. For larger teams, quality assurance and build management are broken into independent teams or even divisions.

If there is a dedicated team, you should clearly define who is responsible for managing builds, updates, testing, and deployment, and communicate that information to the whole team. This way, if an issue arises with a build, the correct people can be informed about it. If you do not have a build team, an individual should be identified who is responsible for creating builds for the team and the client.

Do you need a build tool?

As the Flash Platform matures, a growing number of build automation tools are available to streamline the build and deployment process. The goal of build automation is not only to unify the process from team member to team member and project to project, but also to enable configuration options such as pushing debug builds to testing servers, releasing builds to deployment servers, managing asset locations, application versioning, language localization, and other similar requirements. For most small projects,

build automation can be seen as more overhead than needed, but if your team does establish a build system, it can be leveraged from project to project.

Getting into the benefits and requirements of build automation is beyond the scope of this book, but many different options are available. Adobe has provided a set of Ant scripts for Flex. Ant is a Java-based build language and tool that helps automate the building process. Another tool, Project Sprouts, is a Rake/Ruby-based solution that works with ActionScript 2, ActionScript 3, AIR, and Flex projects.

During the writing of this book, we did an informal survey via Twitter to find out who was using automated builds and what tools they were using. Ant, in collaboration with tools such as CruiseControl, Fx2Ant, and other Ant-based solutions, appear to be the current favorite. But, with any growing community, these technologies and options are evolving at an exceptional rate.

Choosing the tools that should be used, if any, depends on the scope of the current project and the benefits of adopting a build system that will help your team on future projects.

Quality assurance standards

An important part of the overall build and release process is applying quality assurance (QA) to each build to verify features and functionality. One of the challenges of the QA process is making sure that each build, feature, and subfeature is tested in a consistent and comprehensive way.

Developing test cases, plans, and suites

The best way to guarantee a high level of QA is to develop a series of repeatable test suites that encompass a series of test plans, which consist of individual test cases.

Test cases. A test case is a series of well-defined, repeatable steps that execute a specific bit of functionality within an application. Often, test cases evolve from the original use cases defined in the planning phase of the project. For example, one test case for a video player would be test the play functionality. The steps would be as follows: Launch the player, load a valid video, press Play, and verify that the video begins playing. The goal of a test case is to be as simple and targeted as possible, with the minimum number of steps to ensure the expected outcome. A good test case is not intended to test all the functionality of a feature, but a very specific aspect of the functionality of that feature.

Test plan. A test plan consists of multiple test cases that cover all the functionality of specific feature. A test plan should have a series of valid test cases, such as video playing properly, and a series of fail cases. Fail cases are tests that are designed to fail, such as trying to play a nonexistent video file. Fail cases are just as important if not more important than the valid cases. During development, most developers think more about how users should use the feature instead of how users may misuse the feature. By developing fail cases, your test plans will help identify use cases that the developer may have missed.

Test suite. A test suite is a series of test plans that cover either the entire application or large sections of the application, depending on the overall size of the project. Ideally, you or your QA team can have a series of test suites for your entire project that are applied to each build as it is made available.

Writing the tests

Writing a test suite can be an arduous task, depending on the size of the project. The larger and more complex the project, the more tests need to be developed.

EDGE CASES

A common term used by QA is an *edge case*. Edge cases are tests that verify how the feature behaves in potentially uncommon uses. If your job is to test a portable CD player, an edge case would be trying to use it in 120-degree heat or minus 60-degree cold. It is probably not going to happen, but you still need to make sure that it works as expected. A good test plan should always include edge cases because these are often the unexpected bugs that get found and reported by your users.

For smaller projects, the number of tests can still be large, but the detail required for each test may not be as important.

For larger projects, you may have a dedicated QA team. If this is the case, then the QA team usually works closely with the development and project management teams to determine the features, how they should work, and when they will be available for testing. Once the features and test timeline are defined, individual QA team members are assigned to test a feature or a set of features.

For smaller teams, there may not be a dedicated QA team or person; it is up to the team to determine who will handle testing. Ideally, the person who created the functionality should not be the one testing it because having a fresh pair of eyes will often expose issues that were missed by the people who created the functionality. For smaller teams, it is still a good idea to develop a series of test plans that can be run by the assigned tester, whether it's a developer, designer, manager, or even the client.

To help augment your QA team, it may be worth considering bringing in nonteam members to help review and test the application. This could be a small set of potential users, friends, or other company employees, or you could create a prerelease program to invite target users to review the application. Having more eyes on the project will provide new insight into both potential issues and missing features that could improve the overall quality of the application.

Once the testing team has been defined, the assigned authors will begin outlining and writing test cases. For large teams, there could be a standardized process for writing test cases, plans, and suites; however, the basic steps are the same for any sized team. Begin by brainstorming all the possible ways the feature can be used and misused. Usually, the assigned individual does the initial brainstorming by building an outline of test cases. The outline is a simple list of test titles, such as "play valid video," "pause video," and "load invalid video path."

Once the first draft of tests is created, other team members should review the tests to make sure that all the valid fail and edge cases have been defined.

It is also important that the developer of this feature review the test case outline. This does two important things; the developer will have a good insight into the feature and can provide feedback on any possible missing cases, and it gives the developer a preview of all the ways their feature may be used and can help prevent issues before they arise.

After the outline has been defined and approved by the team, the steps of each case should be written out. Each step should be clear and concise and should enable nearly anyone to execute the test by just reading the defined steps. Having a formal test plan, with each test case written out, enables you and your team to reassign QA team members to new features and test each feature in a consistent and repeatable manner, and it also enables nearly anyone to execute a test plan for a feature.

When writing tests, an assortment of tools can be used. Applications such as Adobe Buzzword or Tables allow your team to create detailed testing plans that can be shared and reviewed among the team. Tables enable your team to create columns that track when the test was last run and if it was successful. By having this information in a sharable location, other team members can review the state of the testing pass and take over the test pass if required.

Automated testing

Automated testing is a similar concept to an automated build process. The goal of automated testing is to create a suite of tests that can be executed via an application testing harness, such as FlexUnit, ASUnit, or Flex Monkey. These testing harnesses run small scripts or snippets of code that execute methods and functionality within your application and then verify whether the results of the executed code meet predefined standards.

Automated tests are usually executed at multiple stages of the project. Determining when your team executes the tests depends upon your development and build process. Usually, the developer executes the automated tests before checking in new code to make sure that the updated code does not break any existing functionality. With automated builds, it is also possible for the build system to run all of the tests after a new build is completed to check for potential errors.

Your team's developers, QA engineers, or both can develop automated tests. Who develops the tests depends upon your development methodology and team responsibility. If your team follows Test Driven Development (TDD), then your developers are often responsible for writing and updating your automated tests. QA will sometimes be involved in TDD to write extended tests or manage existing tests. In other methodologies or team structures, the QA team is responsible for writing and managing test suites with support from the developers.

With the release of Flash Builder 4 Premium, FlexUnit is now integrated into the IDE and is making development and management of automated tests much easier (**Figure 12-1**). Now, developers can write, execute, and update test cases and suites easily and effectively during development from within the IDE.

Implementing automated testing is not a requirement for all projects. Your team should determine whether it's feasible and desirable to implement automated testing. For short-duration projects that have limited life spans, automated testing may not be necessary, but if your project is intended to have multiple

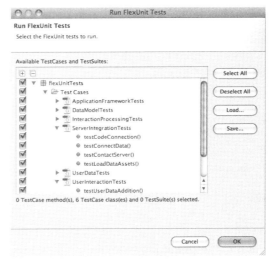

Figure 12-1 Flash Builder 4 has integrated FlexUnit into the IDE.

release cycles or if other teams will be building on top of your code, then you should consider automated testing.

DEFINING APPLICATION PERFORMANCE BENCHMARKS

The stability and usability of an application are not the only guides used to measure a project's success. The performance of the application is just as important to an end user. If the application has slow performance, consumes a perceived excessive amount of system resources, or appears not to function as expected, it obviously can cause frustration.

When planning a project's build and release process, it is important to determine performance standards for the application. These are common questions used to define performance goals:

- What are the minimum system requirements for the application?
- How much memory (RAM) should the application require and how much is too much?
- What is the maximum overall file size of the application?
- How long should it take the application to load?
- What is an acceptable frames per second rate?

Using these questions as a starting point to help define a base performance goal for the application, your team can begin establishing performance metrics before application architecture and development begin. This information will help your developers to make development decisions earlier in the project, which can help mitigate potential performance problems that may occur later in the project.

Frames per second

Frames per second (FPS) are the number of frames the runtime can render per second. The target setting for the SWF is set at compilation and varies from project to project. For more interactive and animation-driven projects, a higher FPS average gives the user a smoother display experience. When the FPS drops below a certain level (because of your project's needs), the application may appear to stutter, slow down, or even hang.

Defining a goal FPS and a threshold FPS can help determine whether an application is performing correctly or whether the development team may need to focus on optimizing certain actions within the application to increase the FPS. Verifying FPS often requires test code to be included in the application so that the tester can verify the current FPS average over time.

File size

For browser-based applications and some AIR applications, overall file size is an important benchmark. File size impacts multiple aspects of the project, from the amount of time it requires to download a file to the amount of bandwidth the application uses. For some projects, file size is critical because of potential max size limits for SWF files. This is common in advertising-based environments, where the ad-hosting provider has a file size cap to control bandwidth consumption.

Load time

Load time is the amount of time an application takes from launch to the instant a user can begin interacting with the application. For Web-based applications, load time is often hindered by the user's bandwidth, SWF size, the number of external assets that need to be loaded, and whether the SWF or assets have been

---

WHAT IS A GOOD FPS?

Understanding how FPS affects your project and the overall performance in Flash Player is important when starting a project. Having a high FPS setting in Flash for a complex animated project may seem like a good idea at first, but this can put unnecessary stress on the player and consume too many CPU resources. Other projects that are focused on data processing may benefit from a lower FPS because animation is not required. Reading up on how FPS and Flash Player work together can help your team make more educated choices for the overall performance metrics.

previously cached on the user's machine. For desktop applications using AIR, load time is hindered more by the application establishing UI elements and connecting with any external Web service if required.

Defining the goal for optimal load time is hard at the beginning of a project, but having a range can help the team optimize throughout the project. During successive testing, it's important to continue to measure and evaluate load time so that the team can optimize it early in the process. Waiting until the end of a project often limits what can be done to minimize load time without having to invest more design and development time late in the game.

Perceived time

Perceived time is defined as how the user experiences (or perceives) the performance of an application. Providing UI feedback and markers to the user can help reduce attention or frustration for slower actions such as processing complex calculations, loading files, or executing an external service call. This includes showing dialog boxes, progress bars, and other visible information to the user as application tasks are performed.

Understanding perceived time can help your team make design and implementation decisions when developing your application. Knowing that a specific operation may take more time will help your team define how to inform the user and decrease the perceived time for an operation.

Memory usage

The larger an application is and the longer the user interacts with it both have the potential to increase memory usage. Implementing functionality and features improperly has the potential to create memory leaks within a Flash application. If this kind of issue arises, the application will continue to consume and use increasing amounts of memory over time. As memory use rises in an application, it and overall system performance begins to degrade.

To help track memory usage, Flash Builder 4 Premium provides a profiler that enables developers and QA engineers to dynamically track the overall application memory usage and pinpoint what parts of the application are using up memory (**Figure 12-2**). By using the profiler, memory leaks and other misuse of system resources can be targeted and ideally resolved before the project is completed.

Minimum system requirements

Defining the minimum system requirements for your project can occur in three ways. First, the features in a feature-driven project can define the minimum requirements, such as video hardware acceleration, 3D acceleration, player requirements, and so on. Second, a technical limitation can drive features, such as deploying to mobile devices or having strict IT requirements that define the technology available for the company. Finally, a combination of desired

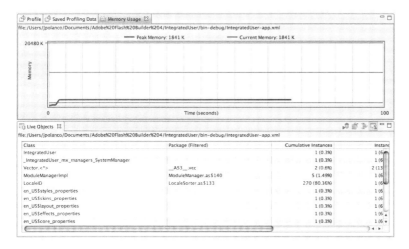

Figure 12-2 Flash Builder 4 has a memory profiler for your application.

features and the limitations of available technology can set your minimum system requirements.

Defining and understanding the target system requirements for your application helps define the application's overall performance goals. For some projects, your client may have outdated systems throughout their user base, and your application will need to function properly for them. Your clients may be on slower networks with slower download speed, and overall SWF size is more important. These kinds of limitations mean that having all the bells and whistles may not be possible for the project and will affect your whole team.

Everyone on your team should understand the project's system requirements so that these potential limitations are kept in mind during the design, development, and testing phases.

MEMORY LEAKS

Memory leaks occur when an object in memory is referenced improperly, preventing the Flash Player from removing it on the next garbage collection (GC) pass. GC is the process of Flash Player that is responsible for scanning the current memory usage of the application and determining whether any objects are no longer needed (referenced) and then removing them if no other part of the application uses the object.

In some situations, an object can be referenced incorrectly preventing GC from removing it, even though it is no longer required by the application. When this occurs, the application has a memory leak because the application will continue to consume more memory over time but not clean up after itself. The longer your application runs, the more memory it uses, eventually causing Flash Player to slow down or even crash.

SUMMARY CHECKLIST

Taking the time to plan your team's build and release strategy is an important aspect of any project. The amount of time and investment required for this strategy depends on the size and complexity of the project and the overall size of your team and the number of external stakeholders. Planning ahead may appear to add more time to the project, but it can save you a significant amount of frustration and delays later.

Before you start the design and development of your project, make sure you have answered the following questions:

✔ What type of project are you building; is it browser or desktop based?

✔ Do you need data and Web services; if so, who manages them, and how do you access them?

✔ How do you plan to distribute your project?

✔ How will you and your client develop, test, and deploy the project?

✔ Do you have a standard system configuration for your developers and testers?

✔ Who is responsible for building and deploying the application?

✔ How are you going to build your project?

✔ Who is responsible for testing your application?

✔ How are you going to track issues as they are found?

✔ Who is going to write your test cases, both manual and automated?

✔ Do you have a set of performance metrics, and how are you going to verify them?

CHAPTER 13

Iterative Build and Release

As with the design and development phases, the build and release process occurs iteratively throughout the project. As new code and content is created and integrated into the application, a new build will need to be created, tested, and deployed.

At first glance, this iterative process appears relatively straightforward. You create a new build, and your team tests the build and tracks and fixes issues; then another new build is created. This process occurs over and over until all the features are done and the issues are fixed. But, as your project moves along the spectrum from smaller-sized to larger-sized, this process can become more complex and time intensive.

The larger the project gets, the ability to find and fix all of the issues can quickly become unachievable. New issues continually keep popping up as your team fixes them, and soon your project deadline and scope grows until no end is in sight. The reality—which you, your team, and your client must consider—is that no application is 100 percent issue-free. You could argue that with smaller projects it may be feasible to achieve perfection, but the odds are that someone will find fault, however minute, with the application.

Because you will never be able to develop the perfect application, a project's success cannot be defined solely by this mark. You must acknowledge that all software has issues, but the goal is to define what issues are important to fix now, what should be fixed soon, and what can be fixed later. This is the hardest part of build and release: defining what is required in your application and what is acceptable to you when the ideal cannot be achieved.

The first step in this process is to find and then bring to light the issues within your application. You can perform this task in many different ways. In this chapter we will present seven common types of testing that can be used in your project:

- *Feature testing* is the process of verifying that the defined features of your application function as designed.

- *Regression testing* is the process of verifying that previously discovered issues are resolved in the current build.

- *Integration testing* is the process of verifying that different features and functionality work together in the application.

- *Continuous testing* is the process of integrating and using automated testing systems within your development and build tools.

- *User interface (UI) testing* is the process of verifying that your UI looks and behaves as designed.

- *Smoke testing* is the process of using a series of simple tests to verify the stability of your application.

- *Stress and performance testing* is the process of verifying that your application can handle real-world situations and behave in a way that your users accept.

In this chapter, we will cover each of these types of testing in more detail. We will also cover features of the Flash Platform that can affect your build and release process as your project moves forward.

CREATING BUILDS, QUALITY ASSURANCE, AND DEPLOYMENT

Once you and your team begin developing the application, you'll need to create new builds regularly so that the new features and assets can be fully tested and reviewed. How and when builds are created for testing depends upon the team and the process defined during the initial planning stages of the build and release process.

With smaller teams and projects, the developers are often responsible for creating builds for testing and client review. For larger projects, the build team is responsible for creating each build. In some situations, the QA team will create their own builds for testing purposes.

TIP ▪ If you do not have a dedicated build team or you have only one person responsible for builds, make sure the responsible person clearly documents the process. This way, if he or she is sick, is unavailable, or leaves the team, another member can use the guide to take over the build process.

Understanding the different types of testing

As builds are created, they should be tested to verify their stability and feature support. You can apply multiple types of testing to each build depending on its intended use.

Feature testing

In the beginning of a project, the most common type of testing is focused on feature development. As developers add functionality to the application, new builds will need to be created so that functionality can be verified. As each build is created, team members responsible for testing will begin a test pass by executing test plans for the features that are currently enabled. The goal of each test pass is to make sure that the developers are building the functionality as it has been defined in the specification.

When feature development begins, not all functionality will be enabled as each build is made available. Keeping the QA and development teams in sync is important in order to know what functionality is available and ready for testing. This means that test plans will be incrementally tested as development progresses.

With any project, features evolve and change as the application grows. When changes occur, the test plans need to be updated to include new tests that verify the updated functionality. Old tests that do not accurately represent the features should be updated or removed to keep the test plan valid.

Once the developer thinks that all of the functionality has been integrated into a build for a feature, the feature is considered *feature complete*. At this point, a full test pass is performed on the build. This means that every test in the feature's test plan is executed to make sure there are no issues with the feature. If any bugs are found, they should be logged into the bug-tracking system, and the developer should be made aware of the issues.

Regression testing

As the developers resolve bugs, it is important to verify that each issue was indeed fixed. The process of verifying that the new build has fixed the issue is regression testing.

A challenge of regression testing is to know which build has fixed the bug. Bug-tracking software helps manage this process by allowing developers to mark the bugs as fixed and reassign the issue to the person who initially logged the bug. Without a tracking system, a new build could be released, and the logger of the bug may mistakenly think the issue is fixed or re-report the issue. Team communication is important to help prevent wasting time on tracking down known or preexisting issues.

One way that the build team can help solve this is to create incremental build numbering so that each build is assigned a unique number. The build is then tagged with this number. Possible methods of tagging include changing the SWF name (in other words, mySwf_1537.swf becomes mySwf_1548.swf), using an About dialog box that shows the version number, or even creating a hidden view that can be accessed through a shortcut enabled by the developers. By having a unique build number, the developers can note which build will have the fix, and then the tester can perform a regression test on the proper build.

Integration testing

As project development continues and features are completed, a more robust form of testing should occur. The focus of this testing is to make sure that different features that interact with each other do not cause any unexpected errors. This is especially important for features that are dependent on other functionality to work.

Ideally, when creating specifications and test plans for features, you want to define all the possible use cases and dependencies. During the writing process, we tend to focus more on the basic functionality of a feature and not how it may interact with other features. A common example is a drop-down menu, which controls settings in the application.

When writing the test plan, we would consider accessing the menu, rollover states, clicking items, and so on. Yet, there may be another feature later that requires the functionality in the menu to be disabled during certain times, but when the original test plan was created, we did not consider this nor did we test for it.

These types of missed use cases often turn into trickier bugs to discover, so it's important to consider how each feature interacts with other functionality as it is developed and tested.

Automated integration testing is possible but is often time-consuming and troublesome because large and complex aspects of the application need to be configured so that the test suite can execute properly. It is usually more suitable to have manual testing of integration points than to invest large amounts of time and effort into building complex testing systems.

Continuous testing

With larger projects or when working with teams that have a well-defined automated process, your team can take advantage of continuous testing. Continuous testing is the process of running automated test suits on every build that is created. Continuous testing is more commonplace with traditional software and server development but is growing in popularity with Flash Platform development teams. Because of the advancement of the Flash Platform and third-party technologies, it's becoming easier to enable continuous testing in your project, which can help streamline your team's build and release process.

MANUAL TESTING

With the introduction of automated testing, the traditional practice of having an individual execute a test plan is now considered *manual testing*. Manual testing is more time consuming because it can be executed only as quickly as the person can follow the test plan, yet manual testing can catch more elusive issues that automated testing may not discover.

For example, when performing a manual test, the tester may see behavior or user experience issues that are not technically incorrect but may cause a user problems. The tester can then raise this issue to the team, and they can react to it. Without manual testing, this smaller or nonobvious issue can be missed because the automated system is just checking to make sure the application is behaving functionally as designed.

The first step of implementing continuous testing is to create a series of automated tests that can be accessed, executed, and managed by your development team. The easiest way to do this is to have a series of FlexUnit tests that are accessible in a code repository. When a developer is ready to check code into the repository or to release a new test build, he or she will run the automated tests to make sure that the changes have not created any new issues.

When developers make a change to an application—adding or modifying functionality, for example—the change can create unintended consequences that cause new issues within the application. These new issues may not be apparent to the developer.

If the developer uses automated testing before a new build is created, he or she will likely catch an issue before it is released for testing or review. Otherwise, the injected issues will be found later during the QA pass, by the client, or potentially by an end user. Another benefit of continuous testing is that it frees the testing team members to focus on more challenging issues such as UI and integration testing.

For teams that are adopting automated build systems such as Ant or Project Sprouts, the build technologies allow you to execute automated tests as builds are created. The build system compiles the new build, runs it through the automated testing system, and then can report issues via e-mail or other communication systems if errors are found.

User interface testing

With most Flash projects, the initial development does not include the final look and feel of the application. This process of applying the final design requires extensive testing to make sure everything is correct.

For smaller teams, the designer should thoroughly review the UI to make sure that it's correct and that it behaves as expected. Any needed changes or tweaks are then designated as bugs and assigned to either the developer or the designer, depending on what needs to be fixed.

For larger teams, the QA engineers work closely with the designers to make sure that the QA team is testing the UI correctly and that they understand the designers' vision so that they can log the issues correctly.

UI testing can be time-consuming and often has to be done manually. Testing manually is usually the default choice because verifying the UI includes checking the layout of the UI and testing user interactions such mouse clicks, scrolling, and other actions. There are automated testing systems that can help, such as FlexMonkey. These systems allow testers to create automated tests that simulate user interactions and compare screenshots of previous versions to verify correct designs and UI.

Automated UI testing requires a lot of resources to manage and update the tests as the application development continues. As with any automated system, any changes to the UI or interactions require updates to the test to make sure that the tests do not fail because of the new modification. Many of the automated systems use screen capturing to verify the UI, and if a UI layout changes, no matter how small, it will cause the tests to fail. UI test automation should be considered an important augmentation to your testing strategy but is not a replacement for full manual UI test passes.

Smoke testing

As your Flash project development continues, you will want to release builds for client review. Before releasing the build, it's important to perform a quick sanity check to make sure the application's core functionality is working correctly. This is smoke testing.

A smoke test is a series of basic tests that cover the most used and most common functionality of your application. For a game, the smoke test could be based around user controls, score management, saving games, loading games, and so on. For a dashboard, it could be logging into a test account, loading test data, verifying that the UI renders the data, and making sure the navigation controls function properly. A smoke test should be quick and efficient, focusing on the most important aspects that make the application work.

Stress and performance testing

In the initial planning phase of build and release, you defined a set of performance goals. As the project progresses, it's important to begin spot-checking performance in new builds. The initial goal of spot-checking is to see whether there are any glaring performance issues within the current functionality. You will not want to spend too much time focusing on performance during initial feature development because the implementation of the functionality will evolve over time.

Once features become complete and the application becomes more stable, then performance testing should begin. As new builds are released, a benchmark is set to determine the current state of the performance. If areas of functionality are not performing to your defined benchmarks, bugs should be logged with notes of what the target goal should be.

As the project comes to completion, a full performance test should begin and stress testing should be considered. Stress testing is the process of making the application handle potentially excessive use, which may occur once the application is released.

For a data-driven application, this could be loading large amounts of data at one time. For a game, it could be having a large number of characters or assets on-screen. For multiuser applications, it could be making sure that a significant number of simultaneous connections are handled properly. Other types of stress testing could include letting the application run for multiple hours or days and making sure it still behaves correctly as time progresses.

Using a bug scrub process

As your various testers find issues within your application, they will submit bugs to your team. In the beginning of a project, these bugs are often handled ad hoc with developers fixing them as they have time during feature development. Often, these bugs are known by the developers and are caused by the initial state of flux a project goes through during the development process.

THE ART OF LOGGING GOOD BUGS

One of the challenges of managing a bug base is maintaining a high quality of detailed bug reports, which are made by your team, client, and users. Inexperienced bug reporters often leave out a lot of details, and their bugs end up being one-sentence statements such as "it doesn't work when I click the button." The problem with this kind of report is that it does not help QA or the developer reproduce or fix the issue. Usually when this happens, your team has to go back to the bug reporter and ask detailed questions about what the bug is and how to replicate it.

A good bug report should have a lot of details; ideally it should be a step-by-step process of how to re-create the bug. If the bug is intermittent (meaning it doesn't happen all the time), the reporter should provide notes about what they were doing when the bug occurred. Ideally, the notes will point the developer in the right direction so he or she can solve the issue.

To help guide reporters, consider using bug note templates. Adobe does a great job of this in its public bug bases. When creating a new bug, its note field is prepopulated with a "steps to reproduce" section, an "actual results" section, an "expected results" section, and a "workaround" section. By having this information in the notes, it guides the reporter to fill in the details and standardize the process.

It is also worth taking the time to train bug reporters on other settings in the bug-tracking tool. Define what priority, severity, reproducibility, and other categories mean for your team and why you use them. This may require that you and your team take some time to define these definitions yourselves before implementing them in the system. Having a well-defined bug-logging process will improve the quality of bugs reported and save time for you and your team.

As the project moves forward, new feature development becomes less of the focus, and the team begins to spend more and more time fixing issues. Prioritizing these issues is an important aspect of the QA and build process. Many bug-tracking systems enable users to assign priority levels to the bugs. Unfortunately, the people logging the bug often just use the default priority or assign the bug the highest priority even if it is technically not true.

To help organize and prioritize bugs, you may need a bug scrub process. *Bug scrubbing* is the process of having a few assigned team members review the bugs currently open (meaning the bugs that are not fixed) and verify that they are assigned a valid priority or severity.

For larger teams, this process also includes multiple steps beyond simple prioritization. One workflow for larger teams is to first have the bug go through a *triage* process depending on who logged the bug. If the client or a user logged the bug, the issue is assigned to a QA member for triage. The QA triage process is to make sure the logged bug is a valid, repeatable bug, not a duplicate of a known issue, or something that has already been fixed in a more recent build. Once triage confirms that the bug is valid, then the bug scrub team assigns the bug to the appropriate developer based upon the team's current workload, individual experience, and other contributing factors.

The bug scrub should occur at regular intervals throughout the project. During initial development, the bug scrub can occur as needed, such as when a large number of unassigned bugs have built up. Later in the project, the bug scrub should start occurring regularly, such as once a week, once a day, or even multiple times a day. As you get closer to the release of the project, you will probably want to have bug scrub meetings more often.

Defining your testing process

The process of testing an application is very organic; it changes over time and evolves to your needs and project size. How you test, when you test, and who is responsible for testing changes as the project goes on, and you will need to work closely with your client to set expectations on what kinds of issues should be resolved and what can be deferred until a later time.

Your project won't require all of these types of testing—it's up to you and your team to determine what testing strategies work and make the most sense for your project.

USING FLASH PLATFORM FEATURES FOR TESTING

When deploying and testing builds on the Flash Platform, you need to consider some important details that could impact the overall process. They include debug build vs. release build settings, browser caching, runtime shared libraries, local shared objects, AIR configuration folders, and AIR versioning. In the following sections, we will examine each of these issues and explain how they can impact your build and release process during development.

Debug vs. release builds

When creating builds for testing and internal review, you need to consider which publish settings should be used to create the application. The compiler supports two types of SWFs and AIR files: debug and release.

Builds, defined

A *debug build* contains additional functionality to allow external debuggers such as Flash Builder, Flash Professional, and the command-line debugger to connect and communicate with the application. This functionality allows you to set breakpoints, profile the application, and inspect the state of the player.

A *release build* does not contain this additional functionality, which means that external debugging sessions cannot be used with the created SWF or AIR file. This means that release builds are smaller than debug builds because they do not contain all of the debug information. Because you cannot debug a release build, it is usually a good idea to distribute debug builds when testing applications. Using release builds for performance testing is recommended because the build represents the final size of the

application and will demonstrate the actual load time a user will experience. Release builds can also be used for client review and of course will be used for final deployment, which we will discuss in Chapter 14.

AIR debug builds

Unlike a debug SWF file, which can be given to anyone with Flash Player, providing a debug version of an AIR application is much more challenging. This is because of how AIR files are created and launched. Under the hood, an AIR application is simply a SWF file with additional information and assets that are bundled into a single file. When debugging an AIR application, a debug SWF is created, and the AIR Debug Launcher (ADL) handles running the application.

When creating an AIR release file, the build process packages up the XML configuration file, the generated SWF, and any other external assets that are required for the application to run into a single AIR file. This file can then be passed to anyone with the AIR runtime, and they can install the application and run it.

When this release bundling process occurs, the default settings create a release build of the included SWF file, which removes the debugging functionality. To maintain the debug functionality, you can pass along the unpackaged AIR files, and testers can use the ADL command-line application to launch the AIR application in debug mode. As you can probably tell, passing along unbundled AIR builds for testing is not a common or easy process.

In most cases, it is easiest for the build team to create release builds that can be used for testing and review. If debugging is later required, then the unpackaged version can be provided and launched via ADL.

Browser and server caching

When testing and even developing applications that are browser-based, the browser and server cache can play havoc with your team. By default, Web browsers try to cache downloaded files so that the next time a user requests a file, the browser doesn't have to get the file from the server again. This caching helps increase performance and limit requests to the Web server.

Browser caching affects the loading and unloading of SWF files and assets. This includes both the main application SWF and any children files that may be loaded by your application. During the testing process, a SWF or asset may need to be changed and then reloaded in the browser. Sometimes, hitting Refresh in the browser will update the file; in other cases, the browser will use the old file that was stored in cache. When this occurs, it can make the application behave in unexpected ways because it could be loading old files.

The best way to guarantee that the requested files are indeed the ones you expect is to clear the browser's cache between each refresh. This option is available in all browsers and usually resides under Preferences or the Option menu. For browsers that support plug-ins or extensions, such as Firefox, there are developer tools that allow you to quickly clear the browser's cache with a single button click. These kinds of tools are indispensible during development and testing.

You also need to consider data caching. When your application requests data from your server, the data being returned by either the browser or the server may be cached. Some server configurations mark file dates and may not return new data unless it is older than a specified time range. It is important that you disable server caching during development so that the most up-to-date data and files are always returned to the application.

Runtime shared libraries

Runtime shared libraries (RSLs) are special external SWF files that contain code that can be shared across browser-based Flash applications. RSLs are not used in AIR applications, so they should be considered only for browser-based applications.

If you are familiar with SWC files, RSLs are similar because they are shared code libraries that are bundled into a single file. Unlike SWC files, an RSL is intended to externalize the library content from the application itself and is loaded into the application at runtime.

One of the challenges that face browser-based applications is overall file size. Because all content has to be downloaded to the end user's machine each time it is viewed (outside of browser caching), trying to minimize file size helps end-user perceived performance and limits the amount of bandwidth your servers use.

Until RSLs were supported, all of the logic and functionality had to be included in the main SWF file, which added to the overall size. On top of that, if you had multiple applications with the same functionality, each SWF would have to include the same code, which increased the file size of each SWF.

With the release of RSL support, applications can now externalize these libraries so that they can be shared across applications. An added benefit is that browsers can cache the RSL file and it will be redownloaded only if the RSL file changes. Having the browser download only those files that have changed helps mitigate your application's overall file download size.

Because of this functionality, RSLs will be cached by the browser like any other SWF or asset. When testing an application, it's important to clear the cache of RSLs just as much as any other file type.

Unsigned vs. signed RSLs

RSLs come in two flavors, unsigned and signed. An *unsigned* RSL is the standard RSL format that is generated by the compiler. An unsigned RSL has the .swf file extension, and Flash Player can verify the contents by using a SHA-256 hash to make sure that the loaded RSL is indeed the one the application expects.

A *signed* RSL is a special RSL that has been approved by Adobe and is digitally signed to validate its content. A signed RSL has the .swz file extension. Unlike an unsigned RSL, a signed RSL is not stored in the browser's cache but instead is cached in a special Flash Player cache. This is important because the Flash Player cache is cleared only when the player is uninstalled. At the time of the writing of this book, only the Flex SDK framework is available as a signed RSL, and Adobe has not announced any plans for allowing third parties to sign and distribute SWZ files.

In most cases, you do not have to worry about signed RSL files. But when doing performance and load testing, it is a good idea to clear all RSLs to test initial load times for users who have never viewed a Flex application before and therefore do not have any SWZ files cached.

Flash Builder 4 and RSLs

In Flex Builder 3, the Flex SDK libraries were compiled into the main SWF by default, but you could turn on Flex Framework RSL support via the project preferences. Once enabled, your application would leverage the signed SWZ files for the framework and reduce the size of your main SWF file.

In Flash Builder 4, RSL support is turned on by default, and all of the framework RSLs are provided as separate files for deployment. This makes it much easier for Flash Builder projects going forward to leverage RSLs, browser caching, and the file size optimization. This also means that the cache not clearing on refresh may impact the testing and review of browser-based Flex applications.

Local shared objects

Local shared objects (LSOs) are Flash Player data objects that allow applications to store data on the user's machine. They are very similar to a browser's cookie functionality and enable you to store configuration data and other important information in a specialized data cache.

Unlike browser cookies, you cannot clear LSOs directly from the browser. To clear an LSO, you can browse to the Adobe Flash Settings Manager to clear out existing LSO data, you can have your developers provide functionality within the application's code base to clear the data, or you can delete the files from your machine. LSO files have the filename extension .sol.

The LSO data should be cleared regularly during the testing process to make sure that previous settings or other data stored in the LSO do not create issues. Often during development, the data structure and information stored in the LSO will change. These changes can cause issues when upgrading from build to build, because the newer or older build may not expect the data in the format that is stored in the LSO. In some situations, such as when you want to verify that LSOs are being correctly written and stored, you will not want to clear the LSO between tests.

This means that if your application leverages LSO storage, then it will be important to clear out existing LSO data between each build or test case, depending on how the LSO data affects the process. Only when verifying version upgrading, such as a 1.0 to 2.0 upgrade, where legacy data is expected, should you keep the LSO data as is.

AIR application data storage

When developing AIR applications, developers can save application-specific data in multiple ways. The most common include the application storage

---

SOL FILES

The SOL files are where Flash Player stores the application's serialized data. The location of the SOL file is dependent on both the OS you are running and which application type was used to store the data.

When saving content via Flash Player, the locations of the SOL file are under Flash Player's preferences folder inside the #SharedObjects folder.

- **For Windows:** The location is C:\Documents And Settings\{user name}\Application Data\ Macromedia\Flash Player\#SharedObjects\{playerID}\{domain name}\{server path}\.

- **For OS X:** The location is /Users/{User Name}/Library/Preferences/Macromedia/Flash Player/#SharedObjects/{playerID}/{domain name}/{server path}/.

- **For AIR:** When viewing content of an AIR application, the SOL file is stored in the AIR application storage folder in the #SharedObjects folder. For the location of the storage directory, see the next sidebar "Application Storage Directory Location."

directory, the encrypted local store, SQLite, and custom folder locations.

Each of these options has different implications on your testing and review processes. The developers need to inform the testers which storage locations are being used, how the data is being used, and when it should be cleared for testing purposes.

Application storage directory

The application storage directory is a unique location for every AIR application. This folder allows developers to store and retrieve information easily from the AIR API and guarantees that each AIR application has a unique location without requiring the developer to define a custom location scheme.

A common use case for this location is application settings, such as window size, window location, application state, and so on. Depending on the data being stored in this location, you may need to clear out the folder between builds or test cases if the data impacts the current build or test goals.

Encrypted local store

Similar to the application storage directory, the encrypted local store is used to save application-specific data to the user's machine. Unlike the application storage directory, anything saved into the encrypted local store is processed through AES-CBC 128-bit encryption to help protect the data.

The encrypted data store is designed to be used to store sensitive data, such as usernames, passwords, account details, and so on, in your application. Unlike the application storage directory, the data location is managed by the OS and is not easily removable. This means that your developers should implement a way for the application to reset the encrypted data for testing and review purposes.

SQLite

AIR provides the ability to manage data using a SQLite database within your application. This database can be provided with the install of your application or can be created dynamically the first time the application is run. Just like any of the previous data stores, managing the SQLite data is an important aspect of the build and release process.

Unlike the previous stores, there is no default location for AIR-supported SQLite databases. The SQL engine in AIR allows developers to create a DB file that contains all the information for the database. An application can access as many DB files as it needs, and the files can be stored anywhere on the user's machine. When testing, reviewing, and deploying AIR builds, it is important for the developers to clearly define the location of the DB files so that they can easily be found if they need to be removed during testing.

Custom folder locations

AIR has the ability to access almost any folder on a user's machine; not only can it access folders but it can also create and remove folders on the user's machine. This means that developers have the ability to store data files in different locations. Ideally, you should use the standardized locations defined earlier, but this does not mean you have to.

APPLICATION STORAGE DIRECTORY LOCATION

Similar to LSOs, the location of the directory depends on both the OS and the ID of the AIR application.

- **For Windows:** The location is C:\Documents And Settings\{user name}\Application Data\ {application ID}.{Publisher ID}\Local Store\.

- **For OS X:** The location is /Users/{User Name}/Library/Preferences/{application ID}.{Publisher ID}/Local Store/.

If your team decides to store data in a custom location, you must clearly define where this data lives. Just like SQL databases, the location is important so that any data can be found and removed for testing and deployment purposes.

AIR versioning

When distributing builds of AIR applications—especially when using auto update—it's important to keep in mind when an AIR application can update or override an existing version.

One of the options within the AIR configuration XML file is the current version of the application you have built. This value can be a number such as 1.0 or a string such as alpha 1. The AIR updating system supports the processing of these values to tell users which version they currently have installed and which version will be installed if they update to a new version.

As we mentioned in the previous chapter, it is a good idea to create incremental version numbers with each build, or at least with each review build, so that you can verify which build you are running and take advantage of the auto-update ability of AIR.

When updating an AIR application that has been previously installed, the version is checked, and the user is told which version is being installed. If the user attempts to install a new version or the same version of the application, they will be informed that their current installation will be overwritten. The user will not be able to install an older version of the application over a newer version; they must uninstall the new version before installing the old version.

Signing builds

All AIR release builds need to be digitally signed with a key to verify the identity of the publisher, this can be done with either a temporary key or an official code signing certificate. During development and testing, the AIR build tools and Flash Builder provide the ability to create a temporary key (P12 file) to enable you to create a build. When it is time to distribute the file, you will want to use a code-signing certificate to verify your company as the publisher. We will discuss code signing in Chapter 14, "Deploying Your Finished Product."

When trying to update or reinstall over an existing installation, the key that was used for both versions must be the same. For example, let's say that build 0.7.6 of the application was installed last week on the client's machine, and the client now wants to install the new build, version 0.7.7, for testing. The easiest way is to double-click the AIR file for 0.7.7. The installer will launch and ask the client whether they want to update to the new version.

Now, let's say that version 0.7.6 was built using a temporary key generated by Aaron and version 0.7.7 was built using a temporary key generated by James. If the client tried to install version 0.7.7, they would get an error (**Figure 13-1**) stating that AIR could not update to this version. The reason is that a different key was used by each version. To install 0.7.7 in this case, the client would have to uninstall 0.7.6 before installing 0.7.7.

This becomes a bigger issue if you are using the auto-update feature to help distribute builds for testing and review. The user would get the same error described above, but it would be displayed after the auto-update has downloaded and tried to update the system.

When creating builds, it is a good idea to have one person generate a temporary key file and then have all builds use this key to make sure that you can seamlessly update.

Figure 13-1 AIR certificate version error

SUMMARY CHECKLIST

The iterative build and release process evolves over the course of the project and becomes a bigger and bigger focus the closer you get to release. Understanding the parts of the process, how they change, and how the Flash Platform affects this process is critical to making your project successful.

Before you start the iterative process, make sure you have answered the following questions:

✔ Who will handle and manage feature testing during development?

✔ Will you use continuous testing, and if so, which team members will be responsible for the process?

✔ Has your team reviewed feature interdependency and planned an integration testing strategy?

✔ Who is responsible for creating, managing, and running your project's smoke tests?

✔ When will stress and performance testing begin, and who will handle it?

✔ When will your build team create debug and release builds for your project?

✔ Are your team members and client aware of potential browser and server caching issues?

✔ Will your project require or leverage RSLs?

✔ Does your project need LSOs, and if so, what will they be used for and when will they be created?

✔ Will your AIR application be storing data on the user's machine? If so, how will it do that? Will it use the application directory, LSOs, the encrypted data store, SQLite databases, or custom locations?

✔ How and when will you increment AIR versions?

✔ Who is responsible for managing the test keys for your AIR application?

CHAPTER 14

Deploying Your Finished Project

Congratulations, after all of your project development, testing, and reviews are complete, it is time to deploy the application to your users or client! In this chapter, we will cover issues you need to consider when deploying your application, and we'll describe a process for reviewing your project's success up to this point.

CREATING AND SECURING YOUR FINAL BUILD

Determining when your application is ready for live deployment depends on multiple factors. It could be that your time deadline has been reached, the defined feature set is complete and all the known bugs have been fixed, or outstanding issues have been deferred to the next release. When your team or client determines that a build is ready for release, you can begin to finalize the build for live deployment.

Traditionally this build is referred to as the *gold master candidate* (GMC). This term comes from the days when a master CD was made from a gold plate from which all other CDs where replicated. Another term for this build is the *release candidate* (RC) or the *release to manufacturer* (RTM) build. At this point—barring any last-minute issues that may arise during the final deployment process—your application is ready to go live.

Once you have reached this milestone, you and your team will need to deploy your application to the live environment. For a browser-based application, this means posting all of the files and assets to the live server.

For AIR applications, this process is slightly different depending on how you intend to distribute the application to your users. This could include sending the AIR file to your client directly, having IT manage deployment, or making the file available on shared drives. It could also mean putting the AIR file on a live server and using an AIR installer badge for one-click installs.

Understanding AIR certificates

Before we talk about pushing your files to the servers, we will explore how the AIR certification process works. This is important because it can impact your client's installation experience. If you are not building an AIR application, you can skip this section and begin reading "Verifying Your Finished Project," below.

In the previous chapter, we discussed the digital key requirements for AIR applications. The digital key is used to identify the publisher of an application and allows your users to determine whether the AIR application is indeed provided by whom they expect.

Because AIR applications have the ability to access and edit a user's file system, the digital key is an important security measure. To help prevent users from installing a malicious and potentially dangerous installation, Adobe has created a digital signature and certification process for AIR applications.

When an AIR application is signed with a temporary key—such as one created from Flash Builder—the user will see a warning during installation informing them that the publisher could not be verified (**Figure 14-1**). This warning is to tell users that the application was not signed by an approved digital certificate key and therefore the publisher's identity could not be determined.

Code signing and certificate authorities

To remove the warning shown in Figure 14-1 from the AIR installation process, you and your company will need to purchase a code signing certificate (CSC) from a respected certificate authority (CA). A CA provides digital keys that allow AIR to verify the publisher's identity and guarantee that the code was indeed created by the claimed source. The process of getting a CSC is relatively easy, but there could be multiple hurdles based upon the structure of your project, company, and client.

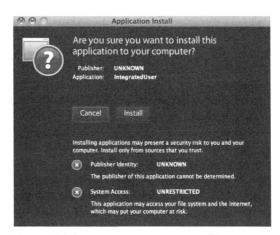

Figure 14-1 Are you sure you want to install?

Before you attempt to purchase a CSC, you need to determine who should sign the application. Are you creating an AIR application for a client, and if so, should your client provide the CSC, or do they want you to sign the AIR application? Does your company or client already have a CSC, and if so, should you use the existing one or get a new one just for your team or department? If your company has an existing CSC, is there a set process for using it, and if so, who needs to manage this process?

Finally, does your project even need a CSC? For many projects, you don't need to worry about getting a CSC. Is this an internal application, and your IT department does not require a signed application? Does your user base expect the application to be signed? We recommend getting a CSC in most cases, but there are situations in which an unsigned application is acceptable.

Purchasing code signing certificates

There are multiple CAs that offer AIR-specific code signing certificates, such as VeriSign and Thawte. When purchasing a CSC, you need to know if the CA sells CSCs to organizations or to individuals. In most cases, you need to have an established corporate identity to purchase a CSC. Usually, CSCs are intended for organizations, but Adobe is working with CAs to allow individual CSCs to be issued to individuals.

CAs often require multiple verification points, such as an e-mail address using your company's domain, a corporate Web site, and an established business phone number. Each CA may have a different set of requirements, so we recommend that you check with the CA to determine what they require before issuing a CSC.

Code signing certificate security

Once you have obtained a CSC, it's important to keep it safe and secure. The CSC is used to define and determine your company's identity, and if the digital key fell into the wrong hands, a malicious developer could create harmful applications and make it look as though they were created and distributed by your company.

Large companies often have established guidelines to help issue, manage, and secure the company CSCs. For example, a company may require that any department-issued CSC be stored on a dedicated signing machine, which is confined within a secure server location that only authorized personnel may access. This procedure ensures that only authorized builds can be signed and distributed with the issued CSC.

If your company has an established CSC procedure, we recommend working closely with the managing department as soon as you know that your team is building an AIR application. In some cases, the bureaucratic process of obtaining a CSC can take considerable time to approve, and any delay can impact your final release.

Smaller companies rarely require this type of procedure. We recommend that your CSC be managed securely, be it a dedicated machine or a predetermined team member responsible for creating release builds of the application.

Installing an AIR badge

One of the powerful distribution techniques of AIR is the ability to create an installer badge that enables a user to install both AIR and your application with a single click. The installer badge is a small, embeddable SWF application that points to both the location of your AIR application and the AIR runtime.

The AIR SDK provides the ability to create a custom installer badge for your application in order to meet your project's design and functional requirements. It can be used with different SWF detection kits and allows for a seamless installation process for your users.

Adobe also provides a tool called Badger (**Figure 14-2**), which helps you and your team automate the AIR badge creation process for your application. The Badger tool is built with AIR and provides an assortment of configuration options for your badge. Once created, you can place the badge on your servers so that your clients can then access and install your AIR application.

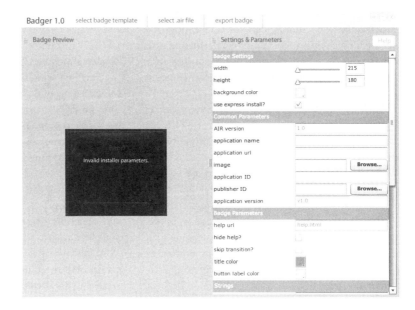

Figure 14-2 Badger

VERIFYING YOUR FINISHED PROJECT

After you've created a release build (and its associated assets) and posted it on your distribution platform—whether on a server or via another distribution method—your team will need to perform a verification test pass to make sure that the release is functioning as intended.

Verification testing

The goal of the verification process is to make sure that your production environment is running exactly the same as your test environment. It is a good idea to run all the smoke tests and ideally perform a full test pass on the live production server. The following are common issues to look out for.

Missing external assets. With browser-based Flash applications, there are often many external assets, such as video and images. When moving files over to the production server, it's easy to miss a folder or a specific image. With AIR applications, the assets are included within the AIR file, but during the build process, some can be missed. Verify that all of the required assets are included in the build.

Invalid URLs and references. Referencing assets, data services, and other URL-based calls may need to be updated when moved to the production servers. Common errors include having assets linked directly instead of relatively such as *http://dev.company.com/ myFolder/myImage.jpg* should be *./myFolder/myImage.jpg*.

Missing or invalid cross-domain XML files. When accessing different domains or subdomains from Flash Player, a cross-domain XML file is required to allow Flash Player to connect to the location. Often when testing or in development, the cross-domain is not required or is set to accept all calls. Once on the production server, the cross-domain becomes much more important and can cause connection issues if not configured correctly.

All-access cross-domain. Similar to the missing or invalid cross-domain files, it is good practice to configure the cross-domain on your servers to allow only proper access to your content. During development we often set access to *, allowing anyone or any application to access our content. Properly configuring your cross-domain should be done during the final deployment process.

Debug build posted. To help minimize the overall SWF size and to prevent people from debugging your files, make sure to always post a release build for your project.

Clearing existing configurations. When the application uses LSOs, data stores, or other ways of storing configuration data, it is important to remove or reset this data on the test machines before the final test pass. Clearing user data before testing mimics your user's configuration and helps verify that the first run of the application behaves correctly.

Stress and performance testing

Similar to verification testing on the production environment, you and your team should also do a full stress and performance test of your application. This test pass is used to verify that your production environment and subsequent services are behaving correctly and mirror your development and testing platform's performance.

Once you have performed your verification and performance testing, your project is now ready for your client and the end users. At this point, you can inform your client, customers, or users that the new version is ready and live for their use.

LOOKING BACK ON YOUR PROJECT

Once your final release is posted, tested, reviewed, and approved, the first thing you and your team should do is take a well-deserved break and celebrate the completion of the project. Even on small projects, we invest a lot of time and energy into making each project the best it can be. Taking a break, even a small one, and focusing on the fact that you have reached this important goal helps boost your team's morale.

After your team has had a chance to relax and regroup, it is a good idea to plan a postmortem meeting with your entire team. The goal of the meeting is to review what went right with your project, what could have gone smoother, and what just didn't work at all.

As we mentioned in previous chapters, no project is the same, and what worked great for one project may not be ideal for another. The Flash development process is a constantly evolving process that needs be fine-tuned by you and your team. Having a postmortem meeting can help plan and improve the next project.

It's often easy to dismiss the postmortem meeting with excuses such as "the project went fine," "we don't have time to meet," or even "we won't be working with that team again." However, without discussing what went wrong—and more importantly what went right—then there is a good chance the same issues will continue from project to project. Taking the time to review is worth the effort in the long term and is unfortunately overlooked by many teams. No matter how big or small your team is, having a postmortem will help you improve your project development process and get a better insight into what works and what doesn't.

Gathering your team

When setting up a meeting to discuss how the project went and what can be improved, it's important to have as many of the team members participate in the meeting as possible. For larger teams or projects that span departments or companies, this may not be possible or even reasonable.

If you cannot have everyone in the same room (or on a conference call), then attempt to gather representatives of each team, department, or company. You may also need to have multiple postmortem meetings with different members so that everyone gets a chance to give their perspective of how the project went.

When planning this meeting, it is important to consider the comfort of you and your team so that it encourages open communication. A lot of people, especially developers who tend to be introverted, will not feel comfortable contributing to these types of meetings. If you think your team may have this, consider ways of creating a forum for feedback that helps the team members share their thoughts without being exposed or identified.

What worked?

The first topic to discuss is what went right for the project. Have the teams look at what stood out to them as a successful aspect of the project and the process.

- Did the iterative development and unit testing processes catch issues early?
- Did the creative briefs clearly define the overall design requirements so that the designers could work efficiently?
- Was there good communication between different teams, departments, and companies?
- Did the team take advantage of new features enabled by Creative Suite 5?
- How did the tools help the team and can they be improved?

Knowing what you and your team liked about the project is critical because it helps identify the strengths of the current project process. Make sure that you define not only what worked but why it worked. Too often we can see something that we know is working but not understand why. Without this, it may not be the same in the next project. Once you understand what worked and why, you can use this information as building blocks for the next project.

What took less time than expected?

When looking at what went well with the project, make sure to look at items that took less time than the team expected. Did this happen because of over estimation, a new workflow, or a new technology or feature you adopted?

By looking at what went smoothly, you can help refine your estimations and planning to take advantage of these improvements. If a small change or technology improved your performance, could this be leveraged by different members or even other teams? After reviewing your project metrics, you may choose to invest more time and energy into the enhancements that improve your processes.

What didn't work?

In addition to knowing why something worked out well, you need to discuss what didn't work. This is often a tricky subject to talk about with your team,

especially if there is conflict among the members. It's easy to turn a constructive meeting into a blame game, where team members point fingers at each other.

The goal of figuring out what didn't work is not to cast fault but to determine why things went wrong.

- Was there a communication breakdown between team members?
- Was the initial deadline too short?
- Were the client's expectations set too high?
- Did the client constantly change the scope of the project and, if so, why?
- Was the technology investment larger than expected?

Once you determine what went wrong, it's important to figure out the exact cause of the issue and how it can be solved in the future.

- If the client kept changing their mind yet wouldn't change the deadline, can your team change the requirements for how a client signs off on each step?
- If communication failed among members, how can it be improved?
- Where there too many meetings and distractions for the team?
- Did the your team take shortcuts that actually backfired?
- Did your team take too much time on a specific area, such as an inordinate amount of time planning the system architecture for the code base?
- Where their tools or processes that were missed that could have improved the project?

Everyone will have a different opinion of what didn't work and why. For some people what was a huge issue could be a perceived as a good thing by another team member. Balancing this is an important aspect during the project process and having an understanding of everyone's perspective is really important.

Even if you are a one-man team, reviewing what you felt went wrong is very important. Make sure you ask yourself, what would you *not* do again and why?

What took too much time?

When reviewing what your team considers went wrong, also take the time to consider what took longer than expected. When we make estimates, we try to anticipate typical issues that could arise but we can never predict them all. When reviewing what took too much time, look at why it took more time than expected.

Look for possible trends that you can consider for the next project.

- Did the build process consume more time then you expected?
- Were the design and development teams on the same page?
- Were there features or technologies that took more investment then expected?
- Were there steps or requirements that were missed or not documented during the planning process?

There will never be "silver bullet" solutions for these kinds of issues, nor will your team be able to foresee and prepare for all the unknowns that come up during project development. But understanding items that took more time than expected can help you reduce or even prevent these issues from happening again.

What can be fixed?

Not everything that went wrong on a project can be fixed. A bad client may always be a bad client. A technology limitation may not be improved by the time your next project starts. Yet, it is important to focus on what can be fixed the next time around.

Whenever an issue is raised, have the team look at how it can be solved or at least improved so it's not as painful next time. If there was a successful workaround to a technology limitation, make sure to note it because it may occur in future projects until the core issue is solved. Some issues will be easy to fix and some will be difficult. But reviewing what is right and wrong with your process will help you improve it.

SUMMARY CHECKLIST

As your project wraps up and your application is ready to be deployed, your team needs to complete the last few steps before the project is given to the client. Taking the time to verify the final build is just as important as the process of getting it there.

Once the project is complete, make sure to go over what went right and wrong with the project. It is too easy to skip this step and start looking at the next project and the future. This wrap-up meeting should be done as soon as possible after the project is done, but make sure to give your team a little bit of a breather to collect themselves after all of their hard work and effort.

Before moving onto maintenance, make sure you and your team can answer the following questions:

- ✔ If you are building an AIR application, do you need and have a AIR code signing certificate? If so, does your company have an established process for obtaining the certificate?
- ✔ Do you need an AIR install badge? If so, who is responsible for creating it?
- ✔ Have you considered and defined a final verification process? If you and your team are responsible for managing the live distribution system, who will handle the final process?
- ✔ Who should be involved in your project's postmortem meeting?
- ✔ Why is it important to understand what went right and wrong with the project?
- ✔ How can your team improve the process?

PART VI

MAINTENANCE

CHAPTER 15

Maintaining Projects After Deployment

As we discussed in Chapter 2, projects and applications can have different life spans for you and your clients. Some projects, no matter the spectrum, end when you deliver the code to the client and your team's work is finished. On other projects—especially larger-spectrum projects—you may continue to update the application with new features, updates, and patches.

The process of maintaining a project varies based on the type of application you have developed and the amount of continued involvement your team will have after final deployment. In this chapter, we will cover the common types of project maintenance, how technology updates impact the application, adding or changing functionality, and considerations for when your application's use comes to an end.

UNDERSTANDING TECHNOLOGY IMPACTS

As the Flash Platform evolves and changes over time, these changes can impact your existing project and how you will update and maintain your application. You might want to add new features or update your application's security to provide better stability for your project. Understanding how the technological changes affect your application will help you take advantage of these changes to create a smooth and reliable maintenance and update process.

Flash Player versions

Adobe periodically releases new iterations of the Flash Player; these updates come in three forms: *major revisions*, *minor revisions*, and *security updates*. A major revision is when the player number changes, such as Flash Player 9 becoming Flash Player 10. Major revisions are used to mark significant changes in the player including extensive new features, API updates, and large overarching changes to the system.

A minor update is when Flash Player changes or adds a dot version, such as Flash Player 10 becoming Flash Player 10.1. A minor update means that new and updated functionality has been added to the player but no fundamental changes across the entire player have been made. Examples of this kind of change include memory improvements, performance improvements, user interaction support, and new media format support.

A security update is when a subnumber is added to the player to indicate a change in the version to fix known issues and potential security risks. For example, Flash Player 10.0.11 becomes 10.0.32.

NOTE ▪ In the past, when Macromedia handled Flash Player development, it tended not to use minor revisions for Flash Player when adding new functionality but focused on using major revisions to identify new and improved functionality. Adobe is changing this process and will be using minor revisions more often to define new functionality and improvements to the player and save major revisions for when sweeping changes occur.

Backward compatibility

When a new version of Flash Player is released (major, minor, or security), your existing application will be viewable by users running the new player. But, your application will not be able to leverage the new or improved features of the player unless you create a new build for the updated version.

For example, say your project was originally developed in Flash Player 10 and your client wants to take advantage of a new improvement in the next major release. If a user views your application in the most up-to-date player, they will not automatically see the improvement offered by this version. To get this improvement, you will need to recompile your application targeting the newest version of the player and then republish your SWF or AIR application.

The reason Flash Player does this is to help prevent updates from "breaking the Web." If a developer created an application that leveraged a feature in a previous version that has been removed or changed in a new version of the player, this would mean that when someone views the content in the new player, the older content would no longer function correctly.

To prevent this from occurring, Flash Player has the ability to run any SWF, going back to version 1.0, with the same feature set that was available at the time the SWF was created. The only time that the Flash Player development team makes a change that could impact previous versions is when a known security issue is discovered that could be taken advantage of by malicious developers.

If this occurs, Adobe will inform the development community of the issue, including any potential impacts the security update could have on applications. In these rare cases, it may require your team to update the application if the change conflicts with or impacts the existing functionality.

Player version penetration and adoption

Understanding the adoption rate for Flash Player can help guide you and your client in deciding when to take advantage of the newest features available in the player. It may be worthwhile to wait a few months after the release of a new player before deploying features that require the newest player, or your client may have the demand to quickly adopt a new version, making this less of a concern for feature updates.

Whenever a new version of Flash Player is released, whether it's a security update or a major revision, not everyone will download the new player the day it comes out. A key metric used by Adobe to help determine what player has the widest support is *player penetration*.

Player penetration is the percentage of computers that are connected to the Internet that have Flash Player installed. This percentage is then segmented by player version. For example, at the time of this writing, 98.9 percent of users in mature markets (United States, Canada, United Kingdom, Germany, France, Japan, Australia, and New Zealand) have at a minimum Flash Player 9 installed, yet 94.7 percent have Flash Player 10. (See *www.adobe.com/products/player_census/flashplayer/version_penetration.html*.)

Another metric is the *adoption rate*. The adoption rate is the length of time it takes a new release of the player to reach a target percentage. Currently, it takes approximately six months for a new player to reach more than 80 percent of the mature market. With each subsequent release of the player, the adoption rate is becoming quicker because of features such as autoupdate and wide adoption of the Flash Player technology on social networks and media distribution sites.

Understanding your target market can also help you decide when to adopt a new version. Your client and users may not be early adopters of the player or they may have limitations (such as IT requirements) when installing new technologies. Or you may have a young user base that quickly updates to the latest and greatest technologies, so taking advantage of the newest player is not a concern.

NOTE ■ When Adobe tracks player penetration, it studies the overall version of the player. For example, the Player 10 segmentation is looking at all revisions of version 10 and not subdividing by security revisions. This means that if one user has 10.0.11 and another user has 10.0.32, the tracking system considers both versions to be version 10. When considering player versions, take into

account the exact version you are targeting (and its release date) to help determine when your audience will have the player version available.

AIR versions

Similar to Flash Player, new versions of AIR are able to run older AIR applications, but older applications cannot automatically leverage new or improved functionality without being recompiled for the new version of AIR. Except, in some cases, a new version of AIR may have improvements for preexisting applications—such as improved memory management or performance—that make it possible for those applications to leverage the new AIR features.

AIR supports self-updating applications. This feature allows you and your team to release new versions of the application, which then notifies the existing versions that a newer version is available. The user can then decide whether to download and auto-install the newest version.

If you want your users to be informed of newer versions of your application, auto-update *must* be implemented before final deployment. During the development and build and release planning process, you should consider whether you want your application to auto-update.

AIR certificate updates

During the life span of an AIR project, you may need to renew, update, or even change the original certificate that was used to sign the application. There are several reasons this may occur. If it does, it can affect updates to your application.

You may need a new certificate if the original one expires. Code signing certificates are valid for a predetermined amount of time, usually one or two years. If your certificate is not renewed within this time frame, it will expire and you will need to obtain a new certificate from the certificate authority. The new certificate will have a different signature than the original certificate. If you attempt to update your application using the new certificate, the AIR installer will see the new certificate as a different version and will not allow

AIR 2.0 AUTO-UPDATE SUPPORT

With the release of AIR 2.0, developers can use the Native Process API to access and integrate OS functionality via command-line integration. This means that AIR applications can now launch and communicate directly with other native applications via the host OS. To enable this functionality, the AIR file must be packaged as an OS native application installer, such as a DMG or EXE file.

Because the AIR application is installed via an OS installer, instead of the AIR installer, the provided auto-update functionality in AIR is disabled for Native Process applications. If your team is building a Native Process application, you need to consider how the application will be distributed and updated when new features are added.

the new version to overwrite the existing application on the user's machine.

Your client may need to update the original certificate because of incorrect data, a misspelling, a company identity change, and so on. Again, the new certificate will be different from the original that was used to sign the application.

In either case, expired or updated, AIR provides the ability to migrate your application from the old certificate to the new certificate. To do this migration, you will need both the old and new certificates. When it's time to build and sign your application, you will have to sign the new version of the application with both of the certificates. This will allow AIR to verify the identify of the new application and properly overwrite it with your updated application. Once you have migrated your certificate to the new version, you will no longer need to sign future applications with the old certificate.

EXPIRED CERTIFICATES

Beginning with AIR 1.5.3, you can use an expired certificate for up to 180 days for the migration process. In previous versions, once the certificate expired, you could no longer use it for migration, which meant that your users would have to uninstall the old version before being able to install the new version.

Flex SDK and RSL versions

Over time, the Flex SDK is updated with both major and minor versions. Unlike Flash Player, new versions of the SDK are not automatically distributed to users nor will your application use a new version even if it is available on the user's machine.

Similarly, third-party Runtime Shared Libraries (RSLs) that your team creates will not be automatically leveraged by your application. In fact, if you enable RSL verification and the downloaded RSL's signature does not match what was used during creation of the application, then your application will not run.

For example, say you have an RSL called MyLibrary.swf. If you updated your RSL and republished it with the same name but did *not* update your application to use the new RSL, then the newer version of the RSL SWF would not match the version listed in the application, and the application would throw an error.

To leverage new Flex SDKs and RSLs, you need to recompile your entire application and point to the new libraries so that the verification ID is included in the application. Just like in Flash Player, this process is required to help prevent breaking existing applications as the API and features change in the different libraries.

Third-party library updates

Similar to the Flex SDK and RSLs, third-party libraries (SWC and source versions) that you use in your application can be updated with newer versions. These updates can offer new features or improved

> ### VERSIONING YOUR RSLS AND MODULES
>
> It is a good idea to avoid generic names when creating your RSLs and modules, such as our example MyLibrary.swf. Because the name is not unique, it may be possible to override an existing RSL with the incorrect version. We recommend that you name your RSLs and modules with a unique identifier, such as the version number, so that you can tell which version is being used and also allow multiple versions to live side by side. For example, MyLibrary_v0.9.8.swf and MyLibrary_v1.3.2.swf can be in the same directory, and older applications can still leverage the older library while new applications can leverage the newest RSL.

performance to the existing API. For example, if you are using a third-party tween animation library, such as Tweener, a new version could be released that dramatically improves animation performance.

Unlike RSLs—code that is external to your application—SWCs and source based libraries are compiled into your application. This means that you will need to recompile your application using the new versions of the libraries. Once you have recompiled the application, you will then need to redeploy the SWF or AIR files to your users.

FIXING ISSUES AFTER DEPLOYMENT

No matter how much testing is done during the deployment process, there is always the potential for undiscovered issues in your application—whether they are minor bugs, major bugs, usability issues, or performance related. The number of potential issues increases along with the complexity and size of your application. With small one-off projects, the bugs found post-deployment may be so minor or rare that updates are not required. But with larger projects, fixing issues after deployment is an important part of the maintenance process.

In determining how and when bugs should be fixed and updated, you'll need to consider the type of application and the importance of the issues being fixed. For browser-based applications, distributing new versions rapidly is much more convenient than trying to push multiple updates via AIR. With a browser-based application, you just have to update the SWF on the servers. But with an AIR application, you need to leverage the auto-updater, which requires your users to be notified, and then they have to choose to update. Constantly flooding your users with updates may not provide the best user experience.

Not only does the type of application impact how and when bug fixes are distributed, but the testing impact and available resources also play significant roles in the update process. Before a new version is distributed to your users, it should go through a proper testing process to make sure that the fixes are not creating new issues. To help minimize the testing time, you need to carefully determine what should be included in a new release.

Critical fixes

If a critical issue is found—such as the application crashes, loses data, or is unable to be used as intended—you'll want to get the fix out to your users as quickly as possible. It may be worth having an update that just contains this fix. These kinds of updates, or *hot fixes*, are important to your users because these critical issues drastically impair your application's usability and stability.

When a critical bug is found, the team needs to review the issue, determine its cause, and then review the potential impact of the fix. Some fixes are isolated and do not affect other aspects of the application. Other fixes may touch different parts of the application and require a more intensive testing process.

Once the fix is determined and implemented by you or your team, it's important to run a complete regression test pass on the feature or features the fix involves. It is also a good idea to run all your smoke tests just to make sure the fix does not have some other unintended consequences. After the fix has been confirmed, you can then deploy the updated application to your users.

Grouping issues

As issues arise, not all of them will be critical bugs that need to be solved right away. To help limit the number of releases you put out yet still get fixes to your users in a timely matter, it's a good idea to group and then prioritize issues for each update.

When an issue is found, the priority of the issue should be defined. Is it high priority, which means that a lot of your users will experience it or that the people that do find the issue are badly impacted? Is the issue medium priority, meaning that it affects some of your users but it can be worked around relatively easily? Or is the issue low priority, meaning that only a handful of people will ever see it or the issue is so minor it doesn't dramatically affect the user experience?

As the issues are prioritized, you will group them in order of importance and then plan a schedule of how and when the issues will be fixed, tested, and then deployed. Once you have scheduled the releases and decided which bugs get fixed when, your team will begin a micro-version of the overall project process. This includes planning the fixes, assigning designers and developers to the tasks, implementing the fixes, testing the application, and then deploying it to the users.

MAKING CHANGES AND ADDING FEATURES

After your project has been deployed, it may require additional features or changes. The source of these changes can vary greatly; they can include design changes, content updates, or new functionality.

When considering updates to an existing application, it's important that these changes get the same attention to detail that the original project received. If the update process is ignored or not prioritized, a previously successful project could be pushed into the "failed" category because of poorly defined updates, under-scoped feature additions, or rushed decisions that did not consider technology and resource dependencies.

If you are making basic changes, then you may need a small project spectrum process. If you are making significant changes to the application, then you should consider using the large spectrum project process.

Making design changes

As an application matures, the overall design of the UI evolves and may even be changed drastically to fit the needs of users, features, and brand. When modifying or adding new features, you'll also need to update the UI to support the new interactivity.

After the original deployment of your application, user feedback can drive changes to the existing UI. What may have seemed intuitive during the initial design and development phase may not meet all of your users' needs. If this is the case, then the current application's design may need to be updated to resolve these usability issues.

Other design changes that are commonly required post-deployment are brand and identity changes. Many application designs focus on meeting the client's overall style and branding requirements. If the

---

WEB SITE DEVELOPMENT VS. APPLICATION DEVELOPMENT

In the past, when creating content-oriented Web sites, a project would not be released until all issues were resolved. With today's rich media orientation and increasing complexity, Flash Platform–based application development is more similar to software development then traditional Web site development. This means that not all issues will be found at the time the project is released, and some issues can and will be deferred to be resolved in later versions.

This approach to development, and specifically updates, requires a different attitude toward how and when bugs need to be resolved. With the new distribution ability of AIR and the ease of changes that can be made to browser-based applications, updates and fixes are easier to distribute post-release than ever before.

client decides to change or improve their brand experience, the new look will need to be applied to existing applications.

All of the changes described in this section could be small modifications or drastic redesigns. Whenever a design change is required, you'll need to revisit the planning, design, development, and build and release processes to properly implement and then deploy the updates to the end user.

Making content updates

Some projects require the application to be updated on a regular basis. These updates can include all forms of media such as images, video, audio, and text. Ideally, you scoped the requirement for content updates during the initial project development, allowing for easy updates via externalized content or leveraging content management systems.

Sometimes, however, an update will be required that was not included in the original project scope. In this situation, you'll need to determine whether the content update will become a regular process or whether this is a one-off change.

If you anticipate that you may need to update content at regular intervals, it may be worth the time and investment to rearchitect and develop functionality to allow easy content updates. This includes externalizing all media content and providing a configuration XML file that is loaded by the application at runtime to determine what media needs to be loaded and where it is located. By externalizing your content, you can easily update the files and the configuration XML to point to the new assets, without having to recompile your SWF each time an asset changes.

In other cases, the content changes could be minor and infrequent enough that it makes sense to just update the content within the application and rebuild a new version.

When updating content, allow sufficient QA testing before releasing the new version to the user. With applications that are designed to support content updates, this testing process may be a simple verification that the content update was made in conjunction with your smoke tests.

With larger changes, especially where a rearchitecture is required, you should invest time in the planning, development, and build and release processes. These kinds of large functional changes have the risk of creating new issues, and they should be fully tested before deployment.

Adding new functionality

With projects on the large end of the project spectrum, multiple releases are often planned during the initial project planning phase. The most often considered changes are updating and adding new features and functionality to the application.

Changes to the application can be business-driven, client-driven, or user-driven, or they can be features that were not included in the initial release because of time or monetary limitations. As these improvements and new features are defined, your team will need to plan a design, development, and release schedule to determine when and how the new features and improvements will be added.

Leveraging source control

When making updates of any kind to an application, you can leverage features of your code repository to help your team streamline the update process. Modern source control systems enable your team to take a snapshot of the current state of the depot (or code repository) so that you can return to it at any time. This process is often referred to as *tagging*.

A good time to tag the depot is at the time of release, before any new development or changes are made. By tagging each release, you and your team can easily return to the state of the code base at the time of release so you can compare it to changes that are made after the release.

Another feature of code repositories is the ability to create *branches*. A branch is similar to creating a clone of the code depot. This allows you and your team to be able to work on the original depot and the clone depot (branch) separately.

A common use case for branching is to allow new feature development to begin in one location while bug fixing or critical updates occur in another.

For example, suppose that shortly after an application is launched, users find a few critical bugs. At the same time, new feature development needs to begin and the changes required will take significantly more time then the bug fixing.

To meet the new feature schedule and get the critical fixes out as soon as possible, you can create a branch within the depot. The branch (remember, it's a clone of the original depot state) will be used to allow developers to fix the critical issues and deploy them to the users. At the same time, the developers can work on new features in the original depot without the risk of impacting the critical fixes development.

Once the fixes are completed and released from the branch, the depot allows developers to merge their changes back into the original depot so that their bug fixes and changes are integrated into the new feature development. Typically, branching and merging are leveraged with larger teams that have multiple developers on a project with a multistaged release cycle.

RECOGNIZING END OF LIFE

Projects, and the applications they create, will not exist forever. Some—such as advertising projects—have very short life spans. Others evolve over time, but eventually they too will lose their usefulness to you, your clients, or your users. When this occurs, the project enters the final phase, or meets its *end of life.*

When planning your project's end of life, you and your team will need to determine whether people are still using the application. If so, informing your existing users that the application is going away is an important step. You will want to provide some advance notice to the users before you stop supporting an existing application.

For browser-based applications, you can display information in the HTML or in the application to warn users that the application will become unavailable in the near future. Other forms of communication—such as e-mail or direct contact—are also desirable if your have the resources and client information to perform these tasks.

BRANCHING CODE DEPOTS

When a code depot is branched, it is actually not cloning the entire depot; the repository is handling all this virtually. Modern code repositories are optimized to minimize overall depot size so that as you make branches, changes, and updates, only the changes to the files are tracked. That way, you don't have hundreds of versions of the same file within the depot.

For AIR-based applications, the users can continue to use the application on their desktop, but you may want to inform them that support for the application will no longer be provided. This information could be listed on your Web site or your team could post a final application update to the users, which would contain the information about the end of support for the application.

If your browser-based application contains data that is important to your clients, you should consider a process to allow the users to retain or save the data once the application is removed from the site. For example, you could allow users to download the data in a format that is flexible yet useful for them, such as comma-separated lists, SQL files, or spreadsheets.

Once your set time for customer and user notification has passed, you can then remove the content and application from your servers. Consider enabling URL redirects, which take users to a landing page informing them that the application is no longer available. This helps inform users who may have missed the previous announcements.

SUMMARY CHECKLIST

Projects have different life spans. The way that you, your team, and your client manage the process depends on the particulars of your project. Some projects require updates to resolve issues, while others continue to add new functionality and improvements over time.

Eventually, all projects come to an end. When that time comes, it's worth considering how you and your client should handle it.

✔ Will your project and the associated applications require ongoing maintenance?

✔ Do you, your team, and your client have strategies for updating the application as issues come to light?

✔ Will your project have multiple cycles of ongoing feature and functionality development?

✔ How often do you plan to update the application?

✔ When the application's end of life is near, does your team have a strategy to inform the users?

Glossary

ActionScript. The programming language used to create Flash Platform–based applications.

ADL. AIR Debug Launcher; the program that allows developers to test and debug their AIR applications.

Agile development. An iterative development methodology.

AIR. Adobe Integrated Runtime; allows Flash and JavaScript-based applications to be run on a user's computer as a native program. This allows the AIR-based applications to access the computer's file system and other desktop-based functionality.

AMF. Action Message Format; an optional binary protocol used by AIR and Flash Player to compress data into a smaller format when communicating with other applications and servers.

API. Application Program Interface; a series of methods that are made accessible so that developers can write code that interfaces with these API methods to perform predetermined functionality.

architecture (development). The process of planning the best way to write code and how it will interact with other aspects of the application, such as server data and media content (video, audio, graphics, text, and so on).

architecture (information). The process of planning the best way to create user interactions and designs to create an engaging and easy-to-use experience for the user.

ASDoc. The ActionScript code commenting format that allows for tools to parse and generate documentation from the code.

Beta software. A prerelease version of the application to allow users to interact with the existing content. Beta software is still in development and is used to find user issues (both design and code based) and to get customer feedback on the current progress of the application.

build (application). A specific version of an application that was created at a specific time and date.

CA. Certificate authority; companies that provide, authenticate, and manage CSCs for customers.

CAPTCHA. A challenge and response test, often using visually modified text, to verify that a human is interacting with the system instead of an automated system. CAPTCHA is usually used to protect Web forms from being used to send spam messages. (CAPTCHA stands for the long-winded Completely Automated Public Turing test to tell Computers and Humans Apart.)

client-side. Any application running locally on a user's operating system, such as a Flash Platform application (Flash Player, AIR, or mobile).

CMS. Content Management System; a server-based application that is responsible for organizing data and allowing individuals to easily add, update, and remove content with a specially designed UI.

component. An isolated suite of code that represents a common user interface feature.

contributor. A member of the project team or other entity that provides input and content (design, code, testing, media, data) to the project.

cross-domain file. An XML file that is located on a server that informs Flash Player if the SWF has permission to access content located on the server.

CSC. Code signing certificate; the file that allows AIR applications to be digitally certified that it was created by the person claiming to be the author.

CSS. Cascading Style Sheets; a format and technology that is used to define visual styles in code for layout purposes.

DACI. Driver, Approver, Contributor, and Informed; a methodology for managing a project and its teams and for solving critical problems.

DAMs. Digital Asset Management system; similar to a CMS and used to store and manage large assets such as graphics, video, and audio.

deserialize. The process of converting data into an uncompressed format.

design asset. An image, vector, audio, or media file that encompasses part of the design for a project. This usually is a Web-optimized version that is ready for the developer to integrate into the project.

design comp. Visual design file that contains the full-fidelity design of a screen or element of a project created in Photoshop, Illustrator, or Fireworks.

design pattern. A common, reusable solution to a coding or functionality problem.

discipline. A set of knowledge that when used together completes a unique set of tasks based on experience, tool skills, and instincts.

E4X. ECMAScript for XML; the default XML processing system built into Flash Player 9 and higher.

feature set. A breakdown of all the features within the application to meet the high-level vision, use cases, and technical requirements.

FPS. Frames Per Second; the number of frames Flash Player can play per second.

GMC. Gold Master Candidate; a term used to refer to the final build of an application before it is released to the users.

high-level vision. Defines the overall basic goals for the project—the who, what, why, when, and how.

HTTP. Hypertext Transfer Protocol; a Web-standard protocol for enabling client and server data communication.

HTTPS. Secure Hypertext Transfer Protocol; an encrypted version of HTTP to provide security and privacy for the data being transferred.

HTTPService. Flex class used for communication over basic HTTP in plain text.

IDE. Integrated Development Environment; a development tool (Flash Builder) that provides the developer with many different features in a unified application to create software faster and easier.

iterative development. The process of creating an application in small, recurring steps to enable shorter phases and allow flexibility to update the project's end goals to meet current or rapidly changing needs.

JSON. JavaScript Object Notation; a text-based protocol that allows for data to be read and stored in a machine-readable way.

feature specification. A document, or process, of taking a predefined feature set and defining a set of functional requirements that will be created for the project.

Flash Platform. An ecosystem of tools, technologies, and services that revolve around Flash Player and AIR. Tools include Flash Professional, Flash Catalyst, and Flash Builder. Technologies include Flash Player, Live Cycle Data Services, BlazeDS, and ColdFusion. Services include Acrobat.com and Flash Platform services.

Flash Player. An application that allows Flash-generated (SWF) content to be played in a browser or on the desktop.

Flex. An SDK provided by Adobe to rapidly create complex Flash-based applications.

framework. A predeveloped code base that provides a starting point for building an application, with the intentions of decreasing the overall code time and increasing developer productivity. A framework provides a lot of common functionality that occurs in most project types.

FXG. Adobe's graphic markup language that defines simple to complex graphical content in an XML-based syntax.

FXP. A file format that contains an archived Flex project that has been saved into a single file. Flash Catalyst CS5 uses this file format as the default format, and FXPs can be imported into Flash Builder 4.

LCDS. LiveCycle Data Services; server-side enterprise solution from Adobe to provide client-side applications with data scaled for heavy usage and for optimized performance with the Flash Platform.

linear development. The process of creating an application in a step-by-step approach by first completing all planning, then completing all design, then completing all development, and finally testing the application.

LSO. Local Shared Object; how Flash Player stores data on the client's machine, similar to browser cookies.

metadata tag. Information applied inside a Flex class to provide additional information to the mxmlc compiler.

milestone. A target goal for a project based on time, functionality, or both.

MVC. Model View Controller; a common design pattern used by developers and frameworks.

MXML. The Flex markup language that allows for laying out Flex-based content in a parent-child structure.

mxmlc. The Flex SDK compiler.

OSMF. Open Source Media Framework; an SDK provided by Adobe to create video- and audio-based applications.

push communication. Communication messaging method initiated by a server to a client.

QA. Quality assurance; the process of verifying that the application behaves as designed and meets the requirements defined for the project.

refactor. The process of rewriting code with the intention to consolidate the code, reduce duplicated logic, and organize the structures in a beneficial way.

RemoteObject. Flex class used for RPC communication over the AMF protocol.

role. A function of someone on a project team who completes a set amount of tasks or responsibilities.

RSL. Runtime shared library; a SWF file that contains code that can be shared by multiple Flash Platform applications.

RTM. Release to manufacture; the process of distributing the final build to the user.

scope (project). The size, sophistication, and magnitude of your project.

SDK. Software development kit; a set of tools and documentation that allows developers to create applications and software using the included content.

serialize. The process of converting data into a compressed format.

server-side. Remote server code and functionality consumed by a client-side application; in other words, the *back end*.

skin (Flex/component). The design UI elements that define the look and feel of a Flex or Flash component. Skins have the unique ability to be changed to meet the required UI needs without having to update or change the internal logic of the component.

skinning. The act of stylizing a component or application to meet the design and UI requirements.

Spark. Flex 4 component architecture.

SOAP. Simple Object Access Protocol; an XML-based protocol for server and client communication.

stakeholder. Someone who has a vested interest in the success of the project. They may be a member of the project team, the client, another division, or even a third- party entity.

style guide. A document that outlines all the rules for the design throughout the project including color usage, typography rules, logo treatments, and others.

SWC. A file format that contains a library of code that can be used by other developers in their Flash Platform projects.

SWF. A file format generated by Flash Professional, Flash Builder, and the Flex compiler. The SWF format is a binary file that represents Flash assets and logic that is interpreted by Flash Player to display the generated content.

SWZ. A digitally signed RSL file.

team sync. The process of project teams regrouping to share important information related to each role and discipline.

technical requirement. Defines the project's technology needs (client-server) to make both the user and the project successful.

TDD. Test Driven Development; the process of writing automated tests before the functionality is created. This enables better tested and functional features during the development process.

UI. User interface; the design elements that are displayed on the screen to the user to provide a visual-based system for interacting with the application.

unit test. A piece of code that is used to test other code.

use case. Defines the steps a user will take to accomplish a goal for a specific piece of functionality within the application.

UX. User experience; the overall UI design and user interaction design (such as scrolling, mouse movement, and so on).

Waterfall development. A linear development process where each phase of the project must be completed before the next phase may begin.

Web service. SOAP-based HTTP communication protocol.

widget. A very small application that provides a limited set of functionality, such as a banner ad or a simple chart that represents a set of data.

wireframe. A low-fidelity representation of your design that is used to capture early feedback from peers and clients before completing final designs.

XML. Extensible Markup Language; a text file format that allows for machines to read in and assign meaning to the data contained in the text file.

XP. Extreme Programming; an iterative development methodology.

Index

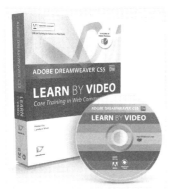

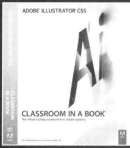
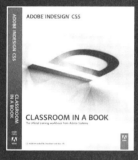

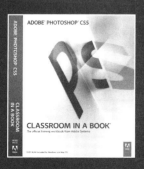

WATCH
READ
CREATE

Meet Creative Edge.

A new resource of unlimited books, videos and tutorials for creatives from the world's leading experts.

Creative Edge is your one stop for inspiration, answers to technical questions and ways to stay at the top of your game so you can focus on what you do best—being creative.

All for only $24.99 per month for access—any day any time you need it.